Ethics in Finance

Foundations of Business Ethics
Series editors: W. Michael Hoffman and Robert E. Frederick

Written by an assembly of the most distinguished figures in business ethics, the Foundations of Business Ethics series aims to explain and assess the fundamental issues that motivate interest in each of the main subjects of contemporary research. In addition to a general introduction to business ethics, individual volumes cover key ethical issues in management, marketing, finance, accounting, and computing. The books, which are complementary yet complete in themselves, allow instructors maximum flexibility in the design and presentation of course materials without sacrificing either depth of coverage or the discipline-based focus of many business courses. The volumes can be used separately or in combination with anthologies and case studies, depending on the needs and interests of the instructors and students.

1 John R. Boatright, *Ethics in Finance*, second edition
2 Ronald F. Duska and Brenda Shay Duska, *Accounting Ethics*
3 Richard T. De George, *The Ethics of Information Technology and Business*
4 Patricia H. Werhane and Tara J. Radin with Norman E. Bowie, *Employment and Employee Rights*
5 Norman E. Bowie with Patricia H. Werhane, *Management Ethics*
6 Lisa H. Newton, *Business Ethics and the Natural Environment*
7 Kenneth E. Goodpaster, *Conscience and Corporate Culture*

Forthcoming

George Brenkert, *Marketing Ethics*

Ethics in Finance

SECOND EDITION

John R. Boatright

Blackwell
Publishing

© 1999, 2008 by John R. Boatright

BLACKWELL PUBLISHING
350 Main Street, Malden, MA 02148-5020, USA
9600 Garsington Road, Oxford OX4 2DQ, UK
550 Swanston Street, Carlton, Victoria 3053, Australia

The right of John R. Boatright to be identified as the author of this work has been asserted in accordance with the UK Copyright, Designs, and Patents Act 1988.

First edition published 1999
Second edition published 2008

1   2008

Library of Congress Cataloging-in-Publication Data

Boatright, John Raymond, 1941–
    Ethics in finance / John R. Boatright. — 2nd ed.
        p. cm. — (Foundations of business ethics)
    Includes index.
ISBN 978-1-4051-5599-1 (hardcover : alk. paper)
ISBN 978-1-4051-5600-4 (pbk. : alk. paper)
1. Business ethics.   2. Finance—Moral and ethical aspects.   I. Title.

    HF5387.B63 2007
    174′.4—dc22

                                                                    2007003772

A catalogue record for this title is available from the British Library.

Set in 10.5 on 12.5 pt Minion
by SNP Best-set Typesetter Ltd., Hong Kong
Printed and bound in Singapore
by Markono Print Media Pte Ltd

The publisher's policy is to use permanent paper from mills that operate a sustainable forestry policy, and which has been manufactured from pulp processed using acid-free and elementary chlorine-free practices. Furthermore, the publisher ensures that the text paper and cover board used have met acceptable environmental accreditation standards.

For further information on
Blackwell Publishing, visit our website at
www.blackwellpublishing.com

Contents

Preface

In the eight years since the publication of the first edition of *Ethics in Finance*, much has changed and much has remained the same. The highly publicized scandals at Enron, WorldCom, Tyco, Global Crossing, Parmalat, and other companies, as well as investigations into conflict of interest in securities analysis, irregular trading in mutual funds, and bid-rigging in insurance brokerage have brought renewed attention to the problem of misconduct and the need for ethics in finance. In particular, the collapse of Enron and the destruction of its auditor Arthur Andersen have prompted a wave of new regulation, most notably the controversial Sarbanes–Oxley Act.

Although a new edition of *Ethics in Finance* is needed to reflect these recent developments, the scandals that have occurred in the United States and elsewhere since 1999 raise few novel issues in finance ethics. Indeed, many of the scandals were mainly instances of accounting fraud. The misconduct we have witnessed, while egregious, is merely familiar kinds of misconduct in new forms. Thus, the basic framework of the first edition is still adequate for understanding the broad range of ethical issues in finance.

Accordingly, the second edition retains the six-chapter layout of the original. The main changes involve additional discussions of some recent developments and an expansion of some of the more theoretical material. In particular, chapter 2 contains a more lengthy treatment of the duties of fiduciaries and agents, and a new section on conflict of interest in place of the former section on philosophical ethics. Chapter 3 includes new discussions of soft-dollar brokerage and the problems of market timing and late trading in mutual funds. The section on bankruptcy in chapter 5 has been expanded to cover personal as well as corporate bankruptcy. Chapter 6, on the theory of the firm, has been substantially rewritten for greater clarity and completeness.

In addition to the people who were acknowledged in the first edition of *Ethics in Finance*, the second edition has benefited from the help of W. Michael

Hoffman and Robert E. Frederick of Bentley College, the editors of the series Foundations of Business Ethics, and my editor at Blackwell, Jeff Dean. The School of Business Administration at Loyola University Chicago has provided critical support for the preparation of the second edition. I am especially grateful for the resources of the Raymond C. Baumhart, S.J., Chair in Business Ethics, which was created to honor a former president of Loyola University Chicago and a pioneer in the field of business ethics. To Ray Baumhart, then, I owe a special debt of gratitude. I also wish to express my appreciation to the former dean of the Loyola business school, Robert L. Parkinson, Jr., and the current dean, Abol Jalilvand, for their enthusiastic support. As always, I am indebted to my wife Claudia, whose affection, patience, and encouragement have been essential for my work.

John. R. Boatright

Preface to the First Edition

Writing a book on ethics in finance is a special challenge. The difficulty does not arise from a lack of subject matter, despite the cynical view that there is no ethics in finance. To the contrary, financial activity is governed by detailed rules, and a high level of integrity is expected of people who bear great responsibility. As a field of study, however, finance ethics is barely formed, and so the first task for a writer in this area is to define the subject. Whereas most textbooks present standard material, this one is forced by necessity to be original. Hopefully, *Ethics in Finance* will help create the field of finance ethics.

Not only is finance ethics still being formed, it is also highly diverse. People trained in finance enter many different lines of work, in which they encounter a variety of ethical dilemmas. The situation of a stockbroker is different from that of a mutual fund manager, a market regulator, or a corporate financial officer. In addition, finance ethics encompasses issues in financial markets, financial services, and financial management, each of which involves different ethical concerns. Financial markets, for example, are characterized by differences in information and bargaining power, which lead to abuses such as fraud and manipulation. In many financial transactions, one party acts as an agent for another and thus may face agency problems, such as conflicts of interest. A financial manager, who has a fiduciary duty to serve the shareholders' interests, must still balance these against the interests of other groups. Finally, financial activity occurs in a larger social setting, and ethical issues arise about the impact of this activity on the whole of society.

A book on finance ethics must also identify the relevant principles for resolving many different kinds of ethical issues. The dilemmas of individual conduct in finance cannot be settled merely by appeals to personal morality; rather, they involve an understanding of the obligations that attach to specific roles. For example, a stockbroker should be honest, of course, but how much information he or she ought to provide depends on his or her role in a complex system. Financial markets are judged primarily by considerations of fairness or equity (which may conflict with efficiency), whereas ethics in the financial services industry revolves largely around the duties of agents to principals. And financial managers are generally fiduciaries who have an obligation to manage assets for the benefit of others, such as the shareholders of corporations. Therefore, finance ethics must include, at a minimum, principles of role obligations, fairness in market exchanges, the duties of agents and fiduciaries, and the welfare of society as a whole.

Many ethical issues in finance have already been addressed by law and industry regulation. Securities law provides not only detailed rules for market transactions but a regulatory body, namely the Securities and Exchange Commission (SEC), to formulate and enforce rules. Exchanges, such as the New York Stock Exchange, and industry associations, such as the National Association of Securities Dealers (NASD), set their own rules and discipline members for violations. The role of ethics in such a highly regulated environment is problematic. Why is it not sufficient merely to obey the relevant rules? One answer to this question is that ethical principles lie at the heart of much regulation. Rules against fraud and manipulation in securities markets, for example, attempt to enforce ethical standards, and issues not yet settled by law or self-regulation are debated, in part, as matters of ethics. Much of this book is devoted, therefore, to an examination of existing regulation and proposals for regulatory reform. In addition, regulation, whether it be by government or industry, is a rather ineffective, uncertain guide, and so a commitment to high ethical standards, and not merely to legal compliance, is essential.

The first two chapters of this book provide a foundation for those that follow. The first chapter is an overview of the field of finance ethics, while the second, on "Theoretical Perspectives in Financial Ethics," introduces the main ethical principles that underlie the discussions of more practical problems. Chapter 3 examines the relation of a finance professional with individual clients, whereas the focus of chapter 4 is on the investment decisions of bankers, fund managers, and others, who are generally acting as institutional investors. Chapter 5 considers ethics in financial markets, and especially financially driven corporate strategies, such as bankruptcy and hostile takeovers. The final chapter is devoted to the theory of the firm as a nexus of contracts, which is central to modern finance.

John R. Boatright

Acknowledgments

I am pleased to acknowledge that the second edition of *Ethics in Finance* contains copyrighted material that is published in other works.

The section of chapter 2 on conflict of interest was previously published as the chapter "Financial Services" in Michael Davis and Andrew Stark, *Conflict of Interest in the Professions* (New York: Oxford University Press, 1999), © 1999 by John R. Boatright.

Portions of chapters 2 and 3 incorporate material from entries on "Fiduciary Duty," "Soft Dollar Brokerage," and "Bankruptcy" that was written for Robert W. Kolb, ed., *Encyclopedia of Business Ethics and Society* (Thousand Oaks, CA: Sage Publications, 2007).

Chapter 6 includes material from John R. Boatright, "What's Wrong—and What's Right—with Stakeholder Management," *Journal of Private Enterprise*, 22 (2006), © 2006 by John R. Boatright.

Abbreviations

ATR	annualized turnover ratio
BCCI	Bank of Credit and Commerce International
CalPERS	California Public Employees' Retirement System
CAPM	Capital Asset Pricing Model
CRA	Community Reinvestment Act (1977)
ENE	"early neutral evaluation"
ERISA	Employee Retirement Income Security Act (1974)
ETI	Economically Targeted Investment
FIRREA	Financial Institutions Reform, Recovery, and Enforcement Act (1989)
FTC	Federal Trade Commission
HMDA	Home Mortgage Disclosure Act (1975)
ICA	Investment Company Act
ICI	Investment Company Institute
IPO	initial public offering
LBO	leveraged buyout
LDC	less-developed country
M&E	"mortality and expense risk"
NASD	National Association of Securities Dealers
NPV	net present value
PDAA	predispute arbitration agreement
PRI	Program Related Investment
REIT	real estate investment trust
RI	relationship investing
SEC	Securities and Exchange Commission
SRI	socially responsible investing
SRO	self-regulating organization
SWM	shareholder wealth maximization

Chapter One

Financial Ethics: An Overview

The public's perception of ethics in finance is shaped by news stories of major scandals, such as these events from the past several decades.

- Wall Street was shaken in the late 1980s by the securities-law violations and the junk-bond market manipulations of Dennis Levine, Martin Siegel, Ivan Boesky, Michael Milken, and others. In 1990, Michael Milken pleaded guilty to six felonies and was sentenced to ten years in prison. Previously, Milken's firm, Drexel Burnham Lambert, collapsed after officials admitted to six felonies and agreed to pay $650 million. James B. Stewart, the author of *Den of Thieves*, calls their activities "the greatest criminal conspiracy the financial world has ever known."[1]
- Salomon Brothers was nearly destroyed in 1991 by charges that traders in the government securities division had attempted to execute a "squeeze" by rigging several auctions of US Treasury notes. The total cost of this scandal—including legal expenses and lost business, on top of a $290 million fine—has been estimated at $1 billion. The firm discharged the people responsible for the bid-rigging, as well as CEO John Gutfreund, who was unaware of the activity at the time. Gutfreund's offense was that he sat on the news for more than three months before reporting it to the Treasury Department.
- After losing $1.6 billion on derivative transactions in 1994, Orange County in California sued its financial adviser Merrill Lynch for concealing the amount of risk that was involved in its investments. In 1998, Merrill Lynch settled the suit for more than $400 million. In 1996, Procter & Gamble (P&G) settled with Bankers Trust after the bank agreed to forgive $200 million that P&G owed on failed derivative transactions. P&G's charges that Bankers Trust had misrepresented the investments was bolstered by damaging tapes, including some in which bank employees used the acronym ROF for "rip-off factor" to describe one method for fleecing customers.

- Unauthorized trading by individuals has caused great losses at several banks and trading firms. Nick Leeson, a 28-year-old trader in the Singapore office of Barings Bank, destroyed this venerable British firm in 1995 by losing more than $1 billion on futures contracts that bet the wrong way on the direction of the Japanese stock market. The same year, a Japanese trader in the New York office of Daiwa Bank admitted to hiding losses of $1.1 billion over an 11-year period. In 1996, the acknowledged king of copper trading was fired by Sumitomo Corporation for losing an estimated $2.6 billion. Sumitomo sued a number of banks, including Chase Manhattan, UBS, J. P. Morgan, and Merrill Lynch, for issuing derivative securities that enabled the trader to hide the losses. In 2002, Allied Irish, Ireland's largest bank, reported losses of $750 million in currency trading that had been hidden by an employee who entered bogus offsetting trades.

- The usually staid mutual fund industry was roiled in 2003 when New York State Attorney General Eliot Spitzer brought charges against a number of mutual fund sponsors, including Bank of America, Putnam Investments, Janus Funds, and Strong Capital Management. These companies had allowed favored traders to make trades after the close of the business day and also to make rapid, in-and-out trades. Late trading is illegal, and most funds discourage rapid trading and have rules that prevent the practice by ordinary investors. In the case of Strong Capital Management, the founder, Richard S. Strong, not only permitted an investor, Canary Capital, to engage in rapid trading, but engaged in the practice himself. He made 1,400 quick trades between 1998 and 2003, in violation of a fiduciary duty that he, as the manager of the Strong family of funds, had to the funds' investors.

- Also in 2003, ten major investment firms paid $1.4 billion to settle charges that their analysis of securities had been slanted in order to curry favor with client companies. At the height of the Internet and telecommunications boom, the firm's securities analysts had issued reports of companies such as WorldCom and Global Crossing that subsequently collapsed. Glowing analysts' reports induced millions of people to invest billions of dollars, much of which was lost when the market bubble burst. The analysts were, in many cases, compensated for their ability to bring in investment banking business, which created a conflict of interest with their duty to offer objective evaluations of companies. Two analysts, Jack B. Grubman at Salomon Smith Barney, a part of Citigroup, and Henry Blodget of Merrill Lynch, paid large fines and agreed to lifetime bans from the securities industry for their roles in pushing companies that they knew were troubled. William H. Donaldson, then chairman of the Securities and

Exchange Commission, commented, "These cases reflect a sad chapter in the history of American business—a chapter in which those who reaped enormous benefits based on the trust of investors profoundly betrayed that trust."[2]

- The biggest scandal of all, the fall of Enron in December 2001, involved many ethical lapses. An important part of the Enron story is the set of off-balance-sheet partnerships that served both to generate phantom profits and to conceal massive debts. These partnerships were formed by Enron's chief financial officer (CFO) Andrew Fastow. For Fastow to be at once the CFO of the company and the general manager of the partnerships and thus to negotiate for both sides in deals constitutes an enormous conflict of interest—a conflict that he took advantage of to reward himself handsomely. Aside from the fact that many of the partnerships violated accounting rules and should have been consolidated on the company's books, Enron guaranteed some of the partnerships against losses with a commitment to infuse them with more stock in the event they lost value. Because the partnerships were capitalized with Enron stock to begin with, a decline in the price of Enron stock triggered massive new debt obligations. The end for Enron came quickly when investors realized the extent of the company's indebtedness.

These scandals not only undermine the public's confidence in financial markets and financial institutions but fuel a popular image of the financial world as one of greed. A 2002 Harris poll revealed that 61 percent of respondents agree that "most people on Wall Street would be willing to break the law if they believed they could make a lot of money and get away with it."[3] In addition, 57 percent believe that "Wall Street is dominated by greed and selfishness" and that people on Wall Street are not as "honest and moral as other people"; and 56 percent believe that "Wall Street only cares about making money and absolutely nothing else." These results are virtually unchanged from polls conducted annually since 1996. This image is not entirely undeserved, of course. Ivan Boesky delighted a commencement audience of business school students at the University of California at Berkeley with the assurance that greed is "all right." "I think greed is healthy," he said. "You can be greedy and still feel good about yourself."[4]

Although these examples of egregious wrongdoing and naked greed rivet our attention, they give a misleading picture of the level of ethics in finance. People in finance engage in an array of activities that involve the handling of financial assets. Not only does the welfare of everyone depend on the care and use of these assets, but millions of financial transactions take place each day with a high level of integrity. However, there are ample opportunities in finance for some people to gain at others' expense. Simply put, finance concerns other people's money (OPM), and OPM invites misconduct. Professionals in the financial services industry—such as stockbrokers, bankers, financial advisers, mutual fund and pension managers, and insurance agents—have a responsibility to the clients they serve. Financial managers in corporations, government, and other organizations have an obligation to manage the financial assets of their employers well. Everyone else involved in finance, from financial analysts to market regulators, fills positions of trust that carry certain duties.

The ethics of an occupation or a profession is best understood not by examining the worst conduct of its members but by attending to the conduct that is commonly expected and generally found. What are the standards that people in finance ought to observe? How should the inevitable ethical dilemmas in financial activities be resolved? These fundamental questions are not easily answered, and the attempt to answer them is the main task of this book. This chapter lays the groundwork for the ones that follow by explaining the need for ethics in finance and providing an overview of the main problems of finance ethics. A comprehensive treatment of ethics in finance is, of necessity, long and involved because of the diversity of financial activities and the range of ethical issues that they raise. However, there is little that is unique to financial ethics. The ethical dilemmas of finance take different forms in other areas of business and the professions, such as medicine and law. Thus, our discussion of ethics in finance can be facilitated by drawing on the well-developed fields of business and professional ethics.

The Need for Ethics in Finance

Some cynics jokingly deny that there is any ethics in finance, especially on Wall Street. This view is expressed in a thin volume, *The Complete Book of Wall Street Ethics*, which claims to fill "an empty space on financial bookshelves where a consideration of ethics should be."[5] Of course, the pages are all blank! However, a moment's reflection reveals that finance would be impossible without ethics. The very act of placing our assets in the hands of other people requires immense trust. An untrustworthy stockbroker or insurance agent, like an untrustworthy physician or attorney, finds few takers for his or her services. Financial scandals shock us precisely because they involve people and institutions that we should be able to trust.

Financial ethics is about far more than trust. However, a complete account of the need for ethics in finance is not possible in a few words. First, finance is not a clearly identifiable occupation or profession. Like medicine, law, engineering, accounting, and so on, finance involves a highly technical body of knowledge, but people who are trained in finance engage in a much wider range of activities. Accountants, by contrast, do much the same work in every setting, and the different accounting functions—public and management accounting or external and internal auditing—raise similar ethical problems that can be identified and addressed in a code of ethics. Thus, accounting ethics, like the ethics of medicine, law, and engineering, focuses on the ethical problems of a relatively uniform activity. Although codes of ethics exist for some specific fields in finance, such as financial advisers and insurance underwriters, the idea of a single code of ethics for everyone in finance is impractical.

Second, the ethics of finance is concerned not solely with the ethical problems of individuals in a specific occupation or profession but also with problems in financial markets and financial institutions. Because market regulation is concerned with fairness, financial ethics must address the question, What are fair trading practices? The financial services industry handles vast assets for clients. The ethical treatment of clients and the responsible handling of assets raise many issues in financial ethics. Finance is also a function in every business enterprise and in most nonprofit organizations and governmental units. Corporate financial managers are responsible for myriad decisions, from how best to raise and invest capital to the planning of mergers and acquisitions. Public finance, on the other hand, is concerned largely with raising and disbursing funds for governmental purposes. These tasks raise ethical dilemmas of personal conduct, as well as broad questions of public policy, when corporate and public financial decisions affect society.

Markets, clients, and personal dilemmas

Finance is concerned broadly with the generation, allocation, and management of monetary resources for any purpose. It includes *personal finance*, whereby individuals save, invest, and borrow money in order to conduct their lives; *corporate finance*, whereby business organizations raise capital, mainly through the issue of stocks and bonds, and manage it in order to engage in economic production; and *public finance*, whereby governments raise revenue by means of taxation and borrowing and spend it to provide services for their citizens. This financial activity is facilitated by *financial markets*, in which money and financial instruments are traded, and by *financial intermediaries*, such as banks and other financial service providers, which facilitate financial transactions.

Ethics in finance consists of the moral norms that apply to financial activity broadly conceived. That finance be conducted according to moral norms is of great importance, not only because of the crucial role that financial activity plays in the personal, economic, political, and social realms but also because of the opportunities for large financial gains that may tempt people to act unethically. Many of the ethical norms in finance are embodied in laws and government regulation and enforced by the courts and regulatory bodies. Ethics plays a vital role, however; first, by guiding the formation of laws and regulations and, second, by guiding conduct in areas not governed by laws and regulations. In general, moral norms reflect the conduct in financial activity that follow from fundamental ethical principles.

Despite the diversity of financial roles and activities, an understanding of the need for ethics in finance can be developed around four broad themes.

(1) *Ethics is needed in financial markets.* Financial transactions typically take place in markets and presuppose certain moral rules and expectations of moral behavior. The most basic of these is a prohibition against fraud and manipulation, but, more generally, the rules and expectations for markets are concerned with fairness, which is often expressed as a level playing field. The playing field in financial markets can become "tilted" by many factors, including unequal information, bargaining power, and resources. In addition to making one-time economic exchanges, participants in markets also engage in financial contracting whereby they enter into long-term relations. These contractual relations typically involve the assumption of fiduciary duties or obligations to act as agents, and financial markets are subject to unethical conduct because of opportunistic behavior by fiduciaries and agents. Finally, market transactions between two parties often have third-party effects, which is to say that they affect others. This is especially true of investment decisions by corporations and financial institutions. Thus, fairness in financial markets includes some consideration of the social impact of financial activity and the responsibility of financial decision makers to balance the competing interests of various groups.

(2) *Ethics is needed in the financial services industry.* The financial services industry is the most visible face of finance and the aspect that affects ordinary citizens most directly. As an industry, it has an obligation to develop products that fit people's needs and to market them in a responsible manner, avoiding, for example, deceptive or coercive sales tactics. In addition, organizations that provide financial services typically deal with individuals as clients. A reputation for ethical behavior is crucial in gaining the confidence of clients, but, more importantly, a firm owes certain duties to clients. For example, a stockbroker or an insurance agent is (or should be) more than an order-taker or a peddler in a buyer–seller environment. Such a person is offering to put special skills

and knowledge to work for the benefit of others. The people who make such offers become fiduciaries and agents who have an obligation to subordinate their own interests to those of clients. Some financial service providers may even be characterized as professionals who have stringent professional duties like those of physicians and lawyers. The main duties of professionals are to perform services with competence and due care, to avoid conflicts of interest, to preserve confidentiality, and to uphold the ideals of the professions.

(3) *Ethics is needed in financial management.* Financial managers, especially chief financial officers or CFOs, have the task of raising capital and determining how that capital is to be deployed. In a sense, a CFO, like an investment manager, is making investment decisions and developing a portfolio, but these decisions are not about which securities to hold but about what business opportunities to pursue.

Financial managers are also agents and fiduciaries who have a duty to manage the assets of a corporation prudently, avoiding the use of these assets for personal benefit and acting in all matters in the interest of the corporation and its shareholders. Specifically, this duty prohibits unauthorized self-dealing and conflict of interest, as well as fraud and manipulation in connection with a company's financial reporting and securities transactions. The major exchanges, the New York Stock Exchange and NASDAQ, as well as the Securities and Exchange Commission (SEC), require publicly held companies to have a code of ethics for their senior financial officers. Section 406 of the 2002 Sarbanes–Oxley Act specifies that companies adopt a code of ethics for senior financial officers with standards that are "reasonably necessary to promote (1) honest and ethical conduct, including the ethical handling of actual or apparent conflicts of interest between personal and professional relationships; (2) full, fair, accurate, timely, and understandable disclosure in the periodic reports required to be filed by the issuer; and (3) compliance with applicable governmental rules and regulations."

Every firm must also have a financial structure in which its capital is divided between equity, debt, and other types of obligations. All of these decisions are guided by a single corporate objective: to maximize shareholder wealth. This objective has been criticized by some who hold that it unjustly neglects the interests of other corporate constituencies. So the ethics of financial management must include a justification of the objective of shareholder wealth maximization.

(4) *Ethics is needed by finance people in organizations.* The vast majority of people in finance are employees of an organization, and they and their organizations encounter the full range of ethical problems that occur in business. These include personal ethical dilemmas, such as the situation

of the financial manager of a corporation who is instructed to overstate the return on a project in order to gain its approval, or the analyst in a brokerage firm who is pressured to withdraw a planned "sell" recommendation for the stock of a company that is also a client of the firm. Individuals who are aware of or involved in unethical and/or illegal conduct face the difficult dilemma of whether to become a *whistleblower*. Consider, for example, the situation of an employee of an investment banking firm who learns that a bribe was made to city officials to secure the business of underwriting a municipal bond offering. What is such a person obligated to do—or free to do? Now that finance is global, people in finance encounter the dilemmas that result from different practices and standards in other countries, Organizations, too, face all of these problems and must develop procedures and policies that address such topics as reporting alleged misconduct and operating abroad.

Ethics and finance theory

The need for ethics, as it has been explained so far, focuses on the practice of finance, but finance is also a theoretical body of knowledge upon which the practical application depends. Many important decisions are based on finance theory, but the contribution of theory is usually thought to be purely technical. The theory of finance is limited to answering questions about what will happen if certain decisions are made. Decision makers can be guided by this knowledge in choosing the most effective means to a given end, but the choice of ends—which belongs to the realm of ethics—is separate from finance theory. In short, finance theory, as commonly conceived, is concerned with means; ethics with ends.

Most finance theorists would insist, moreover, that finance is an objective science that depends solely on observable facts and assumes nothing about moral values. Finance theory, in other words, is completely value-free. The point is often expressed by saying that finance theory is a *positive* science which contains only statements that are verifiable by empirical evidence. Positivists hold that all sciences should exclude normative statements, which is to say statements that express a value judgment.[6]

This picture of finance theory as a purely technical, value-free science that is concerned solely with means and not ends oversimplifies a more complex reality. Financial managers often make decisions that involve both means and ends without being aware of the value commitments that are implicit in the choice of ends. The general assumptions and specific doctrines of finance theory also shape managers' perceptions of what needs to be done and how best to proceed. Thus, even if finance is concerned only with technical matters, it is very easy to slip from saying "This is" to "This ought to be." For example, the fundamental tenet of finance that the objective of the firm is to maximize shareholder wealth is very much a normative statement about what businesses *ought* to do. A complete account of the need for ethics in finance must consider, then, the ethical consequences of acting on the basis of finance theory.

Why the law is not enough

Finance is perhaps the most heavily regulated area of American business. Not only is the basic framework established by major legislative enactments, but Congress and state legislatures have also created innumerable regulatory bodies with the power to set and enforce rules. Many questionable industry practices are challenged in court, so that the judiciary plays a prominent role in determining the boundaries of acceptable conduct. And most markets and exchanges have their own private rule-setting and rule-enforcement bodies. In view of this extensive regulation, people in finance might well assume that law is the only guide. Their motto might be: "If it's legal, then it's morally okay." This motto is inadequate for many reasons. As a former SEC chairman observed, "It is not an adequate ethical standard to aspire to get through the day without being indicted."[7] A certain amount of self-regulation is necessary, not as a replacement for legal regulation, but as a supplement for areas which the law cannot easily reach and as an ideal for rising above the law.[8]

First, the law is a rather crude instrument, and it is not suited for regulating all aspects of financial activities, especially those that cannot be reduced to precise rules. For example, a law against conflicts of interest would be difficult to draft, and indeed such conflicts are not illegal except when they involve the violation of a fiduciary duty or constitute fraud. Because of the variety of conflicts, rules designed to prevent them can be effective only if individuals obey the spirit as well as the letter of these rules. Second, the law often develops as a reaction to activities that are considered to be unethical. It would be perverse to encourage people in finance to do anything that they want until the law tells them otherwise. Besides, the law is not always settled, and many people who thought that their actions were legal, though perhaps immoral, have ruefully discovered otherwise. Third, merely obeying the law is insufficient for managing an organization or for conducting business because employees, customers, and other groups expect, indeed demand, ethical treatment. The attitude that only the law applies to financial activities invites even more legislation, litigation, and regulatory attention. Self-regulation—by individuals, organizations, and markets—is not only a more effective means for securing ethical conduct on some matters but also a shrewd strategy for avoiding more onerous legal regulation.

Ethics and Financial Markets

Market transactions constitute a large portion of financial activity. Many of these are one-time trades that take place in organized exchanges, such as stock markets, commodities markets, futures or options markets, currency markets, and the like. We have already noted that the main ethical problems in market transactions arise from unfair trading practices, such as those involving fraud and manipulation, and from the unlevel playing field that can result from unequal information and other inequalities. Furthermore, financial activity includes long-term contractual relations, in which individuals and organizations become fiduciaries and agents, with the duties or obligations that attend these roles. These aspects of ethics in financial markets are discussed at greater length in the next chapter.

Financial contracting raises some additional ethical problems that are not easily settled. In the standard model of contracting, the terms of a contract specify the conduct required of each party and the remedies for noncompliance. In short, there is little "wiggle room" in a well-written contract. However, many contractual relations in finance and other areas fall short of this ideal, because actual contracts are often vague, ambiguous, incomplete, or otherwise problematic. The result is uncertainty and disagreement about what constitutes ethical (as well as legal) conduct. This section examines four areas in which financial contracting gives rise to ethical problems. These areas consist of the following: implicit contracts, imperfect contracting, remedies for breaches, and the balancing of competing interests.

Implicit contracts

The main terms of contracts are typically expressed in writing or in spoken words. No matter how detailed the agreement, however, some understandings still remain unexpressed and must be inferred. The law recognizes both *express* (written and oral) contracts and *implied* contracts, the latter of which include all manner of legally enforceable agreements. Beyond what is legally enforceable as a contract lie innumerable tacit understandings that have moral, if not legal, force. Financial affairs and business generally would be impossible if every detail of a transaction had to be specified in an express contract. Much is left implicit out of necessity. However necessary implicit contracts may be, they are the source of two ethical problems. One is that whatever is left implicit is subject to differing interpretations and disagreements, and the other is that insofar as they cannot be legally enforced, implicit contracts may be breached with impunity.

Corporations make innumerable implicit contracts with employees, customers, suppliers, and other stakeholder groups. Thus, companies are able to attract talented employees with promises of job security and loyal customers with warranties and other guarantees. Companies often gain valuable community support with pledges to be good corporate citizens. Employees and their employers may interpret guarantees of job security differently, so that a laid-off employee might consider the action to be a breach of an implicit promise. Similarly, customers might accuse a manufacturer of bad faith in failing to replace an arguably defective product. Because they can be broken without legal consequences, implicit contracts facilitate opportunistic behavior. One alleged abuse of implicit contracts occurs in successful hostile takeovers when raiders are able to finance the deal by capturing the value of the implicit contracts that the target firm has made to various groups, most notably employees and local communities. The raiders do not necessarily deny that the former managers made certain promises, but contend that the new management is not bound by these commitments.

Imperfect contracting

Although the parties to a contract attempt to strike the best bargain possible under the circumstances, they often fail to do so because of inherent limitations in our cognitive abilities. The most notable of these limitations are incomplete knowledge, bounded rationality,[9] and lack of knowledge of future contingencies. That is, contractors seldom possess all of the information that they need to make rational choices; they usually lack the ability to process even the information that is available to them; and no one can anticipate and plan for all eventualities.

One of the problems that imperfect contracting creates is that the parties may fail to negotiate contracts that produce the maximal benefit for each. Another problem is that it is difficult in some situations to specify the terms of a contract precisely because the relation itself may be too complex and uncertain to permit careful planning. Both of these problems are cited in arguments for the fiduciary duty of management to serve the interests of shareholders. Employees, customers, suppliers, and other constituencies can write reasonably precise contracts that have predictable results. Shareholders—according to this argument—cannot write such precise contracts, and so considerable managerial discretion is required to serve the shareholders' interests.

Remedies for breaches

Contracting involves two elements: (1) the planning of the relation, with attention to all of the situations that can be foreseen; and (2) the specification of the remedies that are available in the event that one party fails to perform accordingly. There is some evidence that individuals and business firms carefully plan the relation but neglect to provide for breaches.[10] As a result, many ethical and legal disputes concern the available remedies. Suppose, for example, that an employer who has made guarantees of job security as part of an implicit contract terminates a group of employees with three months' severance pay. If the implicit contract includes no provision for severance pay, then employees may grumble about inadequate compensation, while the managers may feel that they have treated the employees fairly. The ethical issue is as follows: What is fair compensation? And in the absence of any contractual agreement, some standard must be sought in more general ethical principles.

A closely related problem is the standard for performance. Remedies can be invoked only when one party has failed to live up to the agreement, but whether this has occurred may be disputed. If the terms of a contract are utterly precise, then noncompliance may be easy to determine, but contracts for more open-ended situations may call not for specific actions (such as "Do X!") but a best effort ("Try to do Y!"). Whether a party has met the "best effort" test requires some standard.[11]

The balancing of competing interests

Financial decision makers often have an identifiable obligation, such as a fiduciary duty, to serve the interests of a particular party, but this obligation does not exclude a responsibility to consider the impact of a decision on others. The extent of this responsibility, however, is open to question. If the primary obligation of a corporate finance officer, for example, is to serve the interests of shareholders, then should the fact that a decision will result in layoffs or plant closures be taken into account? It is tempting for financial managers to make purely financial judgments and leave the more difficult task of balancing interests to others, but such a neat division of responsibility is not always possible.

Furthermore, financial institutions serve many publics and wield immense power in our society. At one extreme, financial institutions have produced devastating social harm through reckless, "public be damned" activities, some of which constitute criminal conspiracies. For example, banks played a significant role in the stock-market bubble that finally burst in 2000 by their eagerness to underwrite securities offerings and to promote these securities, in some cases through biased analysis. Virtually every American bank and many foreign ones financed Enron's complex transactions, some of which were recognizable as fraudulent. Just as manufacturing firms have an obligation to avoid destructive consequences, such as polluting the environment, so too must financial institutions take care that their form of business does not inflict similar harm. Even in their normal activities, financial institutions are called upon to balance competing interests, not only in the distribution of benefits and harms but, perhaps more significantly, in the distribution of financial *risk*. Whose interests should be taken into account in making these decisions? How should competing interests be reconciled?

Many of the harms that business firms inflict on society are *externalities* or spillover effects, which are costs of production that are not borne by the producer but passed along to others. Pollution is a common externality from manufacturing, but financial activities are also capable of producing externalities. Of all financial activities, decisions about investment (which are considered in chapter 5) have the greatest potential for socially harmful consequences. Consider, for example, the impact that bank lending practices have on community development. Insofar as banks engage in *redlining*—the alleged practice of denying mortgages and home-improvement loans for properties in deteriorating neighborhoods, figuratively outlined in red on a map—they actively contribute to the process of urban decay. Banks have also been accused of discrimination by treating racial groups differently in the loan approval process. Both redlining and loan discrimination are addressed by federal legislation, such as the Home Mortgage Disclosure Act (HMDA) of 1975 and the Community Reinvestment Act (CRA) of 1977, but evidence of redlining and discrimination persists. On an international scale, the lending practices of multinational banks and global financial institutions such as the World Bank have an enormous impact on less-developed countries (LDCs). The decision to finance a dam or pipeline, for example, can advance or hinder economic development, support or undermine a government (which may be a corrupt, dictatorial regime), improve or degrade the environment, and protect or threaten the way of life of indigenous peoples. Lending institutions like the World Bank now have very sophisticated procedures for evaluating the many different consequences of their loan decisions.

The Financial Services Industry

The financial services industry provides a vast array of financial services and products to individuals, businesses, and governments. The industry itself primarily comprises major financial institutions, such as commercial banks, savings and loan companies, securities and investment banking firms, mutual fund and pension fund providers, financial planners, and insurance companies. Private partnerships, such as hedge funds, and publicly traded investment management firms, such as Warren Buffet's Berkshire Hathaway, further expand the definition of a financial services firm. In the United States, these institutions have been separated to some extent by law. The Glass–Steagall Act of 1933, for example, prohibited commercial banks from engaging in investment banking, and vice versa, but these legal barriers have been broken by new financial instruments that blur the lines between different financial institutions. The repeal of the Glass–Steagall Act in 1999 permitted further consolidation in the financial services industry, and the globalization of finance to countries with diverse legal systems allows institutions to operate differently abroad.

Firms in the financial services industry fulfil many useful purposes. They enable individuals, businesses, and governments to save and borrow, to invest for a return and to have access to capital, to insure against misfortune, and to effect major changes, such as mergers and acquisitions. These benefits are made possible by specialized services, such as the research of a stock analyst, the guidance of an investment planner, or the investment ability of a mutual fund or pension manager. The financial services industry also provides benefits through the creation of innovative products. Thus, insurance serves to reduce risk by pooling assets; money-market funds allow small investors to invest in large-denomination commercial paper, while mutual stock funds enable people of limited means to hold a diversified portfolio; and home-equity loans turn an otherwise illiquid asset into a liquid liability. In recent years, securities that bundle a group of assets, such as a pool of mortgages and derivatives, which are contracts whose value is "derived" from some underlying asset, have created new opportunities, as well as far-reaching changes.

In providing these services and products, financial services firms operate primarily as financial *intermediaries*, which is to say that they use their capital to support the provision of services rather than to trade and invest on their own behalf. For example, banks receive their revenue largely from fees charged to customers. As intermediaries which still operate in markets, financial services firms encounter virtually all of the ethical problems of market transactions and financial contracting that are presented above. Because financial services are provided to clients in a contractual relationship, most ethical issues are concerned with a firm's obligation to clients, whether these be individuals or organizations. Some practices in the client–provider relation are clearly unethical and even illegal, but others are more controversial; and every practice involves a gray area in which the lines of acceptable and unacceptable conduct are not easily drawn.

This section examines, first, the ethical problems in the financial services industry that concern the treatment of individual clients and the general public. This is followed by a consideration of the ethical issues that arise in managing financial services firms, including the special concerns of institutional investors, such as mutual fund and pension fund managers.

Serving individual clients

The ethical objections to so-called bucket-shop or boiler-room operations are obvious. In these scams, cold-calling con artists attempt to sell securities of dubious value to naive investors, using high-pressure sales tactics and false or deceptive sales pitches. Respectable brokers and agents eschew such unsavory practices. They employ much more refined ones instead.

False and misleading claims

The ethical treatment of clients requires salespeople to explain all of the relevant information truthfully, and in an understandable and nonmisleading manner. One observer complains that brokers, insurance agents, and other salespeople have developed a new vocabulary that obfuscates rather than reveals:

> Walk into a broker's office these days. You won't be sold a product. You won't even find a broker. Instead, a "financial adviser" will "help you select" an "appropriate planning vehicle," or "offer" a menu of "investment choices" or "options" among which to "allocate your money." . . . [Insurance agents] peddle such euphemisms as "private retirement accounts," "college savings plans," and "charitable remainder trusts." . . . Among other linguistic sleights of hand in common usage these days: saying tax-free when, in fact, it's only tax-deferred; high yield when it's downright risky; and projected returns when it's more likely in your dreams.[12]

Salespeople avoid speaking of commission, even though this is the source of their remuneration. Commission on mutual funds is "front-end" or "back-end loads"; and insurance agents, whose commission can approach 100 percent of the first year's premium, are not legally required to disclose this fact—and they rarely do. The agents of one insurance company represented life insurance policies as "retirement plans" and referred to the premiums as "deposits."[13]

Deception

False claims are capable of being disproved—although individual clients may not have easy access to the evidence—but deception is often a matter of interpretation. Promotional material for a mutual fund, for example, may be accurate but misleading if it emphasizes the strengths of a fund and minimizes the weaknesses. Past performance figures can be carefully selected and displayed in ways that give a misleading impression. Deception can also occur when essential information is not revealed. Thus, an investor may be deceived when the sales charge is rolled into the fund's annual expenses, which may be substantially higher than the competition's, or when the projected hypothetical returns do not reflect charges that are revealed elsewhere in the promotional material. As these examples suggest, true claims may lead a typical investor to hold a mistaken belief. Whether the claims are responsible for the false belief, however, or whether the investor has jumped too quickly to a false conclusion, is obviously a matter for further investigation.

Concealment of information

Deception aside, what information *ought* to be disclosed to a client?, Salespeople are not obligated to provide complete details on every product, and clients have some responsibility to seek out information on their own. Questions about disclosure arise in virtually all buyer–seller relations, and several different principles apply. For example, in many states, the seller of a house is required by law to reveal hidden termite damage. The rationale for a legal obligation to disclose the damage is twofold: first, the information is *material*, that is, it concerns a fact that has a significant bearing on the buyer's decision; and, second, the information cannot be readily obtained by the buyer. Of course, the buyer could hire a termite inspector, and so the law reflects the judgment that a buyer should not have to incur this expense when the information can be provided at less cost by the seller. In short, legislators have determined that a housing market is more efficient under a rule of seller disclosure than under a rule of *caveat emptor* ("let the buyer beware").

The Securities Act of 1933 requires the issuer of a security to disclose all material information, which is defined as information about which an average prudent investor ought reasonably to be informed or to which a reasonable person would attach importance in determining a course of action in a transaction. The rationale for this provision of the Securities Act is both fairness to investors, who have a right to make decisions with adequate information, and the efficiency of securities markets, which requires that investors be adequately informed. Most financial products, including mutual funds and insurance policies, are accompanied by a written prospectus that contains all of the information that the issuer is legally required to provide.

Churning, suitability, and risk

In addition to the obligation of any seller to avoid deception and to provide sufficient information, people in the financial services industry have additional obligations which derive from their role as fiduciaries or agents. The most prominent of these obligations are: to avoid excessive trading that generates commission but does not benefit the client (called "churning"), to recommend only suitable investments, and to disclose the level of risk.

Churning may be committed by a broker who executes multiple trades or trades with higher than usual commission for the purpose of generating more commission. In addition, an insurance agent may engage in what is called "twisting" by advising a client to exchange an old life insurance policy for a new one when there is little additional benefit for the policyholder but a handsome commission for the agent. Although the ethical and legal wrongs of churning are easily identified, the definition is not as self-evident. Clients who suffer losses from frequent trades often claim that their accounts were churned, but clients who gain are seldom known to complain about a broker's active trading. How can we determine whether a broker executed unwise trades solely for the commission or engaged in aggressive trading that merely turned out badly? The problem of defining churning is addressed in chapter 3.

Suitability and risk disclosure are closely related. The obligation to recommend only suitable investments for a client includes judgments of the appropriate level of risk among many other factors. In addition, brokers, agents, and other salespeople have an obligation to inform clients about the riskiness of investments. Both obligations are problematic for at least three reasons. First, is the relation merely a buyer–seller relation or an agent–principal relation? If a customer places an order with a broker to buy 100 shares of IBM stock, then, under most circumstances, the broker is being paid to execute the order and has no obligation to judge the suitability of the investment or to disclose any risk. On the other hand, if a client asks for investment advice, then the broker has an obligation to recommend only suitable investments and to explain the risk involved. Many relations fall between these poles, so that the obligations of the broker are unclear. The nature of the relation may also be a source of misunderstanding, as when a client believes that he or she is obtaining investment advice while the broker views his or her role as that of a salesperson.

Second, how far do these obligations extend? If a broker has refrained from recommending an unsuitable investment and advised the client of the significant risk, what is the broker's obligation for a client who insists on making the investment anyway? To refuse to make the trade and thereby protect a client from his or her own poor judgment would be *paternalistic*. Paternalism—which may be defined as limiting people's liberty for their own good—is generally suspect and in need of justification. Thus, requiring people to save for their retirement through Social Security is criticized for interfering in people's investment decisions, but the system is upheld on the grounds that many people lack the discipline to save. On the other hand, legalized gambling permits people to throw away their life savings at the roulette tables of Las Vegas. Should unsophisticated investors be allowed to make similar bets on complex derivatives, for example? Or do they deserve to be protected by investment professionals, who, after all, would not wish to be compared with Las Vegas croupiers?[14]

Third, judgments of suitability and risk are obviously open to interpretation. Whether an investment is suitable for a client depends on the client's financial objectives and risk preferences, the total risk and reward of the investment, and a comparison with other available investment opportunities. Although some investments are clearly unsuitable for any given client, others may fall into a gray area in which reasonable disagreement is possible. How unsuited need an investment be to be unsuitable?

The integrity of products
The financial products that firms offer to their clients and the general public should meet certain standards of integrity. Not only should they be accurately represented—which is to say, firms should avoid false, misleading, or deceptive claims and disclose relevant information, including the level of risk—but they should also be fairly priced and offer sound value. In addition, financial services firms perform a valuable function when they create innovative products that meet special needs.

An example of a controversial financial product is viatical settlements. Also called accelerated benefits or "living benefits," viatical settlements are purchases of the life insurance policy of terminally ill persons who would prefer a cash payment before death to the payment that would otherwise go at death to a beneficiary. The amount of the payment is some percentage of the face value of the policy, based on an estimate of the life expectancy of the policy holders. The purchaser, which may be an insurance company or a private investor, gains if the policy holder dies sooner than expected but may suffer a loss if the policy holder (known as a viator) lives longer. Viatical settlements are morally troubling because they appear to be bets on the life expectancy of the terminally ill. However, they provide a way for people facing death to realize the value of an asset that they may desperately need. That is, a terminally ill person, who purchased a life insurance policy in order to benefit a survivor, may now have a greater need to pay medical bills or otherwise spend money while alive. Thus, viatical settlements are potentially a great benefit for policy holders with a terminal illness. They are also subject to potential abuse inasmuch as the purchaser may take advantage of a policy holder's desperation. Whether viatical settlements are ethical, therefore, depends, in part, on the percentage of the face value that is offered to the policy holder, as well as on the consent of the beneficiary and the disclosure of all relevant information. Most states have laws on viatical settlements in order to prevent abuses, and a national organization, the Viatical Association of America, also has a Code of Ethics and Standards of Business Practice.

Managing financial institutions

Financial services firms are themselves businesses, and as such, they confront managers with typical business problems. However, the nature of the business raises special ethical concerns in the management of financial institutions. And institutional investors, such as mutual funds and pension funds, because of their large holdings, face additional ethical issues about their investment decisions.

Institutional clients

The obligations of financial services firms to individual clients that are discussed above apply to institutional clients as well. Although institutional clients are usually more sophisticated and better able to protect their own interests, they are still owed accurate and complete information and competent, reliable service. The losses on derivative transactions by Orange County, California, and by Procter & Gamble show that even sophisticated investors may be unable to understand complex financial instruments and are vulnerable to fleecing as much as naive individual investors. In addition, the size and complexity of transactions with institutional clients create special opportunities for misconduct that show the need for additional safeguards. For example, the constant need of cities to float bonds creates a lucrative municipal bond-underwriting business for many firms, and the greatest amount of business goes to the firms with the best relations with countless city governments. Until the practice, known as "pay to play," was restricted by an industry agreement, political contributions to city officials were essential for gaining access, and the leading firms still devote great resources to currying favor with city officials who are in a position to throw business their way.

In one widely publicized incident, Mark S. Ferber, a politically well-connected partner in the distinguished firm Lazard Frères, was selected to oversee the financing of a $6 billion project to clean up Boston harbor, and in this capacity he had the power to recommend the firms that would raise the money. In a secret agreement, Merrill Lynch, which obtained much of the business, agreed to split the underwriting fees with Lazard Frères, and over a four-year period, the two firms split $6 million in fees. In addition, Mr Ferber received $2.6 million in retainer payments, while Merrill Lynch garnered millions more from other clients of Mr Ferber which were steered to Merrill Lynch. An SEC commissioner described the fee-splitting arrangement as outrageous and declared, "I hire an investment adviser to give me prudent objective advice and they have a financial incentive to skew the business to a particular party? That's troubling, and if I were a client, I'd have a fit."[15]

Merrill Lynch and Lazard Frères denied that the secret agreement was improper or that they had any obligation to reveal it. Mr Ferber said, "I'm not telling you it's pretty. But there is no violation of my fiduciary responsibilities."[16] A federal judge disagreed and sentenced Ferber to 33 months in prison, in addition to a $1 million fine and a lifetime ban from the securities industry. Merrill Lynch and Lazard Frères each paid $12 million to settle charges brought by the SEC. In a parting shot, the judge chastised the firms and their lawyers for creating an environment that fostered rampant graft and corruption. As for the obligation to disclose conflicts of interest, the judge concluded, "And if this sorry lot of municipal bond attorneys do not understand it, let me spell it out: it is required that every potential conflict of interest be disclosed in writing and in detail."[17]

Conflicts of interest

Because financial institutions act as fiduciaries and agents, they frequently encounter conflicts of interest. This problem is covered in chapter 2. Of the many instances of conflict of interest in financial services, two are worth noting here. First, research analysts who work for brokerage and investment banking firms are torn occasionally between the integrity of their research and the interest of the firm. Brokerage firms are loath to offend powerful clients by lowering a "buy" recommendation to "hold" or (worse) "sell." Analysts who uncover unfavorable information that could cause a drop in the price of a client's stock are not infrequently pressured by their firm to keep quiet—or threatened after the fact with retaliation by the errant company. One writer observes "Because of a 'shoot the messenger' syndrome, it is always risky for an analyst to issue a negative report. He or she may be coerced by the investment bankers and could be cut off from the company contact."[18] In firms that underwrite initial public offerings (IPOs), the evaluation of the analysts is often lower than the rosy projections of the corporation's finance department and the firm's investment banking group. A firm that underwrites an IPO cannot issue a recommendation on the stock in the first 25 days, but after this "quiet period," the research department is expected to issue a "buy" recommendation as a "booster shot."[19] Reputable firms attempt to shield their research analysts from improper pressure, but the conflicting interests of researchers and underwriters are an unavoidable source of tension.

A second instance of conflict of interest that has received great attention concerns personal trading by fund managers. In 1995, John Kaweske, a former money manager for Invesco Funds Group, paid $115,000 to settle an SEC complaint that he had not reported 57 personal trades for himself and his wife, as required by the company's rules. Although it is not illegal for fund managers to trade, the SEC holds that they should not use their position for personal gain. Mutual fund companies are required by law to have policies and procedures on personal trading, although the details are left to each company. At Fidelity Investments, for example, fund managers are barred from buying or selling a stock for their own portfolio within seven days of trading the same stock for their funds; they must hold personal stocks for at least two months; and they cannot sell short any stock that Fidelity owns. The Fidelity policy has been criticized for encouraging fund managers to invest in stocks that are *not* in their portfolio, and that is a problem because managers can save the best prospects for themselves. The problem of personal trading by fund managers and the possible solutions raise complex issues that are covered in chapter 3.

Supervision and arbitration
Wrongdoing can occur in any organization. A key test of ethics is the organizational response. Do supervisory managers look the other way or even wink and nod at unethical sales practices by subordinates that benefit the firm? What controls are in place to detect and punish those who violate company rules? Do compensation systems and other incentives foster unethical and even illegal behavior? A legal obligation of anyone in a supervisory capacity in a securities firm is to supervise subordinates with an appropriate degree of care.

Many rogue traders, such as Nick Leeson at Barings Bank, insist that their activities were known to and condoned by their superiors, who also stood to gain by the success of these "star" traders. A former Metropolitan Life manager complained that he repeatedly warned his supervisors of widespread misconduct by the company's sales force.[20] The manager reported that nothing was done during the 1987–90 period to prevent the payment of millions of dollars in unearned sales commission that resulted when salespeople short of their goal for the year sold large policies to friends and relatives in late December. Although the buyers had no intention of keeping the policies and would return them within the 10-day free-trial period, the sale was credited for the calendar year, and the salesperson received a year-end bonus.

A major weapon of victims in most industries is the lawsuit. People who are injured by defective products, for example, can sue for actual losses as well as punitive damage. Investors, by contrast, are forced by the securities industry to waive the right to sue and to abide by the results of arbitration. This system is intended to resolve disagreements quickly, fairly, and inexpensively. In practice, however, some investors who have lost their life savings to dishonest and incompetent brokers have been denied any compensation. Opponents of the practice charge that arbitrators, who do not need to know or follow relevant laws, are often industry insiders who fail to obtain critical documents and admit irrelevant information into the process. Arbitrators' decisions, which do not need to be explained, are largely immune to appeal. Employees of securities firms are also required to submit disputes to arbitration. As a result, some women whose charges of sexual harassment have been dismissed by unsympathetic male arbitrators are unable to seek redress in the courts.[21] A congressional critic of arbitration in the securities industry has remarked, "Christians had a better chance against the lions than many investors and employees will have in the climate being created."[22]

Consumers are increasingly losing the right to sue banks, credit card companies, mortgage lenders, insurers, and other providers of financial services.[23] Many consumers are unaware that they have lost the right to sue, and those who object to compulsory arbitration are told to "take it or leave it." Compulsory arbitration can also be a headache for financial services firms. In particular, the securities industry has been concerned about large punitive damages. In response to both industry concerns and the objections of investors, an arbitration policy task force, which was formed by the National Association of Securities Dealers (NASD), issued a report in 1996 that made 70 recommendations for overhauling the system of compulsory arbitration.[24] The recommendations of this task force and the main issues in compulsory arbitration are examined in chapter 3.

Institutional investors
Trading in financial markets is now dominated by institutions such as mutual funds, insurance companies, pension funds, and private trusts and endowments. The managers of these large investment portfolios have the obvious duties of all fiduciaries, and these duties are detailed in specific legislation. Thus, the Employee Retirement Income Security Act (ERISA) of 1974 imposes very specific fiduciary duties on the managers of private pension funds. However, institutional investors encounter two unique problems that result from their role as shareholders of public corporations.

First, should institutional investors make investment decisions solely on the basis of financial factors, or should they consider socially desirable objectives? In 1994, the California Public Employees' Retirement System (CalPERS), which controls $80 billion in assets, announced that it would take into account how a corporation treats its employees in making investment decisions. The decision was based on a study which showed that companies with recommended employment practices outperformed the average for their industries by 7.5 percent, and companies with poor practices consistently lagged behind industry averages.[25] Considering the treatment of employees, therefore, is sound financial decision making, but the use of such factors involves a departure from standard balance-sheet analysis. Writing in support of the CalPERS decision, former Secretary of Labor Robert B. Reich observed:

> [M]easures of success in the capital management business have become more complicated, less dependent on traditional measures of corporate performance, and more reliant on factors previously considered intangibles. . . . The difficulty of measuring these concepts on a balance sheet simply requires analysts to look a little harder to fully assess a company's prospects.[26]

Some mutual funds, pension plans, and endowments go beyond the CalPERS position and engage in *socially responsible investing*. The aim of socially responsible investors is to hold stocks only in corporations that treat employees well, protect the environment, contribute to communities, produce safe, useful products, and, in general, exercise social responsibility. In particular, all socially responsible investors avoid the stocks of companies involved with tobacco, alcohol, and gambling (so-called "sin stocks"), and some screen out companies that are engaged in defense contracting, nuclear energy, and business with oppressive foreign regimes. Socially responsible funds enable people who are concerned with where their money is going and how it is used to invest with a clear conscience. Churches, universities, and foundations want their investment decisions to be consistent with the values that they espouse.

The right of fund managers to engage in socially responsible investing is unproblematic as long as the goals are understood and accepted by the appropriate parties. Thus, pension plans in which contributors are free to choose among socially responsible and conventional stock funds raise no ethical concerns. But do the managers of a pension plan with a single fund have a right to reject all tobacco stocks, for example? Whether fund managers can effectively screen for social responsibility and whether socially responsible funds produce satisfactory returns are further questions that are considered in chapter 4.

Second, as major shareholders in numerous corporations, institutional investors must decide what role they are going to play in corporate governance. In voting on shareholder proposals, the election of directors, amendments to the bylaws or charter, or any other matters, should institutional investors use the same purely financial criteria that guided the initial investment decision? Should they be traditional, passive investors or should they become more active participants in corporate affairs? How closely should they monitor the performance of the officers and directors of a corporation, and what should they do in the event of lagging performance? Dissatisfied individual shareholders have the option of selling their stock and switching their investment to another company. However, institutional investors are often "locked into" an investment and have no choice but to push for major changes. In recent years, institutional investors have forced CEO changes at such giant companies as American Express, Borden, General Motors, IBM, Kodak, and Westinghouse. The term *relationship investing* has been coined to describe this development. The arguments for and against relationship investing, which are examined in chapter 4, concern primarily the impact of this movement on corporate governance. Some proponents believe that more active institutional investors have the potential to restore shareholder control, while opponents are more skeptical.

Individuals in Organizations

The ethical dilemmas that arise for *individuals* in finance are typically not questions that confront the profession as a whole, such as whether a sales practice is deceptive or whether insider trading is unfair. Rather, they test one's own personal values, moral beliefs, and commitment to right action that arise from working in an organization. In short, they are organizational challenges to an individual's *integrity*.

Organizational pressures

Some of the most difficult dilemmas of business life occur when individuals become aware of questionable behavior by others or are pressured to engage in it themselves. In a survey of 30 recent Harvard University MBA graduates, many of the young managers reported that they had received "explicit instructions from their middle-manager bosses or felt strong organizational pressures to do things that they believed were sleazy, unethical, or sometimes illegal."[27] A survey of more than one thousand graduates of the Columbia University business school revealed that more than 40 percent of the respondents had been rewarded for taking some action they considered to be "ethically troubling," and 31 percent of those who refused to act in ways they considered to be unethical believed that they were penalized for their choice, compared to less than 20 percent who felt they had been rewarded.[28] The Harvard graduates do not believe that their superiors or their organizations are corrupt. The cause is rather intense pressure to get a job done and to gain approval. Ethical and even legal restraints can get lost when the overriding message is "Just do it!"

Unethical behavior can also be fostered by the culture of an organization. In *Liar's Poker*, an amusing exposé of the author's brief stint as a trader at Salomon Brothers, Michael Lewis describes the coarse pranks of a group who occupied the back row of his training class.

> There was a single trait common to denizens of the back row, though I doubt it occurred to anyone: They sensed that they needed to shed whatever refinements of personality and intellect they had brought with them to Salomon Brothers. This wasn't a conscious act, more a reflex. They were the victims of the myth, especially popular at Salomon Brothers, that a trader is a savage, and a great trader is a great savage.[29]

In the culture that Michael Lewis describes, ethical behavior is not readily fostered. He continues, "As a Salomon Brothers trainee, of course, you didn't worry too much about ethics. You were just trying to stay alive. You felt flattered to be on the same team with the people who kicked everyone's ass all the time."[30]

Wrongdoing also occurs in large organizations when responsibility is diffused among many individuals and no one person is "really" responsible. In 1985, the now-defunct brokerage firm E. F. Hutton was convicted of 2,000 counts of fraud for a check-kiting scheme in which the firm obtained interest-free use of more than $1 billion over a 20-month period by systematically overdrafting checking accounts at more than 400 banks. This check-kiting scheme began as an attempt to squeeze a little more interest from the "float" that occurs when checks are written on one interest-bearing account and deposited in another. Until a check clears, the same dollars earn interest in two different accounts. No one person created or orchestrated the practice, and yet the firm, through the actions of many individuals, defrauded banks of millions. When the check-kiting scheme began, few people were aware of the extent of the activity, and it continued, no doubt, because anyone who intervened would have had to acknowledge the existence of the fraud and take responsibility for the loss of the extra income. In addition, the participants could assure themselves that their own actions did not do any significant harm.

Leadership and ethics

Although individuals bear some responsibility for their own behavior, the leaders of firms and those in other leadership positions have a responsibility for the environment in which unethical conduct takes place. In a *Harvard Business Review* article, Lynn Sharp Paine writes:

> Rarely do the character flaws of a lone actor fully explain corporate misconduct. More typically, unethical business practice involves the tacit, if not explicit, cooperation of others and reflects the value, attitudes, beliefs, language, and behavioral patterns that define an organization's operating culture. . . . Managers who fail to provide proper leadership and to institute systems that facilitate ethical conduct share responsibility with those who conceive, execute, and knowingly benefit from corporate misdeeds.[31]

The bond-trading scandal at Salomon Brothers, for example, was not due merely to the willingness of the head of the government bond-trading department to violate the Treasury auction rules; it resulted, in large measure, from the aggressive trading culture of the firm, from a poorly designed compensation system, and from a lack of internal controls. At Salomon Brothers, some units had negotiated compensation systems in which members shared a bonus pool equal to a percentage of the total profits, while managers in other units received lesser amounts that were based, in part, on the overall performance of the firm. This system placed no cap on the bonuses of some traders and encouraged them to maximize profits without regard for the profitability of the whole firm. In addition, there were few controls to detect irregular trading by the managers of the most profitable units. The task for the new leadership of Salomon included a thorough overhaul of the whole organization.

In 2004, Marsh Inc., which calls itself "the world's leading risk and insurance services firm," was accused by the New York State Attorney General of cheating its insurance brokerage clients by rigging bids and accepting undisclosed payments from insurance companies that it recommended. As an insurance broker, Marsh advises clients on the choice of insurance companies and policies. By accepting so-called contingency commissions—which are fees of 5 to 7.5 percent of the annual premium on top of a typical 15 percent standard commission—Marsh placed into self in a conflict of interest that potentially hampered its ability to offer its clients unbiased service. This added cost of companies' insurance policies, which is arguably exorbitant for the services provided, is passed along to the public in the form of higher prices. Although contingency commissions appear to be questionable, they have gone largely unquestioned by industry leaders. Jeffrey W. Greenberg, the chairman and CEO of Marsh, issued a statement calling them a "long-standing, common industry practice."[32] Nevertheless, Marsh paid $850 million in 2005 to settle the charges, agreed to forgo the payments permanently, and issued an apology for engaging in the practice. More ethically aware leadership might have recognized the inappropriateness of contingency commissions and ended their use much earlier.

Ultimately, the level of ethics in finance depends on a complex interplay of the personal integrity of individuals, supportive cultures, ethical leadership by people in positions of responsibility, and an understanding of the ethical issues that arise in finance. This book is concerned primarily with these ethical issues, which must be understood in order to settle questions about right and wrong conduct in finance. Knowing how financial activity ought to be conducted is an essential first step toward ensuring a high level of ethics in finance, but this knowledge is of little use without personal integrity, a supportive culture, and ethical leadership.

Notes

1. James B. Stewart, *Den of Thieves* (New York: Simon & Schuster, 1991), 15.
2. Stephen Labaton, "Wall Street Settlement," *New York Times*, April 29, 2003, A1.
3. Harris Poll #60, November 6, 2002.
4. Quoted in Stewart, *Den of Thieves*, 223.
5. Jay L. Walker [pseudonym], *The Complete Book of Wall Street Ethics* (New York: William Morrow, 1987).
6. The physical sciences are generally considered to be purely positive, but whether the social sciences can or should be value-free is a subject of much dispute. Economics, for example, is divided into two distinct branches: positive economics, which is allegedly value-free, and normative economics, which explicitly assumes value judgments.
7. The remark is by former SEC Chairman Richard Breeden, which is quoted in Kevin V. Salwen, "SEC Chief's Criticism of Ex-Managers of Salomon Suggests Civil Action Is Likely," *Wall Street Journal*, November 20, 1991, A10.
8. For a discussion of the limits of law, see Christopher D. Stone, *Where the Law Ends: The Social Control of Corporate Behavior* (New York: Harper & Row, 1975).
9. The term *bounded rationality* is due to Herbert Simon, "A Behavioral Model of Rational Choice," in *Models of Man: Social and Rational* (New York: John Wiley, 1957), 241–60. Because of cognitive limitations, human beings cannot act in complex situations as the rational decision makers presupposed by economic theory. According to Simon, organizations serve to overcome the limited rationality of individual actors.

10. Stewart Macaulay, "Non-contractual Relations in Business: A Preliminary Study," *American Sociological Review*, 28 (1963), 55–67.

11. A proposal for such a standard is presented in Charles J. Goetz and Robert E. Scott, "Principles of Relational Contracts," *Virginia Law Review*, 67 (1981), 1089–150.

12. Ellen E. Schultz, "You Need a Translator for Latest Sales Pitch," *Wall Street Journal*, February 14, 1994, C1.

13. Michael Quint, "Met Life Shakes Up its Ranks," *New York Times*, October 29, 1994, C1.

14. The protection of "at risk" investors can be addressed not only by suitability rules but also by rules for securities transactions. Thus, SEC rules limit private placements and other "exempt transactions"—that is, transactions exempt from some provisions of securities law—to "accredited investors." The rationale for this limitation is discussed in chapter 2. Whether more sweeping restrictions to exclude "at risk" investors from securities markets are necessary is examined in Robert E. Frederick and W. Michael Hoffman, "The Individual Investor in Securities Markets: An Ethical Analysis," *Journal of Business Ethics*, 9 (1990), 579–89.

15. SEC commissioner Richard Y. Roberts, quoted in Leslie Wayne, "A Side Deal and a Wizard's Undoing," *New York Times*, May 15, 1994, Sec. 3, p. 1.

16. Wayne, "A Side Deal and a Wizard's Undoing," Sec. 3, p. 8.

17. Quoted in Craig T. Ferris, "Ferber Judge's Words Are Chilling Indictment of Muni Industry," *The Bond Buyer*, January 21, 1997, 27.

18. Patrick J. Regan, "Analyst, Analyze Thyself," *Financial Analysts Journal*, July–August 1993, 10.

19. W. Powers, "Why Hot, New Stocks Get Booster Shots," *Wall Street Journal*, February 10, 1993, C1.

20. Cynthia Crosson, "Met Brass Had Warnings on Abuses: Ethics Mgr.," *National Underwriter*, January 23, 1995, 3, 41.

21. For examples, see Margaret A. Jacobs, "Riding Crops and Slurs: How Wall Street Dealt with a Sex Bias Case," *Wall Street Journal*, June 9, 1994, A1, A8.

22. Margaret A. Jacobs and Michael Siconolfi, "Investors Fare Poorly Fighting Wall Street—and May Do Worse," *Wall Street Journal*, February 8 1995, A1.

23. Barry Meier, "In Fine Print, Customers Lose Ability to Sue," *New York Times*, March 10, 1997, A1, C7.

24. *Securities Arbitration Reform*, Report of the Arbitration Policy Task Force to the Board of Governors, National Association of Securities Dealers, Inc., January 1996.

25. Statement by Robert B. Reich, in "Should Investors Look Beyond the Bottom Line?" *Business and Society Review*, Fall 1994, 7.

26. Ibid., 7–8.

27. Joseph L. Badaracco, Jr, and Allen P. Webb, "Business Ethics: A View from the Trenches," *California Management Review*, 37 (Winter 1995), 8.

28. "Doing the 'Right' Thing Has Its Repercussions," *Wall Street Journal*, January 25, 1990, B1.

29. Michael Lewis, *Liar's Poker: Rising Through the Wreckage on Wall Street* (New York: W. W. Norton, 1989), 41.

30. Ibid., 70.

31. Lynn Sharp Paine, "Managing for Organizational Integrity," *Harvard Business Review*, March–April 1994, 106.

32. Gretchen Morgenson, "Hat Trick: A 3rd Unit of Marsh under Fire," *New York Times*, May 2, 2004, sec. 3, p. 1.

Chapter Two

Theoretical Perspectives in Finance

In order to analyze and resolve ethical issues in any field, we must first understand the theoretical perspectives that prevail in that field. In medical ethics, this means understanding the physician's role; in legal ethics, the adversary system. Because of the diversity of financial activity, no one perspective is all-encompassing, but two features are characteristic of the financial world, namely *market transactions* and *financial contracting*. The ethical issues in market transactions are commonly framed in terms of *fairness* or *equity*. Since fairness or equity can sometimes conflict with efficiency, a major problem in finance ethics is managing the so-called equity/efficiency trade-off. Financial contracting, by contrast, does not consist merely of one-time economic exchanges but involves the creation of ongoing relationships, in which two parties mutually agree to certain roles. In financial contracts, people often become fiduciaries or agents with certain attendant duties. For this reason, the duties of fiduciaries and agents are prominent in finance ethics. The most significant breach of the these duties occurs in conflicts of interest, in which some interest, usually a personal interest, interferes with the ability of a fiduciary or agent to fulfill the obligation to serve the interests of others.

This chapter is concerned with the three main theoretical perspectives through which most ethical issues in finance are commonly viewed: fairness in financial markets, the obligations or duties of people in financial relationships, and conflict of interest. The first section of this chapter addresses the question of what is fairness, especially in market transactions. These matters are also the subject of much of the legal regulation of markets, especially securities law. The second section deals with the obligations or duties of fiduciaries and agents, which may be characterized, in brief, as candor, care, and loyalty. Furthermore, some problems connected with agents, which are the subject of a field known as agency theory, raise important ethical considerations that are covered in the third section of this chapter. The fourth and concluding section is concerned with conflict of interest.

Equity and Efficiency

Like any market, financial markets require rules and accepted understandings in order to operate properly, and much of the necessary regulatory framework is provided by law. The Securities Act of 1933 and the Securities Exchange Act of 1934, with their many amendments, and the rules adopted by the Securities and Exchange Commission (SEC) constitute the main regulatory framework for markets in securities, and particular financial investment institutions, such as banks, mutual funds, and pension and insurance companies, are governed by industry-specific legislation.

The main aim of financial market regulation is to ensure *efficiency,* but markets can be efficient only when people have confidence in their *fairness.* Efficiency is itself an ethical value because achieving the maximum output with the minimum input—which is a simple definition of efficiency—provides an abundance of goods and services and thereby promotes the general welfare. A society is generally better off when capital markets, for example, allocate the available capital to its most productive uses. People will participate in capital markets, however, only if the markets are perceived to be fair, so that fairness has value as a means to the end of efficiency.

We also value fairness as an end in itself, and because fairness can conflict with efficiency, some choice or trade-off between the two must often be made. This unfortunate fact of life is commonly described as the *equity/efficiency trade-off.* Painful choices between efficiency and fairness (or equity), or between economic and social well-being, are at the heart of many difficult public policy decisions, but we should not lose sight of the fact that fairness contributes to efficiency even as the two conflict.

Fairness or justice is a very broad term, even when its use is restricted to financial markets. The first task of this chapter, therefore, is to identify the different ways in which transactions in financial markets can be unfair and to discover how this unfairness can be corrected. The possible ways in which individual investors and the public at large can be treated unfairly by the operation of financial markets are many, but the main kinds of unfairness can distinguished as fraud and manipulation, inequalities in information and bargaining power, and inefficient pricing.[1]

Fraud and manipulation

One of the main purposes of securities regulation is to prevent fraudulent and manipulative practices in the sale of securities. The common-law definition of fraud is the willful misrepresentation of a material fact that causes harm to a person who reasonably relies on the misrepresentation. Section 17(a) of the 1933 Securities Act and Section 10(b) of the 1934 Securities Exchange Act both prohibit anyone involved in the buying or selling of securities from making false statements of a material fact, omitting a fact that makes a statement of material facts misleading, or engaging in any practice or scheme that would serve to defraud.

Investors—both as buyers and as sellers—are particularly vulnerable to fraud because the value of financial instruments depends almost entirely on information that is difficult to verify. The buyer of a house can at least examine the house itself, but a stockholder buys solely on the basis of information about the firm. Much of the important information is in the hands of the issuing firm, and so antifraud provisions in securities law place an obligation not only on buyers and sellers of a firm's stock, for example, but also on the issuing firm. Thus, a company that fails to report bad news may be committing fraud, even though the buyer of that company's stock buys it from a previous owner who may or may not be aware of the news. Insider trading is prosecuted as a fraud under Section 10(b) of the Securities Exchange Act on the grounds that any material nonpublic information ought to be revealed before trading. However, communicating that information is often not possible in an impersonal market, and so the only recourse for an insider may be to refrain from trading.

Manipulation generally involves the buying or selling of securities for the purpose of creating a false or misleading impression about the direction of their price so as to induce other investors to buy or sell the securities. Like fraud, manipulation is designed to deceive others, but the effect is achieved by the creation of false or misleading *appearances* rather than by false or misleading *representations*.

Fraud and manipulation are addressed by mandatory disclosure regulations as well as by penalties for false and misleading statements in any information released by a firm. Mandatory disclosure regulations are justified, in part, because they promote market efficiency: Better informed investors will make more rational investment decisions, and they will do so at lower overall cost. A further justification, however, is the prevention of fraud and manipulation under the assumption that good information drives out bad. Simply put, fraud and manipulation are more difficult to commit when investors have easy access to reliable information. Mandatory disclosure regulations are generally considered to be preferable to merit regulations, such as state "blue-sky" laws that require approval of offerings from a regulatory agency in order to ensure that the prices of the securities fairly reflect their value. Although many states have enacted "blue-sky" laws with provisions for a regulatory approval based on merit, Congress specifically denied the SEC the authority "to pass on the investment merit" of any security.

Equal information

Fairness in financial markets is often expressed by the concept of a "level playing field," which requires not only that everyone play by the same rules but that they be equally equipped to compete. Competition between parties with very unequal information is widely regarded as unfair because the playing field is tilted in favor of the player with superior information. When people talk about equal information, however, they may mean that the parties to a trade actually *possess* the same information or have equal *access* to information.

That everyone should possess the same information is an unrealizable ideal, and actual markets are characterized by great information asymmetries. The average investor cannot hope to compete on equal terms with a market pro, and even pros often possess different information that leads them to make different investment decisions. Moreover, there are good reasons for encouraging people to acquire superior information for use in trade. Consider stock analysts and other savvy investors who spend considerable time, effort, and money to acquire information. Not only are they ordinarily entitled to use this information for their own benefit (because it represents a return on an investment), but they perform a service to everyone by ensuring that stocks are accurately priced. Efficient pricing reduces information asymmetries because the prices of stocks, bonds, and other financial instruments are available to all, but this kind of equal information is possible only if people with superior information are allowed to trade on it. Thus, information asymmetries are "self-correcting" because people with superior information can reap the benefit only by trading, which registers that information in the market for all to see.

The possession of unequal information strikes us as unfair, then, only when the information has been illegitimately acquired or when its use violates some obligation to others. One argument against insider trading, for example, holds that an insider has not acquired the information legitimately but has stolen (or "misappropriated") information that rightly belongs to the firm. Another argument contends that insiders have an obligation or fiduciary duty to a firm that precludes trading on insider information. (These arguments are examined in chapter 5.) In both arguments, the wrongfulness of insider trading consists not in the possession of unequal information, but in violating a moral obligation not to steal or a fiduciary duty to serve others. Insider trading can also be criticized on the grounds that others do not have the same access to the information, which leads us to the second sense of equal information, namely equal access.

The trouble with defining equal information as having equal access to information is that the notion of equal access is not absolute but relative. Any information that one person possesses could be acquired by another with enough time, effort, and money. An ordinary investor has access to virtually all of the information that a stock analyst uses to evaluate a company's prospects. The main difference is that the analyst has faster and easier access to information because of an investment in resources and skills. Anyone else could make the same investment and thereby gain the same access—or a person could simply "buy" the analyst's skilled services. Therefore, accessibility is not a feature of information itself but a function of the investment that is required in order to obtain the information.

Yet another argument against insider trading is that insiders use information that is not merely costly to obtain but that cannot be obtained by an outsider at any price. In other words, the information is inherently inaccessible. Frank H. Easterbrook and Daniel R. Fischel question this point. They ask, "If one who is an 'outsider' today could have become a manager by devoting the same time and skill as today's 'insider' did, is access to information equal or unequal?" And they conclude that there is "no principled answer to such questions."[2] The information of an insider can also be acquired by sleuthing or bribery, or merely by becoming a "tipee."

The sense of fairness that is expressed by the concept of a level playing field does not require that everyone possess the same information or have equal access to information in an absolute sense. Still, we hold that some information asymmetries are objectionable for one reason or another and ought to be corrected. From a utilitarian perspective, it could be argued that markets are more efficient when information is readily available and that we should seek to make information available at the lowest cost. To force people to make costly investments in information—or to suffer loss from inadequate information—is a dead-weight loss to the economy if the same information could be provided at little cost. Thus, the requirement that the issuance of new securities be accompanied by a detailed prospectus, for example, is intended not only to prevent fraud through the concealment of material facts but also to make it easier for buyers to gain certain kinds of information, which benefits society as a whole. Furthermore, investors, if forced to choose rules for a securities market, would realize that everyone is better off with a free flow of information.

Although efficiency and fairness both support attempts to reduce information asymmetries in financial markets, exactly what fairness or justice requires is not easy to determine. The same arguments that support a free flow of information may also justify people in taking advantage of superior information. In general, securities law aims to protect the reasonable investor from unfair advantage-taking by those with superior information, but whether any given instance of advantage-taking is unfair is open to dispute. Consider, for example, whether a geologist, who concludes after careful study that a widow's land contains oil, would be justified in buying the land without revealing what he knows.[3] A utilitarian could argue that without such opportunities, geologists would not search for oil, and so society as a whole is better off if such advantage-taking is permitted. In addition, the widow herself, who would be deprived of a potential gain, is better off in a society that allows some exploitation of superior knowledge. A difficult task for securities regulation, then, is drawing a line between fair and unfair advantage-taking when people have unequal access to information.

Equal bargaining power

Generally, agreements reached by arm's-length bargaining are considered to be fair, regardless of the actual outcome. A trader who negotiates a futures contract that results in a great loss, for example, has only himself or herself to blame. However, the fairness of bargained agreements assumes that the parties have relatively equal bargaining power. Agreements can be criticized as unfair only when one party takes undue advantage of a superior bargaining position. Whether unequal bargaining power, like unequal information, leads to unfairness is, of course, a matter of dispute.

Unequal bargaining power is an unavoidable feature of financial markets, and exploiting such power imbalances is not always unfair. In general, the law intervenes when exploitation is unconscionable or when the harm is not easily avoided, even by sophisticated investors. Little concern should be expressed, perhaps, for investors without the resources or skills for successful trading, but the success of financial markets depends on reasonably wide participation. If unequal bargaining power were permitted to drive all but the most powerful from the marketplace, then the efficiency of financial markets would be greatly impaired.

Unequal bargaining power can result from many sources—including unequal information, which is discussed above—but other sources include the following.

Resources
In most transactions, wealth is an advantage. The rich are better able than the poor to negotiate over almost everything. Prices of groceries in low-income

neighborhoods are generally higher than those in affluent areas, for example, because wealthier customers have more options. Similarly, large investors have greater opportunities. They can be better diversified; they can bear greater risk and thereby obtain higher leverage; they can gain more from arbitrage through volume trading; and they have access to investments that are closed to small investors.

For example, SEC rules permit private placements and other exempt transactions in which securities need not be registered, but these are limited to "accredited investors," who must meet certain thresholds with regard to personal wealth and investment size. These rules are designed to protect small investors by ensuring that they have access to the information that registration provides, but they also limit their investment opportunities. The private sale of large blocks of securities outside of established markets is also an investment opportunity that is available only to very large investors, which are usually institutions. The advantages of greater wealth are not usually considered to be unfair, in part because small investors can pool their resources and obtain the same benefits, by investing in a mutual fund instead of an individual portfolio, for example. Without such opportunities for small investors, however, markets that favor the wealthy would probably be regarded as unfair.

Processing ability

Even with equal access to information, people vary enormously in their ability to process information and to make informed judgments. Unsophisticated investors are ill-advised to play the stock market and even more so to invest in markets that only professionals understand. Yet the sale of "penny stocks" flourishes, despite concerted attempts to suppress this market, and respected securities firms sell complex, highly speculative partnerships and other investment vehicles to unsuspecting investors. Supposedly sophisticated investors for major corporations and governmental units have been badly burned by derivative instruments. Fraud aside, financial markets can be dangerous places for people who lack an understanding of the risks involved.

Securities firms and institutional investors overcome the problem of people's limited processing ability by employing specialists in different kinds of markets, and the use of computers in program trading enables these organizations to substitute machine power for gray matter. Program trading has been criticized mainly for introducing volatility into trading that is not warranted by the fundamentals of a market, but program trading also serves to reduce the number of investors who have any business in the financial marketplace.

Coercion

The outcome of arm's-length bargaining is considered to be fair only when the parties enter into an agreement voluntarily. Just as coercion and duress invalidate a contract, so too do they undermine the fairness of any transaction. The reason is that contracts and transactions create morally binding obligations. If a person agrees to buy something for more than it is worth, then the person is obligated to pay—and everyone else is obligated not to interfere—because the agreement reflects the will of the parties involved. If we discover that the person had been coerced into the agreement—say, by having a gun held to his or her head—then there is no longer any obligation because this transaction is not what the person, in fact, willed.

When is a person coerced? Coercion is not merely a matter of being under pressure or lacking options. Thus, a person who sells the family silver to avoid foreclosure on a home is not being coerced, nor is an investor who must sell stocks at a loss in order to meet a margin call on a failed investment. Whether offers can be coercive is an especially difficult question, because a person is always free to refuse a true offer (as opposed to the proverbial offer than cannot be refused, which is not a true offer but a thinly veiled threat). An offer can be coercive, however, if the treatment of a person falls below some moral baseline. Robert Nozick proposes the example of a slave owner who offers to stop the beatings if the slave performs some task.[4] Despite the good that is being offered—namely, to stop the beatings—the offer is coercive because the slave ought not be beaten at all. On the other hand, a employer who offers an employee a bonus to perform some disagreeable task is not making a coercive offer because the employee can refuse and not suffer any moral wrong. Roughly, then, an offer is coercive when the recipient has a right to a better offer, even though the offer itself might make the person better off.

Vulnerabilities

Investors are only human, and human beings have many weaknesses that can be exploited. Some regulation is designed to protect people from the exploitation of their vulnerabilities. Thus, consumer protection legislation often provides for a "cooling-off" period during which shoppers can cancel an impulsive purchase. The requirements that a prospectus accompany offers of securities and that investors be urged to read the prospectus carefully serve to curb impulsiveness. Margin requirements and other measures that discourage speculative investment serve to protect incautious investors from overextending themselves, as well as to protect the market from excess volatility. The legal duty of brokers and investment advisers to recommend only suitable investments and to warn adequately of the risks of any investment instrument provides a further check on people's greedy impulses.

Efficient pricing

Fairness in financial markets includes efficient prices that reasonably reflect all available information. A fundamental market principle is that the price of securities should reflect their underlying value. In the absence of efficient prices, investors are unable to form rational portfolios and the market as a whole is unable to allocate capital to its most productive uses. The mandate to ensure "fair and orderly" markets—set forth in the Securities Exchange Act of 1934—has been interpreted to authorize intervention to correct volatility or excess price swings in stock markets. Volatility that results from a mismatch of buyers and sellers is eventually self-correcting, but in the meantime, great harm may be done by inefficient pricing. Individual investors may be harmed directly by buying at too high a price or selling at too low a price during periods of mispricing, or they may be harmed indirectly by lost opportunities when they flee the market out of fear of volatility. Volatility also affects the market by reducing investor confidence, thus driving investors away, and some argue that the loss of confidence artificially depresses stock prices. At its worst, volatility can threaten the whole financial system, as it did in October 1987.

Fiduciaries, Agents, and Professionals

Although fairness in financial markets is an important and complex matter, it does not constitute the whole of financial ethics. Another prominent feature of financial activity is financial contracting, which is not merely a market transaction but the creation of a relation with attendant duties. The buyer and seller of a block of stock, for example, are parties to a market transaction in which the main ethical question is whether the exchange is fair. The broker who executes the trade for either party, by contrast, is acting in a role which requires the broker to serve a client well. The duties of a broker to a client derive not from the rules for market transactions but from a contractual relation in which the broker has agreed to assume certain duties—in return for some compensation, of course.

The contractual relations that occur in financial activity are diverse, and so the duties involved in these relations are not easily summarized. However, two distinct roles are those of fiduciaries and agents. Although finance cannot be generally characterized as a profession like medicine, law, or engineering, some roles might be accorded professional status. And so the basis for the duties of professionals has some relevance to ethics in finance. The section is concerned, then, with the duties of fiduciaries and agents, as well as those of professionals, and in particular with the duties to avoid conflicts of interest and to preserve the confidentiality of information.

Fiduciaries

A *fiduciary* is a person who has been entrusted with the care of another's property or assets and who has a responsibility to exercise discretionary judgment in this capacity solely in this other person's interest. Common examples of fiduciaries are trustees, guardians, executors, and, in business, officers and directors of corporations. Fiduciaries provide a valuable service for individuals who are unable for some reason to manage their own property or assets. Thus, a person saving for retirement might prefer that a pension fund be managed by a professional manager, who assumes the role of fiduciary. A fiduciary is part of a *fiduciary relationship*, in which the other party is the beneficiary of the fiduciary's service. And a *fiduciary duty* may be defined as the duty of a person in a position of trust to act solely in the interest of the beneficiary, without gaining any material benefit except with the knowledge and consent of this person.

A fiduciary relationship has two elements: trust and confidence. Something is entrusted to the care of a person with the confidence that proper care will be taken. A fiduciary relationship can be created by a contract, as when one person (called a *trustor*) creates a trust and another agrees to be a *trustee* who manages the trust. However, a fiduciary relationship, with its attendant duties, can be imposed by legislation. For example, the law governing pensions makes any pension fund manager a fiduciary for the intended beneficiaries, and corporate law makes officers and directors fiduciaries of the corporation and its shareholders.

Broadly, the duty of a fiduciary is to act in the interest of the beneficiary. This duty, which requires the subordination of self-interest, contrasts with market conduct, in which everyone is assumed to act out of self-interest. As Justice Benjamin Cardozo famously observed "Many forms of conduct permissible in a workaday world for those acting at arm's length, are forbidden to those bound by fiduciary ties. A trustee is held to something stricter than the morals of the marketplace. Not honesty alone, but the punctilio of an honor the most sensitive, is the standard of behavior."[5] The main principles of fiduciary duty are candor, care, and loyalty. In general, these principles involve obligations that also apply to market actors but to a higher degree for those in fiduciary relationships.

Candor

In a market, everyone has an obligation of honesty or truth-telling. It is wrong to say something false or to make a material misrepresentation. However, market actors are not required to disclose all information that others might want to know. A fiduciary, on the other hand, has a duty of candor, that is, a more extensive obligation to disclose information that the beneficiary would consider relevant to the relationship. Thus, it would be violation of a fiduciary duty for an attorney or an investment banker to conceal important information from a client (unless doing so would violate a duty to another party). Similarly, the director of a company would fail in a fiduciary duty by remaining silent about matters that are critical to a decision under discussion.

Care

When property or assets are entrusted to a fiduciary—the trustee of a trust, for example—that person should manage what is entrusted with due care, which is the care that a reasonable, prudent person would exercise. Although an extraordinary level of care is not legally required, a fiduciary is expected not to act negligently. Although market actors also have a duty of due care with respect to certain matters, this obligation governs only how the party conducts a chosen activity and not the activities that are chosen. For example, a manufacturer should exercise due care in the design and assembly of its products, but it has no responsibility of due care in the products it chooses to manufacture. A fiduciary, by contrast, has a duty to act in all matters with a high level of care. Generally, a fiduciary has a great amount of discretion in choosing how to care for that which has been entrusted, and the principle of due care for a fiduciary includes how that discretion is exercised.

Loyalty

A duty of loyalty has two aspects: it requires a fiduciary to act in the interest of the beneficiary and to avoid taking any personal advantage of the relationship. In a market transaction, there is generally no obligation to serve the interests of another except to make good faith efforts to abide by the contracts made; and gaining some personal advantage is the whole point of entering into a market transaction. In general, acting in the interest of a beneficiary is acting as the beneficiary would if that person had the knowledge and skills of the fiduciary. Taking personal advantage, by contrast, is deriving any benefit from the relationship without the knowledge and consent of the beneficiary.

An example of personal advantage-taking in a fiduciary relationship is self-dealing, as when a director or executive buys some asset from the company or sells something to it, unless it can be shown that the transaction is fair and would have occurred at arm's length. Insider trading or other personal use of confidential information gained in a fiduciary relationship is also a violation of a duty. It is wrong for a fiduciary to gain some personal benefit, even if the beneficiary is not harmed, because the fiduciary would no longer have an undivided loyalty. To have such a divided loyalty is also a conflict of interest, and so the principle of loyalty entails that a fiduciary should avoid any conflict of interest.

Conflict of interest is difficult to avoid, however, and a requirement that conflict be avoided entirely might not be desirable. For example, many directors are officers or executives of another company, and they often serve on other boards as well. To insist that directors avoid all conflict of interest would deprive companies of knowledgeable and experienced guidance. The principle of loyalty can still be honored, though, if directors act conscientiously to exercise unbiased judgment, disclose all conflicts, and refrain from participating in some decisions.

Agents

An *agent* is a party who has been engaged to act on behalf of another, called the *principal*. The agent may be a person, such as a real estate agent, or an organization, such as an advertising agency. Agency relations are due to the need to rely on others for specialized knowledge and skills. For example, selling a house requires considerable knowledge and skill, as well as time, and so a seller may engage a real estate agent to act on the seller's behalf, doing what the seller would do if that person had the real estate agent's knowledge and skills. An agent can also be authorized to affect a principal's legal relationships. For example, an authorized agent may enter into contracts that bind a principal or assume power of attorney. An agent thus becomes an extension of the principal, acting the principal's place, with a duty to use his or her abilities solely for the principal's benefit.

In some instances, the duties of an agent are simply to work as directed. Employees are agents of an employer, for example, and insofar as employees have assigned tasks, their duty is to complete these tasks with competence and care. Often, it is not possible for a principal to specify in detail what an agent is required to do. Indeed, agents are typically engaged because they know better than the principal what should be done and how it should be done. Thus, the duties of an agent, as well as a fiduciary, tend to be open-ended. That is, the specific acts that are to be performed are not fully specified in advance, and agents and fiduciaries have wide latitude or discretion in the choice of means to advance the interests of others. Aside from a positive duty of an agent to act in the interest of a principal, there is a negative duty to avoid advancing personal interests in the relationship. It would generally be a violation of an agent's duty, for example, to use the principal's property or information for personal gain.

The duty of an agent to act in the interest of a principal is, in general, not as inclusive as the duty of a fiduciary. The duties of both are limited to the scope of the engagement, but the role of an agent is usually narrower than that of a fiduciary. Thus, the duty of a broker who is acting as an agent in the sale of securities is narrower than that of a broker who is acting as a fiduciary in managing a client's portfolio. As an agent–broker, a person may not have an obligation to advise against an unwise trade, for example, but a broker–adviser, acting as a fiduciary, would have such an obligation. The difference between the two cases is the scope of the engagement, that is, the range of services that the client seeks and the broker has agreed to provide.

By agreeing to serve the interest of another, an agent, as well as a fiduciary, has a duty to avoid conflict of interest. Another important duty that gives rise to some difficult ethical dilemmas is the duty of an agent or a fiduciary to maintain *confidentiality*. The need for confidentiality arises from the fact that people in finance, in order to do their work, must have access to sensitive, privileged information, and this kind of information will generally be revealed by those who have it only under a pledge of confidentiality. This willingness can be obtained, moreover, only if the provider is assured that the information will be held in confidence and used only for the purpose for which it was provided.

Sometimes this assurance is provided by an explicit contract, such as a confidentiality agreement. It is also implicit in the agency relation. Section 395 of the *Restatement of Agency* holds that an agent has an obligation "not to use or to communicate information confidentially given him by the principal or acquired by him during the course of or on account of his agency . . . to the injury of the principal . . . unless the information is a matter of generally knowledge." The confidentiality of the physician–patient and attorney–client relationship is recognized in law, so that, except under certain circumstances, these professionals cannot be compelled to reveal confidential information in legal proceedings. The best pledge that people in finance can give, however, is information will not be revealed except as required by law.

The obligation to preserve confidentiality does not end with the agency relation but continues to exist as long as the information is confidential. Confidentiality includes not only an obligation not to *reveal* certain information without the client's or the employer's consent but also not to *use* it for any purpose other than that for which it has been provided. For example, confidentiality is breached in cases of so-called "piggyback" trading, in which a broker copies the trades of a savvy client. Assuming that the trading has no effect on stock prices, the client is unaffected.[6] However, the broker has gained a personal benefit by using knowledge of the client's trades for purposes that fall outside the relationship. The information was provided by the client for the purposes of trading, not to enrich the broker. A further problem for a bank or investment firm with competing clients is that the advisers for one side may possess information that was acquired in confidence from the other side. If the advisers reveal the information to the client or merely use it on their behalf, a breach of confidence has occurred.

The duties of professionals

The conduct of physicians, lawyers, engineers, and other professionals is governed by special professional ethics. Which occupations are professions and which are not is a subject of much dispute. Historically, the three main recognized professions have been law, medicine, and the clergy, although in recent years engineers, architects, healthcare providers, social workers, journalists, and realtors, among many other occupational groups, have claimed professional status. Certainly, not all people in finance are professionals, but some might rightly claim this status, especially those that provide specialized services to clients, such as financial advisers and insurance underwriters. Before we can determine whether anyone in finance is a professional, we need to understand the criteria for a profession.

Three features of a profession are commonly cited:

(1) *A specialized body of knowledge.* Professionals do not merely have valuable skills, like those of a plumber, but possess a highly developed, technical body of knowledge that requires years of training to acquire.
(2) *A high degree of organization and self-regulation.* Professionals have considerable control over their own work, and, largely through professional organizations, they are able to set standards for practice and to discipline members who violate them.
(3) *A commitment to public service.* The knowledge possessed by professionals serves some important social need, and professionals are committed to using their knowledge for the benefit of all.

These three features are closely related and mutually reinforcing. It is because professionals possess a specialized body of knowledge that they are given a high degree of control over their work. For the same reason, we leave it to professionals to determine what persons need to know to enter a profession and whether they know it. There is a danger in giving so much independence and power to professionals, but we have little choice if we are to enjoy the benefit of their valuable specialized knowledge. Consequently, professionals enter into an implicit agreement with society: In return for being granted a high degree of control over their work and the opportunity to organize as a profession, they pledge that they will use their knowledge for the benefit of all. Without this guarantee, society would not long tolerate a group with such independent power.

The standards of a profession include both technical standards of competence and ethical standards. Ethical standards are generally presented in a code of professional ethics, which is not only a mechanism for the self-regulation of a profession but also a visible sign of the profession's commitment to public service. A code of ethics is not an option for a professional but something that is required by the nature of professionalism itself. Developing a code of ethics is often the first step taken by an occupational group that is seeking recognition as a profession.

Is finance a profession? Merely proclaiming an occupation to be a profession does not make it so, and so any group that lays claim to professional status must provide a convincing rationale. The best case is made by financial planners and insurance underwriters, who provide highly technical services that meet some important need. Organizations such as the Institute for Certified Financial Planners (which bestows the designation of Certified Financial Planner on those who meet its standards) and the International Association for Financial Planning have developed codes of ethics that include enforcement procedures. Members of each organization are required to subscribe to the organization's code of ethics, and they can be reprimanded, suspended, or removed from membership for infractions. Organizations in the insurance industry confer the designation Chartered Property Casualty Underwriter, Chartered Life Underwriter, and Chartered Financial Consultant on their members and have detailed codes of ethics. All of the codes stress the commitment of the profession to public service and profess such ideals as integrity, objectivity, competence, diligence, confidentiality, and the avoidance of conflicts of interest.[7]

Agency Theory

Negotiating a contract is merely the beginning of a relation that requires constant monitoring. Once a bargain is struck, steps must be taken to ensure that each party abides by the agreement. Agreements in which one party has agreed to act in the interests of another, which are especially difficult to monitor, are the subject of *agency theory*. An *agency relation* is one in which one person, called the agent, agrees to act for the benefit of another, the *principal*. Agency relations are common. Physicians are agents of patients, as are professionals such as attorneys and accountants with respect to clients. All agency relations are subject to a common problem, however.

The problem with agents

The main problem with agency relations arises when a principal cannot monitor the agent's performance. In many economic exchanges monitoring is easily done. A customer who buys a pair of shoes from a cobbler, for example, can inspect the merchandise before paying, and the cobbler can retain possession of the shoes until the customer pays. The owner of a shoe factory, by contrast, is less able to ensure that the workers have fulfilled a contract that calls for a day's wages worth of labor. Paying by the hour is a solution as long as the output and each person's contribution to that output can be measured. However, in joint production, where individual contribution, as well as the total output, is difficult to determine, workers are more apt to lie down on the job. In such cases, the factory owner is forced to depend on the workers to carry out their part of the bargain. The shareholders of a corporation who hire a manager to oversee production in a factory have an even greater challenge in holding the manager to a contract because of the greater opportunities for a manager to act in his or her own interest.

The agency problem results, in part, from the inability of a principal to observe an agent's actions, but a more systemic source is the existence of *information asymmetries*. Information asymmetries refer to differences in the information possessed by the two parties and, in particular, to the superior information that agents usually possess. Patients lack the knowledge to evaluate fully the medical treatment of a physician, even though patients seek out doctors precisely because of their greater knowledge. Agency theory assumes, furthermore, that every person acts in his or her own self-interest and will give up as little as possible in any exchange. Agents can be expected, in other words, to avoid exertion if they can (called *shirking*) or to engage in *opportunism* by seizing any chance to enrich themselves at the principal's expense. Whatever a principal loses by an inability to monitor his or her agents effectively is known as *agency loss*.

Agency relations cannot be avoided entirely because we must rely on others to some extent, and we create agency relations even when they are avoidable because the benefit is great enough to offset the agency loss. Thus, the gain from hiring workers to work in a factory may still exceed the loss due to shirking. Agency loss can be reduced by investments in monitoring, and economics teaches that rational principals will spend to reduce agency loss up to the point where marginal gains equal marginal outlays. Thus, a factory owner will invest in supervisors as long as each dollar spent improves the productivity of workers by at least one dollar. However, agency loss can also be reduced by structuring relations so that agents are induced to act in the interests of principals without a need for further monitoring. Instead of increasing supervisors, for example, the factory owner can offer bonuses for reaching productivity goals. A bonus system serves to motivate workers and induce them to monitor each other. Paying managers in stock or stock options similarly serves to check their shirking and opportunism by aligning their interests more closely with the interests of the shareholders. Structuring contractual relations in ways that reduce agency loss may involve some expenditures, but these will often be less than investments in direct monitoring.

Agency theory thus shows us the importance of how financial contracts are structured. All of the costs of reducing agency loss plus the costs of the remaining (or residual) agency loss are referred to as *agency costs*, and so agency relations, if they are to be efficient, should be structured so as to reduce agency costs.

Problems of agency theory

Agency theory is clearly a powerful tool for modeling complex economic phenomena. However, any model simplifies as it clarifies. Models, of necessity, make certain assumptions, some of which may not be true but are used for their practical value. Models also focus our attention on certain aspects of the phenomena so that we "see" a complex reality in a particular way. Psychologists call this narrowing of vision a *framing effect*. A framing effect that serves the purposes of financial theory may cause us to miss important ethical aspects of complex economic phenomena.[8] Finally, the assumptions and framing effects of a model might result in mistaken solutions to problems or even incorrect assessments of the problems to be solved.

Egoism

Agency theory accepts the standard economic assumption of *egoism*, which holds that individuals seek to maximize their own perceived self-interest. In other words, we all act selfishly to get the most of whatever it is that we want. Economics does not make any value judgment about the goods that people prefer or about the selfishness that is assumed.

Most philosophers and even some economists contend that egoism is factually false. In *Passions within Reason: The Strategic Role of the Emotions*, the economist Robert H. Frank observes that people engage in altruistic behavior by giving anonymously to charity, by seeking justice for others at great trouble and expense, and by endangering themselves to help others.[9] Proponents of egoism respond that such seemingly altruistic acts still reflect what people want for themselves. This response suggests that Mother Teresa's deepest desire was to help others, so that her kind acts were done for her own (selfish) benefit. However, if nothing would count as nonselfish behavior, then egoism is a meaningless proposition. It makes sense to say that some behavior is selfish only if some nonselfish behavior can at least be imagined.

In view of this criticism, most economists hold that people have at most a general tendency to maximize their own welfare, but that the assumption of universal egoism is close enough to the truth for the purposes of economic theory. A not-quite-true assumption accepted for the purposes of a theory, however, may not be acceptable when applied to particular phenomena. In *Passions within Reason*, Robert H. Frank argues that economic life requires commitment and trust and that the single-minded pursuit of self-interest is ultimately self-defeating. Much of what we want requires the cooperation of others, and we cannot gain the benefits of cooperation without honoring commitments, being trustworthy, and in general having the kinds of feelings that have evolved to make mutually beneficial interaction possible.

The assumption of egoism in agency theory raises problems similar to those encountered in economics. Principals seek to benefit from inducing others to act as agents on their behalf. The inducement usually appeals to the agents' own self-interest (wages to workers, for example), and the main problem for the principal is to protect against shirking and opportunism by agents. The standard solutions to this problem, aside from greater inducements, are increased monitoring and more effective contractual forms (think of the use of stock options to align a CEO's interests with those of the shareholders, for example).

The framing effect of looking at agency relations in this way is apt to lead to a distrust of agents and a reliance on mechanisms of control. Such an approach is warranted in certain situations, but when applied in a business setting it may result in an overinvestment in monitoring and other contractual solutions and a corresponding underinvestment in building trust in an organization, and in fostering traits like loyalty and professionalism. Workers who are committed to their jobs and take pride in a job well done are often more productive than those who are treated as would-be shirkers and opportunists. Professionals, such as doctors, lawyers, and public accountants, are difficult to monitor because of the information asymmetries involved, and so professional ethics is all the more important for protecting principals who engage professionals as agents.

Moral hazard and adverse selection

Agency relations are subject to two additional problems that are difficult to overcome by the standard solutions, namely *moral hazard* and *adverse selection*. Agency relations arise, in part, from a lack of information about the effort or contribution of one party to a transaction. Monitoring under such conditions requires that surrogates be found in order to measure effort or contribution. Thus, managers who cannot tell at a glance how hard someone is working may look at the amount of time a person sits at a desk, with the result that workers spend more effort looking busy than being productive. The use of surrogate measures may be counterproductive by producing incentives that lead to the opposite of the desired behavior. This is the problem of moral hazard.

The term *moral hazard* developed from the problem in insurance that is created when an insured person (a driver, for example) has little incentive to be careful because the risk of an activity is borne largely by others (by the insurer, in this case, and also by hapless people in the driver's path). Moral hazard in insurance can be reduced by contractual means, such as deductibles and copayments, which share some of the risk with the insured, but insurance companies also benefit by seeking out careful, trustworthy people to insure. Similarly, employers reduce the moral hazard problem when they are able to attract loyal, hardworking employees. Potential insurants and employees have an advantage when they can persuade insurers and employers of their suitability, but attempts to do this raise the second problem.

Just as employees may attempt to look busy rather than be productive, applicants for employment have a strong incentive to appear to be suitable candidates, whatever their actual qualifications may be. As a result, potential employees do not present themselves accurately but in ways calculated to appeal to an employer. They send "signals" about their suitability for employment.[10] Employers thus have the daunting task of reading the signals and determining the qualifications of applicants accurately. A failure to do this well leads to *adverse selection*; that is, to the selection of less than the best employees. Insurers face a similar obstacle in determining the insurability of applicants who engage in signaling. Both agents and principals have a vested interest in effective signaling, but achieving this is difficult. However, signals from individuals and business firms with well-earned reputations for integrity and trustworthiness will have an edge.

The problems of moral hazard and adverse selection, which arise from agency theory, can be solved to some extent, then, by discouraging purely self-interested behavior and fostering certain ethical traits, especially those of honesty and reliability. Agency theory reminds us that self-interested behavior and the problems it creates must be taken into account, but to think only in terms of egoism may blind us to other possible solutions to these problems.

Ethical aspects of contracting

Agency theory suggests that the only ethical obligations of people in an agency relation are those that arise from the relation itself. Being a loyal agent defines the whole of morality in a firm built on agency relations, and even then, principals must constantly strive to prevent shirking and opportunism by unreliable agents. In a limited relation between a principal and an agent (a homeowner engaging a realtor, for example), fulfilling the terms of a contract may be the predominant ethical element. However, a complex set of relations, such as a nexus-of-contracts firm, has important ethical aspects that agency theory does not encompass.

First, agency theory assumes that only principals are at risk from the opportunism of agents, but agents are subject to opportunism by greedy principals. Charles Perrow observes that workers bear some risk that is not reflected in the usual description of managers as principals and workers as agents. Such a description overlooks the possibility that managers might lie to workers about the profitability of the business, falsify records of workers' output, and expose workers to hazardous working conditions, all in order to extract more profits.[11] Firms make many implicit contracts with employees that can be broken without legal consequences, so that employees are forced to depend on the good will of management. The designations of principals and agents is, to some extent, a matter of convention, and a case could be made that managers are the agents of employees in some matters. J. Gregory Dees suggests that in situations where employees are at risk, "the traditional principal–agent model of the firm could be reversed, treating the employer as the agent of her employees, providing them with . . . accurate reports of their work, safe working conditions, capital to support their efforts, and compensation in the future for work today."[12] Even in the traditional model, however, the threat of exploitation in a principal–agent relation is reciprocal, so that agents as well as principals need protection.

Second, both agents and principals are bound by the ordinary rules of morality, and so situations may arise in which the obligation of an agent to a principal conflicts with another obligation that does not depend on the agency relation. A manager would face such a conflict if, for example, a project that benefits shareholders pollutes the environment. Conflicts like these often involve *externalities* in which an activity imposes a cost on third parties. Becoming an agent, then, does not free one from all other moral constraints, and, in particular, it does not free one to impose externalities in order to benefit a principal.

Moreover, agents are limited by the same moral restraints that apply to principals themselves, and so principals have no right to engage agents to do what they themselves would not be permitted to do. In addition, two parties may each be an agent of the other in certain matters, and one party can be both a principal and an agent with respect to different parties. (Thus, a manager who acts as a principal in supervising workers may also be an agent for the workers in administering a pension plan, and the same manager is also an agent of the corporation.) Because of this complex web of agency relations, an agent may face conflicting obligations that must be weighed one against the other. For all of these reasons, then, agency relations give rise to many difficult ethical dilemmas involving conflicting obligations.

Third, agency relations themselves must meet certain standards of *fairness*. Shirking and opportunism are two kinds of unfair advantage-taking in agency relations, and much of agency theory revolves around the prevention of these two forms of unfairness. They are not exhaustive, however; principals and agents can be unfair to each other in many other ways. Contract law identifies numerous sources of unfairness in the making of contracts that lead to invalidation, including such tactics as deception, coercion, manipulation, and exploitation.[13] Thus, workers who agree to perform hazardous work when the hazards are not revealed—or, worse, when the hazards are concealed—have been treated unfairly in an agency relation. Contracts can also be unfair in their terms if they unduly favor one side or violate some right. Finally, the breaking of a contract is a form of unfairness to which agency relations are especially vulnerable because they so often involve agreements or understandings that have moral but not legal force. Thus, an employee who is legally dismissed for no good reason can legitimately complain of unfair treatment in the breaking of an implicit contract.

Agency theory achieves much of its power by simplifying the ethical obligations of agents toward principals. For the reasons just given, this model misses not only the obligations that both agents and principals have as members of society but also the many possible conflicts between agency-related obligations that arise in actual agency relations.

Conflict of Interest

Financial services could scarcely be provided without raising conflicts of interest. In acting as intermediaries for people's financial transactions and as custodians of their financial assets, financial service providers are often forced to choose among the competing interests of others—and weigh those interests against their own. Although personal interest plays some role, the conflicts of interest in financial services arise primarily from attempts to provide many different kinds of services to a number of different parties, often at the same time. Conflicts of interest are built into the structure of our financial institutions and could be avoided only with great difficulty. As one person has noted, "The biblical observation that no man can serve two masters, if strictly followed, would make many of Wall Street's present activities impossible."[14] In addition, the inhabitants of Wall Street are motivated primarily by self-interest and can be induced to serve any master only within limits. The challenge, therefore, is not to prevent conflicts of interest in financial services but to manage them in a workable financial system.

The definition of conflict of interest

Although much has been written about the definition of conflict of interest, the issues in the controversy over various definitions have little bearing on the understanding of conflicts in the financial services industry.[15] As a working definition, the following is sufficient: A conflict of interest occurs when a personal or institutional interest interferes with the ability of an individual or institution to act in the interest of another party, when the individual or institution has an ethical or legal obligation to act in that other party's interest.[16] Conflicts of interest are inherent in financial services because of the ubiquitous roles of agent and fiduciary, with their attendant duties to serve the interests of others.

Kinds of conflicts of interest
Three distinctions commonly made among conflicts of interest generally are especially relevant to conflicts in the financial services industry. First is the distinction between *actual* and *potential* conflicts of interest. An actual conflict of interest occurs when an individual or institution acts against the interest of a party whose interest that individual or institution is pledged to serve, whereas a potential conflict of interest is a situation in which an actual conflict of interest is likely to occur. Actual conflicts of interest generally constitute misconduct, but potential conflicts, while best avoided, may need to be tolerated as unavoidable features of certain situations.

Second, a distinction is made between *personal* and *impersonal* conflicts of interest. A conflict of interest is personal when the interest that actually or potentially interferes with the performance of an obligation to serve the interest of another is some gain to an individual or an institution. Thus, a lawyer who stands to benefit personally by acting against the interest of a client is in a personal conflict of interest. However, the interfering interest may also be another person's interest which an individual or institution is duty bound to serve. For example, a lawyer who has two clients with opposed interests also faces a conflict of interest, which may be described as impersonal.[17] This is the classic "two masters" problem.[18]

Impersonal conflicts are more common in the financial services industry, where firms have large numbers of clients. For example, if a broker, in managing a discretionary account, selects an inferior security because it generates a higher commission, the broker is acting in a personal conflict of interest by putting self-interest ahead of the client's interest. However, a broker who manages accounts for multiple clients may be forced to choose among the interests of these different parties when he or she decides how to allocate a security in short supply. Trust officers who manage multiple trust accounts face similar conflicts. This kind of conflict also occurs for brokers and trust officers in the utilization of market-moving information. Which accounts receive the benefit of this information, and in what order? Mutual fund advisers may be forced to decide how to allocate investment opportunities between various funds. The individuals who manage multiple accounts and funds have an incentive to favor those that are more important to them personally or to the firm, because these accounts belong to large customers, for example, or because they generate higher fees and commissions. A mutual fund adviser may allocate an especially profitable investment that is in short supply to a lagging fund in order to boost its performance or to a high-performing fund in order to gain greater publicity.

In many situations, the obligations that are owed to different parties (who may have competing interests) cannot all be fulfilled, in which case some priority must be followed in allocating gains and losses. Not every account or fund can receive a firm's undivided loyalty of the kind we expect from individual lawyers, for example. Moreover, the standard solution for a lawyer with an impersonal conflict of interest, namely to sever the relation with at least one of two competing clients, is not available to a broker or trust officer, who, of necessity, manages dozens, if not hundreds, of accounts, or to a mutual fund company, which generally offers a variety of funds.

Third, a conflict of interest may be either *individual* or *organizational*. Organizations as well as individuals act as agents and assume fiduciary duties, and an organization can fail to serve the interests of a principal or the beneficiary of a trust even when no individual is at fault. For example, if a trust officer in the trust department of a commercial bank learns that a corporate customer of the commercial bank is in financial difficulty, should he or she be permitted or required to use that information in managing trust accounts? On the one hand, a failure to use the information could result in avoidable losses for the beneficiaries of those accounts, but, on the other hand, use of the information would violate the confidentiality that the bank owes to the corporate customer. One solution is to separate the trust and commercial functions by implementing policies on information use or by constructing "Chinese walls" to prevent the flow of information.

Because financial services are delivered primarily by institutions that offer a multitude of services to multiple customers or clients, most of the conflicts of interest in this area are *potential, impersonal,* and *organizational.* They result from the deliberate design of our financial institutions and pose a problem for those responsible for creating, regulating, and managing these institutions.

Why conflicts arise in financial services

In broad terms, a conflict of interest arises for financial services providers when some interest interferes with the performance of an agency or fiduciary duty. Much the same could be said about conflicts of interest in other areas, including medicine and law. However, there is one important difference: The work of most financial services providers does not meet the standard criteria for a profession. Among the criteria for a profession which are lacking in financial services are a high degree of organization and self-regulation, a code of ethics, and a commitment to public service. These criteria are possibly met by financial planners and insurance underwriters, but not by brokers, bankers, traders, and most other people in the financial services industry, who, in the strict sense of the term, are not professionals.

As a consequence, the obligations of financial services providers are not grounded in the structure of a profession. That is, the duties of a physician can be determined by asking what it means to practice medicine, and similarly for the duties of an attorney. By contrast, the obligations of financial services providers as agents and fiduciaries cannot be derived from some general account of a profession but must be sought elsewhere. Instead of the structure of a profession, the grounding for the obligations of financial services providers is found in *financial contracting.* Providers become agents and fiduciaries as a result of specific contracts to perform agreed-on services. Within the limits imposed by law, the obligations created by these contracts can be whatever two parties conclude by mutual agreement. The duties of a broker to a customer or client, for example, can vary widely and be adjusted continuously, and a broker and any given customer may have multiple relations, each with its own contractual terms.

The law defines many roles and specifies the duties that attach to them, especially in the design of financial institutions. For example, mutual funds and pension funds must be established and operated in conformity with the relevant laws. These laws require, among other things, control by trustees, and the duties of these trustees, which vary, are specified in some detail. However, much of the law that defines the relationship between contracting parties may be regarded as default, "off-the-shelf" contracts, whose terms the parties can alter or "contract around" by mutual agreement. In general, the law specifies obligations for common, standardized roles, such as a broker, and for roles in the governance structure of financial institutions, such as trustee of a mutual fund or a pension fund. However, even when the law is fairly specific, much still remains to be negotiated in contracts for financial services.

Because the specific obligations of financial services providers are created by financial contracting, two important practical consequences follow. First, we can seldom determine whether an individual or an institution is in a potential or actual conflict of interest without knowing the precise terms of the contract between the parties. Merely knowing the roles in question is not sufficient, except when their duties are precisely specified in law. As a result, we cannot make many generalizations about what constitutes conflicts of interest for financial services providers, as we can for professionals. Judgments must be made on a case-by-case basis.

Second, self-interest is a legitimate factor in the roles of financial services providers. Unlike professionals, whose work is conducted almost entirely as a professional and is consequently subject in all its aspects to the rules of professional ethics, financial services providers operate, in part, as self-interested economic agents who legitimately engage in financial activity on their own behalf, often while they are serving as an agent or a fiduciary.

For example, a commercial bank with a trust department may be a fiduciary in the management of a corporation's pension fund at the same time that it is acting as a seller in making a commercial loan to the corporation. Similarly, an investment bank might be an investor in a takeover for which it is also raising the capital and thus be both an agent (in its financing activities on behalf of the raider) and a principal (by being an investor on its own behalf). Portfolio managers for mutual and pension funds are generally permitted to trade for their own accounts, and in so doing they are not only fiduciaries for the fund's shareholders but also active traders, competing against them. The potential for abuse in such situations is obvious.

In each instance, we could separate the functions and require those who are agents and fiduciaries to forgo all self-interested activities. Some have suggested removing trust departments from commercial banks, for example, but such proposals for restructuring our financial institutions are generally rejected on grounds of efficiency. The gain is not worth the price. Moreover, it would be difficult, as a practical matter, to insist on wholly altruistic financial services providers. Professionals can be expected to be altruistic because of their commitment to public service. Inasmuch as financial services providers primarily enable other people to make money, they cannot easily be induced to employ their special money-making skills solely for the benefit of others. Persuading them to combine self-interested and altruistic activities is perhaps the best that can be achieved.

The sources of conflicts in financial services

The conflicts of interest in financial services are too numerous to list exhaustively, and they are even difficult to classify because of the range of activities. However, one way to classify the various types of financial activities is by imagining a world of pure market transactions and identifying the need for intermediaries and custodians. To the extent that the agent and fiduciary duties of financial services providers arise from contracting in a free market, this hypothetical device provides a useful typology of financial activities within which the possibilities for conflict of interest can be classified.

If individuals conducted their financial affairs as rational economic agents in a free market, there would be no conflicts of interest because, by definition, each person in a market is legitimately pursuing his or her self-interest. No one has any obligation in a free market to serve the interests of anyone else. Hence, there are plenty of competing interests in a free market but no conflicts of interest. Of course, there are moral constraints on free-market exchanges, such as the impermissibility of force and fraud, but these constraints do not create the conditions for conflicts of interest. However, this world would be unsatisfactory for many reasons, and insofar as rational economic agents are free to form contracts that advance their interests, they would do so. It is from this kind of contracting in a free market that the conditions for conflicts of interest arise.

Financial instruments

In a free market, participants would create an array of *financial instruments* that impose obligations on both parties. For example, few people have enough money saved to buy a home. Thus, instead of exchanging money for a house in a single transaction, the buyer and seller might draft a mortgage, which is a secured long-term loan. Similarly, a farmer and a mill owner might seek to reduce the risk inherent in the grain market. A glut of grain at harvest time would depress prices and possibly ruin the farmer, whereas a shortage would raise prices to the detriment of the mill owner. Instead of waiting until harvest time and exchanging at the market price, which is risky for both parties, they might agree in advance to a futures contract for the delivery of grain at a predetermined price. Mortgages and futures contracts solve two critical problems at once, namely how to create long-term financial relationships and how to manage the risks that result from our lack of knowledge of the future.

The creation of financial instruments also creates the need for a variety of financial intermediaries to handle the complex transactions between contracting parties. More important, intermediaries are necessary because the parties may not be able to contract face to face but may require the services of a third party. For example, when a savings bank collects deposits from customers and lends the to home buyers, the two parties never meet; their "transaction" is mediated by the bank, which combines the functions of saving and lending. Similarly, the farmer and the mill owner might act independently to protect themselves by operating through a futures market. Investment banks, serving as underwriters, handle the many different tasks that are involved when a corporation issues new securities, including the task of finding buyers for the securities. Insurance companies enable large numbers of people to protect themselves from risk by pooling premiums, which are then used to satisfy claims.

Financial intermediaries act as agents, performing transactions and other activities that require specialized skills that are employed for the benefit of others. In so doing, they have an obligation to act in the principal's best interest. Thus, a broker has an obligation to achieve the best execution of a trade, and a fund manager has an obligation to select brokers who will provide the best execution. Both can be swayed by a personal or an institutional interest to make decisions that result in less than the best execution. For example, if the trust department of a commercial bank allocates the commissions for trades in trust accounts to brokerage firms that maintain a customer relation with the bank—a practice known as reciprocation, or "recip" for short—then the quality of the brokerage service might be compromised. Even if a broker customer provides the best execution, the bank has still used its power to allocate brokerage commissions, which ought to be exercised solely for the interest of the beneficiaries of the trust funds, in order to advance the bank's commercial interests. The bank might have been able to use this power in some other way that would secure a benefit to the trust beneficiaries instead of the bank itself.

Insofar as an intermediary is the custodian of funds, such as uninvested cash in a trust or brokerage account, the intermediary is also a fiduciary. Individual accounts often contain positive cash balances from the sale of securities that have not been reinvested and from funds deposited in anticipation of purchases. Although the amount in each account is often small, the aggregate amount is usually quite large. If the trust department of a commercial bank leaves uninvested cash in noninterest bank accounts, then the bank, not the individual trust beneficiary, is benefited. A brokerage firm can also deposit uninvested cash in interest-bearing accounts and claim the interest for themselves, or they can leave it in noninterest accounts in order to gain some other benefit from a bank. SEC Rule 15c-3 stipulates that uninvested cash can be used only to provide some benefit to customers, such as providing funds for purchases on margin and for short sales. However, trust departments and brokerage firms need not credit accounts for any interest or other benefits that they derive from invested cash. Brokerage firms defend these cash management practices on two grounds. First, funds left on deposit are for the convenience of the customer and not the firm—which, in any event, could derive greater income from the commissions generated by new investments. Second, the benefits they derive help keep their fees low, so that customers are credited with the income, albeit indirectly.

Trust departments are in a position to advance the interests of the parent commercial bank in many other ways. For example, in managing trust accounts, a trust department may buy the stock of important corporate clients and hold it when it would be prudent to sell. Trust departments may also cooperate with the management of corporate clients by voting proxies in favor of management and by helping management defend against hostile takeovers. Such practices are known as "customer accommodation." In their other trust activities, such as disposing of assets during probate, a bank can serve or accommodate its customers' interests (and perhaps its own) by selling property or other valuable assets to them. For example, a trust department may be required, in the probate of an estate, to sell controlling interest in a company which had been a bank customer. By selling the controlling interest to another bank customer, a continued relationship is assured.

Financial markets

In addition to financial instruments, free-market participants would seek to build *financial markets*, in which financial instruments could be issued and traded. Securities, such as stocks and bonds, are sold first in a primary market and then traded in a secondary or after market. A bond, for example, can be held to maturity, but a holder may also wish to cash out of this investment, in which case another buyer must be found. Mortgages can be exchanged between institutions and even pooled to form mortgaged-backed securities that trade in markets. The liquidity of a financial instrument, which is the ease with which it can be traded, adds to its value and reduces the risk of holding it—hence the benefit of secondary markets. Many aspects of primary and secondary markets, including the obligations of the various participants, are a matter of law, specifically the Securities Act (1933) and the Securities Exchange Act (1934). Securities markets are regulated by the Securities and Exchange Commission (SEC). However, within the legal framework established by law, the obligations of participants in financial markets are flexible and subject to negotiation.

Primary and secondary markets create many different specialized roles. A major source of business for investment banks is the underwriting of new issues of securities, including not only corporate stocks and bonds but also initial public offerings (IPOs) of formerly private companies. Underwriting itself consists of several distinct roles with accompanying obligations. An underwriter serves as adviser, analyst, and distributor. As an adviser, the investment bank is an agent, providing advice on how to structure and price the offering. As an analyst, the bank serves its own customers and the investing public by certifying the value of the securities. As a distributor, the underwriter also buys the securities for sale to its customers or, at least, conducts the sale, and it may pledge to buy any unsold portion of the offering. The commitment to sell the securities underwritten by an investment bank creates an incentive to sell the stocks or bonds to customers, whether they are suitable investments or not, and there is also a temptation to place any unsold securities in accounts that the firm manages. Because any unsold securities have been judged a poor value by informed market participants, placing them in individual accounts, without the clients' knowledge, would appear to be a violation of a firm's fiduciary duty.

The underwriting role has a built-in conflict of interest by its very nature. As an adviser to a corporate client, the bank should seek to obtain the highest price for the securities, but it serves its investment customers by obtaining the lowest price. However, this is a "virtuous" conflict of interest because the outcome is usually fairly priced securities. The investment bank must act like an auctioneer, seeking to obtain the highest price for the corporate client consistent with selling the whole offering to the bank's customers. The price, therefore, must be fair to both parties. A "vicious" conflict of interest may result, though, from the fact that the underwriter is compensated, in part, by the spread between the amount paid to the issuer and the public offering price. Thus, an underwriter has an incentive to "buy low" from the corporate client and to "sell high" to their customers.

Conflicts of interest arise for organized markets and exchanges. In the United States, there are two national stock exchanges, the New York Stock Exchange and the American Stock Exchange, as well as smaller regional exchanges. The stocks of many smaller companies trade through NASDAQ, an over-the-counter market, operated by the National Association of Securities Dealers (NASD). Other exchanges exist for bonds, commodities, futures, and other financial instruments. These organizations serve multiple constituencies and must balance the various competing interests. For example, the

NASD has recognized a conflict between its role as an association of securities brokers and dealers and as an operator of the NASDAQ market.[19]

Particular roles within organized markets and exchanges give rise to role-specific conflicts. For example, floor traders in commodities and futures exchanges are privy to market-moving information that they can exploit by timely trading on behalf of themselves or others. Such trading constitutes a misappropriation of confidential or proprietary information and is strictly prohibited. A floor trader operates in an *auction market*, which is characterized by large number of buyers and sellers trading small lots.

In an auction market, prices are known to all, and the trader operates purely as an agent in the execution of trades. By contrast, in a *dealer market*, in which large blocks of securities are traded between a few parties, trades are brokered by a dealer, known as a *block positioner*. In a dealer market, both prices and commissions are generally hidden and subject to negotiation, and the dealer may be acting as both an agent for other parties and as a principal for the firm. These conditions create potential conflicts of interest.

One market role worth noting is the *market specialist*, who has responsibility for maintaining a fair and orderly market in one or more stocks. Whenever the numbers of buyers and sellers in a stock market are mismatched, the specialist is expected to buy or sell, using his or her own inventory, in ways that approximate a market with a sufficient number of buyers and sellers. A specialist also holds a "book," which is information about calls and puts and limit orders. Because of the specialist's privileged access to the market and to sensitive information, the possibility exists for abuse. Not only can a specialist manipulate the price of stocks, but he or she is able to engage in trading as a principal with virtually no risk in so-called riskless principal transactions. For example, a specialist with an order to buy a stock when it drops to a certain price can buy the stock just above that price, with the assurance that if the price drops further the stock can be sold to the customer who placed the order. As long as the commission for the sale exceeds the loss on the transaction, the specialist takes no risk.

Advisory and management services

Active trading of securities in markets and the holding of diverse portfolios would lead free-market participants to seek an *investment adviser* and perhaps a *professional manager* for an investment portfolio. For example, a broker acts not only as an intermediary by executing trades but also an investment adviser, recommending suitable securities, and as a portfolio manager if the customer has given the broker discretionary authority to trade for the customer's account. If a broker is compensated only for executing trades, then he or she has an incentive to recommend frequent trading of (possibly) unsuitable securities, and especially to engage in excessive trading in discretionary accounts, a practice known as "churning." Similar practices occur in banking, when loan customers are urged to replace one loan with another, and in insurance, when agents persuade customers to replace one policy with another, in order to generate extra fees and commissions, These abuses are called "flipping" and "twisting," respectively, which are discussed in chapter 3.

Investment advisers, who must register with the SEC under the Investment Advisers Act of 1940, offer investment advice to the public. Because a conflict of interest is created when investment advisers are paid a commission on the investments selected by the client, some advisers attempt to remove this source of conflict by charging a flat fee. Investment banks derive a large portion of their income from advising corporate clients on a wide range of matters, including financial restructurings, mergers and acquisitions, and hostile takeovers. Because investment banks offer other services to the same clients and also have clients with competing interests, their advisory activities create multiple conflicts of interest. Finally, mutual funds, pension funds, and insurance companies provide professional management for large portfolios of securities. Two potential conflicts of interest for portfolio managers arise when they engage in personal trading for their own accounts and when they allocate commissions to brokers for the execution of trades in return for research and other nonmonetary benefits, which are covered elsewhere.

Organizational governance

Because of the complexity of providing financial services and the problem of marshaling vast resources, free-market participants would create large organizations, which require forms of governance. Just as corporate law specifies the form of governance for business corporations, so other pieces of legislation create governance structures for financial organizations. The Investment Company Act of 1940 sets forth the framework for investment companies, including mutual funds, and most private pension plans are regulated by the Employee Retirement Income Security Act of 1974 (ERISA). Each of these acts requires the fund to be under the control of trustees with a fiduciary duty to the shareholders (of a mutual fund) or the beneficiaries (of a pension fund).

The governance structure of any organization creates potential conflicts of interest, not only because of the personal interests of the responsible persons but because of the multiple roles that these persons fill. An investment banker, for example, who is a director of a corporation or a trustee of an endowment fund is offered a plethora of opportunities to advance the interests of one group to the detriment of another group's interests. Individuals who wear two or more hats may be able to compartmentalize their roles and their attendant obligations. A more difficult challenge faces institutions that attempt to fill multiple roles, in which legitimate interests are continually competing.

For example, mutual funds trustees are obligated to represent the interests of the shareholder investors of a fund. However, some are people with a close association with management who also do business with the fund in various ways. Critics have accused these trustees of paying insufficient attention to fund fees and other investor concerns and have called for a greater number of independent trustees on fund boards. Real estate investment trusts (REITs) raise special governance problems, not only because of a lack of independence among the trustees, who are often associated with the sponsoring institution, but also because of the prevalence of outside management of REITs. Unlike mutual funds, REITs can assume debt and leverage its assets, and when management fees are based on total assets of the trust, the managers have an incentive to assume more debt than may be beneficial to the investors. Because of the externalized management structure of REITs, shareholders are usually unable to evaluate the fees, which are not stated separately from REIT returns. As a result, the governance structure of REITs does not provide the degree of accountability that is present in other financial institutions.

Strategies for managing conflicts of interest

Despite the prevalence of potential conflicts of interest in financial services, the occurrence of actual conflicts has been minimized by relatively effective preventive strategies.[20] These strategies are embodied in much of the regulation of the financial services industry and in accepted industry practices. They can be conveniently classified under the headings of competition, disclosure, rules and policies, and structural changes.

Competition
Fierce competition among financial services providers for customers and clients provides a powerful incentive to avoid actual conflicts of interest and even the appearance of conflicts. Because results are critical in this competition, any source of inefficiency must be eliminated. For example, "recip" in commercial banks with a trust department has been virtually eliminated because of the need for returns on trust accounts to compare favorably with those of other trust departments and mutual funds. The allocation of brokerage commissions must be based on "best execution" rather than other institutional interests. In competing for customers by keeping fees low, trust department and brokerage firms must also employ responsible cash

management practices. It has been argued that competition prevents the abuse of soft dollars, because fund managers who misallocate them will pay a price in the marketplace.[21] Competition is still limited in some areas of the financial services industry, and perhaps conflicts could be further reduced by eliminating these barriers, by, for example, increasing the kinds of firms that could serve as trustees of pension funds.

However, competition also contributes to conflicts of interest. It is because of competitive pressures that firms branch out into related services and combine with other service providers. A bank that makes real estate mortgage loans might be tempted to sponsor a REIT, for example, despite the increased risk of conflicts. The entry of retail brokerage firms into underwriting puts them in direct competition with investment banks, thereby increasing competition, but the move also creates conflicts with their retail customer business. The mergers of retail brokerage firms with investment banks, which have been prompted by competitive pressures, give rise to even more conflicts. Furthermore, competition depends for its force on other factors, most notably disclosure. For example, unless fund earnings are properly disclosed, competition cannot exert pressure on firms to reduce conflicts of interest.

Disclosure

Disclosure as a strategy for managing conflicts of interest is generally understood as the disclosure of adverse interests, as when a politician discloses his or her investment holdings. This kind of disclosure is important in financial services. For example, a broker who is acting as a principal in a transaction is required by SEC Rule 10b-10 to disclose this fact to a customer. Section 17 of the Investment Company Act requires detailed disclosure of transaction involving "affiliated persons" who stand to gain personally from a mutual fund's activities. Under the Securities Act, the prospectus for a security must include a description of any material conflicts of interest held by the issuing parties.

However, disclosure in finance includes much more than disclosure of adverse interests. It has been noted that disclosure of performance data of all kinds, including levels of risk, facilitates competition, which in turn reduces conflicts of interest. In addition, conflicts of interest can be avoided by making known a firm's policies and procedures for dealing with conflicts. For example, if a trust department discloses its policies concerning the priority given to accounts or the treatment of uninvested cash, there need be no violation of fiduciary duty because the terms of the contract that create this duty have presumably been accepted by the trust beneficiaries. In this case, an informed beneficiary has no justified complaint if his or her account receives less attention than that of a corporate pension fund. Similarly, an investment bank can reduce conflicts of interest by announcing in advance its policies should two clients be involved in a hostile takeover.

Rules and policies

Specific rules and policies serve to reduce conflicts of interest, whether they are disclosed or not, by prohibiting conduct that constitutes or facilitates conflicts. These rules and policies may address conflicts of interest directly by requiring people to avoid conflicts of interest or by prohibiting the kinds of conduct that would constitute conflicts of interest. Other rules and policies may operate indirectly by creating conditions which reduce the possibility of conflicts of interest. For example, policies on the flow of information in any financial services firm—such as who has access to what information and who must be apprised of certain information—are vital for many reasons, including the prevention of conflicts of interest. Some commercial banks require that only the securities of sound, creditworthy corporations be selected for trust accounts. Not only is such a policy a good practice for a trust department, but it also prevents the possibility of conflict if, for example, the bank is also a creditor of a corporation in danger of bankruptcy. In such a case, the sale of the stock by the trust department might endanger the bank's commercial loans, which creates a conflict of interest.

Rules and policies have many sources, including federal and state legislatures and regulatory agencies, industry associations and exchanges, and financial services firms themselves. These rules and policies need to mesh with each other and be mutually supporting. However, the prevention of conflicts of interest is probably best achieved by financial services institutions themselves: that is, an employee's own firm provides a strong first line of oversight. Every firm is different, and each one can provide better oversight if it has the flexibility to tailor measures to its own circumstances. Also, whether any given action constitutes a conflict of interest is not always easy to determine, and judgment is required for carefully evaluating each case. Thus, broad rules and policies for the whole industry are likely to be less effective than finely crafted ones from each financial service institution.

An example of such company-imposed conflict of interest rules is the complex system governing personal trading by find managers, which is discussed in chapter 3. Although federal law mandates that mutual fund companies regulate personal trading, the exact set of rules is left for each company to develop.

Structural changes

Because so many conflicts of interest in financial services result from combining different functions in one firm, these conflicts could be reduced by structural changes that separate these functions. The existence of separate institutions for commercial and investment banks, mutual funds, and insurance companies is due to laws that mandate this separation, in part, to avoid conflicts. Many conflicts could be eliminated by separating the functions of trust management and commercial banking, of underwriting and investment advising, of retail brokerage and principal trading, and so on. Addressing the problem of conflict of interest by such radical structural changes is probably unwarranted, however, because of the many advantages of such combinations. For example, underwriting a corporation's securities requires an investment bank with substantial sales capability as well as personnel with analytical skills. The trend in the financial services industry is toward more rather than less integration.

Even within multifunction institutions, many structural changes are possible and perhaps advisable. One such change is strengthening the independence and integrity of functional units. In particular, steps can be taken to strengthen the autonomy of trust departments in commercial banks and research departments in investment banks by increasing the sense of professionalism among trust officers and research analysts. Managing the flow of information is an important factor in creating autonomy. This is done, in part, by building "Chinese walls" that create impermeable barriers between functional units. Chinese walls can also be built by policies that prohibit personnel from acting on restricted information, even if it is known. There are some drawbacks to Chinese walls, however. They take away some of the gains from integrating different functions in one firm, and firms may also lose the confidence of customers, who fear, for example, that investment advice does not represent all the information possessed by a firm. However, a customer may also benefit, by being assured that a broker's investment advice is not biased by the need to place unsold stocks in an underwriting. One significant benefit of Chinese walls to firms is increased protection against charges of insider trading.

Finally, financial services providers avoid conflicts of interest by seeking parties with independent judgment in situations in which their own judgment is compromised. Examples of such independent parties include independent trustees on the boards of mutual funds, independent appraisers in determining the value of assets in cases of self-dealing, independent actuaries in the operation of corporate pension funds, and independent proxy advisory services in deciding how to vote shares held by trusts and funds.

Conclusion

The study of conflicts of interest in financial services encompasses the duties of agents and fiduciaries in financial affairs. What are the duties of financial services providers? What undermines these duties? And what can be done to support them? These questions are as old as the biblical warning about serving two masters and as new as the latest Wall Street scandal. No comprehensive answers are possible, but a few generalizations can be made. First, the duties of financial services providers result from contracting in a free market and conflicts arise from the attempt to fulfill all the contracts made. To achieve efficiency in the delivery of financial services, we have knowingly designed institutions that make conflicts of interest unavoidable. In this process, the problems with conflicts have generally been recognized and reasonably effective measures have been developed. Although individual awareness of conflicts of interest and managerial attention to them are important, the prevention of conflicts must also involve government, the industry, and especially financial services firms. At the present time, two main problems remain. These are deciding how to make the trade-off between efficiency and the reduction of conflicts and finding solutions that give the desired results.

This chapter has considered the three main theoretical perspectives in finance ethics—fairness in market transactions, the obligations or duties of people in financial contracting, and conflict of interest—which provide a foundation for examining specific ethical issues in financial markets, financial institutions, and financial management. Although finance ethics involves many complex and difficult issues, virtually the whole of ethics in finance can be reduced to two simple rules: "Be fair (in market transactions)!" and "Keep your promises (made in contracts)!" Since one promise that is often made in finance is to serve the interests of others, the rule "Keep your promises!" includes a third rule, "Avoid conflicts of interest!" However, as the subsequent chapters illustrate, determining what is fair in market transactions, what are the obligations of people in financial relationships, and how to avoid or manage conflicts of interest are very challenging tasks.

Notes

1. Much of this section is derived from Hersh Shefrin and Meir Statman, "Ethics, Fairness and Efficiency in Financial Markets," *Financial Analysts Journal*, 49 (November–December 1993), 21–9.
2. Frank H. Easterbrook and Daniel R. Fischel, *The Economic Structure of Corporate Law* (Cambridge, MA: Harvard University Press, 1991), 254.
3. The example is taken from Anthony Kronman, "Contract Law and Distributive Justice," *Yale Law Journal*, 89 (1980), 472–9.

4. Robert Nozick, "Coercion," in Sidney Morgenbesser, Patrick Suppes, and Morton White, eds, *Philosophy, Science and Method* (New York: St Martin's Press, 1969), 440–72.
5. *Meinhard v. Salmon*, 164 N.E. 545, 546 (1928).
6. Arguably, the client may have "lost" by unknowingly giving away valuable investment advice that might have been sold to the broker.
7. For a comprehensive collection of codes of ethics, including those in finance, see Rena A. Gorlin, ed., *Codes of Professional Responsibility*, 4th edn. (Washington, DC: Bureau of National Affairs), 1999.
8. This point is made in J. Gregory Dees, "Principals, Agents, and Ethics," in Norman E. Bowie and R. Edward Freeman, eds., *Ethics and Agency Theory* (New York: Oxford University Press, 1992), 25–58. Much of the discussion in this section is derived from this work.
9. Robert H. Frank, *Passions within Reason: The Strategic Role of the Emotions* (New York: W. W. Norton, 1988). For other works that challenge the egoistic assumption of economics, see Robert Axelrod, *The Evolution of Cooperation* (New York: Basic Books, 1984); Amartya Sen, *On Ethics and Economics* (Oxford: Blackwell, 1987); and E. S. Phelps, ed., *Altruism, Morality, and Economic Theory* (New York: Russell Sage, 1975).
10. The concept of signaling was introduced by Michael A. Spence, who suggested that employees may seek a certain education, and employers may hire people with that education not because the education needed for the job, but because it is a reliable indicator of successful employment. Michael A. Spence, "Job Market Signaling," *Quarterly Journal of Economics*, 87 (1973), 355–74. Robert H. Frank discusses the importance of morality for effective signaling in *Passions Within Reason*, 96–113.
11. Charles Perrow, *Complex Organizations: A Critical Essay* (New York: Random House, 1986), 227.
12. Dees, "Principals, Agents, and Ethics," 37.
13. In contract law, these sources of unfairness are expressed by the concepts of duress, fraud, and unconscionability. See Dees, "Principals, Agents, and Ethics," 41.
14. Warren A. Law, "Wall Street and the Public Interest," in Samuel L. Hayes, III, ed., *Wall Street and Regulation* (Boston: Harvard Business School Press, 1987), 169.
15. Michael Davis, "Conflict of Interest," *Business and Professional Ethics Journal*, 1 (1982), 17–27; Neil R. Luebke, "Conflict of Interest as a Moral Category," *Business and Professional Ethics Journal*, 6 (1987), 66–81; John R. Boatright, "Conflict of Interest: An Agency Analysis," in Norman E. Bowie and R. Edward Freeman, eds., *Ethics and Agency Theory: An Introduction* (New York: Oxford University Press, 1992), 187–203. For criticism of these works, see Thomas L. Carson, "Conflict of Interest," *Business and Professional Ethics Journal*, 13 (1994), 387–404; Michael Davis, "Conflict of Interest Revisited,"

Business and Professional Ethics Journal, 12 (1993), 21–41, with replies by John R. Boatright and Neil R. Luebke.

16. This definition is adapted from John R. Boatright, *Ethics and the Conduct of Business*, 5th edn. (Upper Saddle River, NJ: Prentice Hall, 2007), 131–4.

17. Rule 1.7(a) of the American Bar Association's *Model Rules of Professional Conduct* labels a situation in which a lawyer represents clients with opposing interests a conflict of interest.

18. *Matthew* 6:24. "No man can serve two masters: for either he will hate the one and love the other, or else he will hold to the one, and despise the other."

19. Speech by Mary L. Shapiro, president, NASD Regulation, Inc., Vanderbilt University, Nashville, Tennessee, April 3, 1996.

20. This is a conclusion of a set of reports on conflicts of interest in the securities markets commissioned by the Twentieth Century Fund and published together in *Abuse on Wall Street: Conflicts of Interest in the Securities Markets* (Westport, CT: Quorum Books, 1980).

21. D. Bruce Johnsen, "Property Rights to Investment Research: The Agency Costs of Soft Dollar Brokerage," *Yale Journal on Regulation*, 11 (1994), 75–113.

Chapter Three
Ethical Issues in Financial Services

The financial services industry still operates largely through *personal selling*. Although more and more investors are sending their money in envelopes to faceless mutual funds and dealing with banks via cash machines and 800 numbers, many people still buy and sell securities through a broker whom they know personally. Most people know their insurance agents personally and deal with financial planners, tax advisers, and other finance professionals face-to-face. Personal selling creates innumerable opportunities for abuse, and although finance professionals take pride in the level of integrity in the industry, misconduct still occurs. However, customers who are unhappy over failed investments or rejected insurance claims, for example, are quick to blame the seller of the product, sometimes unfairly.

There are "bad apples" in every business, of course, but many critics fault the industry itself. Critics cite the need for better training of sales personnel, more stringent rules and procedures, more aggressive oversight, more disclosure to investors, and changes in the compensation system. The full-service brokerage business is facing a crisis as wary customers, who have felt vulnerable relying on individual brokers, now have many options for their investment dollars. Mutual funds and even banks now offer investors the opportunity to invest without the fear of being "ripped off" by a broker.

This chapter examines a broad range of issues facing the financial services industry in building customer confidence and ensuring a high level of integrity in personal selling. A general discussion of unethical sales practices involving deception, manipulation, and concealment is followed by an in-depth look at churning by brokers and similar abuses by insurance agents and loan officials. Many clients of brokerage firms are required, as a condition of opening an account, to submit disputes to arbitration, and this requirement, along with alleged abuses in the arbitration process, has prompted a controversy that is covered in this chapter. The chapter concludes with a consideration of two ethical issues in mutual funds: the problem of mutual fund managers who trade for their own account and the recent scandals involving late trading and market timing by investors.

Sales Practices

Two real estate limited partnerships launched by Merrill Lynch & Co. in 1987 and 1989 lost close to $440 million for 42,000 investor-clients.[1] Known as Arvida I and Arvida II, these highly speculative investment vehicles projected double-digit returns on residential developments in Florida and California, but both stopped payments to investors in 1990. At the end of 1993, each $1,000 unit of Arvida I was worth $125, and each $1,000 unit of Arvida II a mere $6.

Not every investment is a success, of course, and aggressive investors reap higher rewards for assuming greater risk. However, the Arvida partnerships were offered by the Merrill Lynch sales force to many retirees of modest means as safe investments with good income potential. The brokers themselves were told by the firm that Arvida I entailed only "moderate risk," and company-produced sales material said little about risk, while emphasizing the projected performance. Merrill Lynch advised its own brokers that the Arvida funds were appropriate for investors with $30,000 in income and a $30,000 net worth, or with a $75,000 net worth—which is to say, most of the brokers' clients. Left out of the material was the fact that the projections included a return of some of the investors' own capital, that the track record of the real estate company was based on commercial, not residential projects, and that eight of the top nine managers of the company had left just before Arvida I was offered to the public.

Merrill Lynch insists that the brokers acted properly in selling the Arvida limited partnerships to clients, but several questions can be raised about the firm's sales practices. First, were some investors *deceived* by the brokers' sales pitches? The prospectus for an offering is typically scrutinized by the SEC and the issuing firm's legal staff in order to ensure full disclosure of all legally required information. However, investors seldom read all of the fine print and do not always understand what they do read. Much of their understanding of an investment comes from conversations with brokers, and here there is ample opportunity for deception. Second, did the Merrill Lynch brokers have a responsibility to protect the interests of their clients? At one extreme, brokers can be viewed as sellers of a product whose obligations do not extend beyond those of any seller, which include, of course, a prohibition on deception. The other extreme is to view brokers as agents who are pledged to advance the interests of clients to the best of their abilities. However, the responsibilities of brokers lie at neither extreme and vary with the client and circumstances.

What is ethical and unethical in sales practices is difficult to determine in detail because of the many kinds of sellers in the financial services industry. The situation of stockbrokers is different from that of insurance agents or financial planners, for example. Selling is done both by person-to-person contact (including cold calling) and by more anonymous mass-media advertising and direct-mail promotion. However, two issues are ever present, namely whether a sales practice is deceptive and the extent of a seller's responsibility to protect the buyer.

Deception and concealment

Deception is a broad term without clear boundaries. The Federal Trade Commission (FTC) was charged by Congress in 1914 with the task of protecting consumers from deceptive advertising, and the Commission struggles to this day to develop an adequate definition. Federal securities law prohibits practices that would "operate as a fraud or deceit" on a person; the Investment Company Act, which regulates mutual funds, contains similar language; and state insurance laws also prohibit fraud and deception in the sale of insurance. Most legal action has focused on fraud, with the result that the concept of deception in finance lacks a clear legal definition.

Despite the vagueness of the term, some guidelines have been developed for identifying deception. In general, a person is deceived when that person holds a false belief as a result of some claim made by another. That claim may be either a false or misleading statement or a statement that is incomplete in some crucial way. Even if every claim made by Merrill Lynch brokers is literally true, deception is still possible if the clients formed mistaken beliefs because of statements made or not made. Indeed, some investors in the Arvida limited partnerships claimed that the distinction between return *on* capital and a return *of* capital was not clearly explained to them, and that, as a result, they misunderstood the cash-flow projections. In short, the investors complained that the brokers' sales pitches were deceptive.

Conditions for deception
The FTC, the SEC, and other regulators employ a three-factor test: (1) How reasonable is the person who is deceived? (2) How easily could a person avoid being deceived? And (3) how significantly is the person harmed by the deception?

First, some people are more easily deceived than others, and some claims could mislead only a few, rather gullible individuals. Regulations that seek to protect even the most ignorant consumer would prohibit all but the most straightforward of claims and would severely hamper advertising and promotion. Regulators have generally employed a *reasonable person* standard that asks whether a customer or client of ordinary intelligence and knowledge would draw a mistaken conclusion from a claim. For example, advertising for credit cards and bank loans often features a low "teaser" rate that applies for an initial period. Even though the attractive rate is featured prominently in advertisements, a reasonable person, it is assumed, can read the fine print and compare the various offers. On the other hand, a misleading comparison of mutual fund performance that would lead even careful readers to conclude that a poorly performing fund is superior to the competition is arguably deceptive.

Second, potentially deceptive claims that can be easily countered by readily accessible information are less objectionable than claims that most people can accept only at face value. Information on mutual fund performance is so widely available—albeit in confusing abundance—that a single misleading comparison is not as serious as a misstatement of the fees for a particular fund, since this is information that an investor can obtain only from a company's own material. Third, deception that would lead a person to suffer a significant financial loss or some other grave harm is of greater concern to regulators. For this reason, claims about finance and health care receive more scrutiny than claims about, say, clothing or perfumes, and misleading claims for home-equity loans, where a person's home is at risk, are more likely to be considered deceptive than equally misleading claims for credit cards or installment loans.

False and misleading claims, which are generally easy to identify, are morally objectionable because they are forms of dishonesty. More problematical is the concealment of information, because whether a claim is false or misleading is a matter of fact, whereas what information *ought* to be revealed involves a value judgment. Furthermore, the moral objection to concealment is not that concealing certain information is dishonest but that it is *unfair*. Whether a sales practice is deceptive cannot be determined, therefore, without considering the conditions for fair market transactions. (Some of these conditions are discussed in chapter 2, but the focus there is on fairness in financial markets rather than on fairness in sales practices.)

Market theory generally considers economic exchanges to be fair if each party makes a *rational choice*—or at least has the opportunity to make a rational choice.[2] Consequently, sales practices in finance are unfair, and hence deceptive, when they substantially interfere with the ability of people to make rational choices about financial matters. The concept of rational choice in economics is complicated, but the details need not concern us here.[3] It is sufficient to note that economic theory assumes that in any economic trans-action, each party gives up something (a cost) and receives something in return (a benefit). In addition, economic actors make choices that produce (or are expected to produce) the greatest net return for themselves. In short, economic actors are assumed, to be egoistic utility maximizers.

This concept of economic rationality further presupposes that:

(1) both the buyer and the seller are capable of making a rational choice;
(2) both the buyer and the seller have sufficient information to make a rational choice; and
(3) neither the buyer nor the seller is denied the opportunity to make a rational choice (this condition excludes coercion, for example).

All three of these conditions are fraught with difficulties. A misleading claim may constitute manipulation, and thus cross a line between legitimate persuasion and illegitimate coercion. But where should that line be drawn? The capacity for rational choice is an uncertain standard, not only because many people are unsophisticated about financial matters but because even experienced investors may not understand complex transactions. This condi-tion does not specify how people who are unable to make a rational choice should be treated. Who is responsible for protecting vulnerable investors? Should they be barred from certain markets? Finally, what is sufficient infor-mation? And who has an obligation to ensure that an investor is sufficiently informed? (The concept of materiality, which is introduced in chapter 2, provides an answer to the former question, but not the latter.)

Examples for analysis
In order to examine some of the difficulties in the conditions for fair market exchanges that bear on whether claims are deceptive, consider the following situations:

(1) A brokerage firm buys a block of stock prior to issuing a research report that contains a "buy" recommendation in order to ensure that enough shares are available to fill customer orders. However, customers are not told that they are buying stock from the firm's own holding and they are charged the current market price plus the standard commission for a trade.
(2) A broker assures a client that an initial public offering (IPO) of a closed-end fund is sold without a commission and encourages quick action by saying that after the IPO is sold, subsequent buyers will have to pay a 7 percent commission. In fact, a 7 percent commission is built into the

price of the IPO, and this charge is revealed in the prospectus but will not appear on the settlement statement for the purchase.

(3) The names of some mutual funds do not accurately reflect the fund's true investment objectives. One study showed that fewer than two-thirds of the funds classified as "growth and income" performed in a manner that is consistent with that investing style. However, the investment objectives of any fund are stated in the prospectus, and the current portfolios of all active funds are available for inspection.[4]

(4) Insurance companies that sell variable annuities are permitted by the SEC to advertise with charts that project hypothetical returns that do not include "mortality and expense risk" (M&E) charges for insurance coverage.[5] These charges, which range from 1.27 percent to 1.4 percent annually, must be disclosed in the text of all advertising. The insurance industry contends that omitting M&E charges from the hypothetical returns is necessary in order for investors to compare their variable annuities with those offered by mutual fund companies, which do not contain any insurance coverage.

First, we can ask whether any information would have a significant bearing on an investor's purchasing decision. That is, is the information *material*? If an investor decides to purchase shares of stock in response to a "buy" recommendation, it matters little whether the shares are bought on the open market or from a brokerage firm's holdings. The price is the same. An investor might appreciate the opportunity to share any profit that is realized by the firm (because of lower trading costs and perhaps a lower stock price before the recommendation is released), but the firm is under no obligation to share any profit with its clients. To do so, moreover, would invite the charge of favoring some clients over others. (However, the practice of amassing holdings in advance of a "buy" recommendation is criticized as a form of insider trading because a firm buys stock with knowledge of a not-yet-released analysts' report.)

On the other hand, a client might be induced to buy an initial offering of a closed-end mutual fund in the mistaken belief that the purchase would avoid a commission charge. The fact that the commission charge is disclosed in the prospectus might ordinarily exonerate the broker from a charge of deception, except that the false belief is created by the broker's claim, which, at best, skirts the edge of honesty. Arguably, the broker made the claim with an intent to deceive, and a typical, prudent investor is apt to feel that there was an attempt to deceive.

Second, information about the investment objective of a mutual fund is material by any reasonable standard, but has the threshold for full disclosure been achieved by statements in the prospectus? The name of a fund conveys some information, but unless the description is highly inaccurate (such as a speculative junk-bond fund called "The Widows and Orphans Secure Income Fund"), it is questionable whether investors are seriously harmed. Investment objectives are difficult to state in a name, and so it is not unreasonable to expect investors to read the prospectus for this information.

Fund-tracking firms, such as Lipper Analytical, Morningstar, and Value Line, classify mutual funds, so that some of the responsibility for any deception and part of any remedy rests with the classifying by these firms. The SEC and the National Association of Securities Dealers (NASD) have examined the situation and have concluded that the benefits of greater regulation for investors do not outweigh the costs, especially given the practical difficulties of devising adequate guidelines. (For example, nondescriptive fund names would deprive investors of one form of communication about investment objectives.) The debate on whether fund names are deceptive revolves around utilitarian considerations, namely the seriousness of the harm and the costs and benefits of the proposed remedies.

Third, the question of whether insurance companies should be permitted to use charts that omit M&E charges is debated mainly in terms of *fair competition* with mutual funds. Variable annuities are essentially mutual funds with tax-deferred contributions. One SEC official explained: "For purposes of understanding what the tax effect would be, you have to show the returns [of both insurance company and mutual fund variable annuities] net of all charges. It levels the playing field."[6] Critics complain that some M&E charges are ordinary fund management expenses that mutual funds must reflect in charting hypothetical returns. If so, then omitting M&E charges tilts the playing field in favor of the insurance companies. However, both sides agree on the proposition that disclosure rules should promote fair competition between variable-annuity providers and enable consumers to compare the products of these providers in easily understood presentations.

The responsibility to protect

What is the obligation of brokers, agents, or other salespersons in finance to protect the interests of those who buy financial products? Certainly, a broker, for example, should not exploit a naive or inexperienced client, but does a broker have a strong positive obligation, like that of a physician or a lawyer, to act solely for the benefit of others? The responsibility of a broker to protect may not extend this far, but neither is a broker merely a salesperson. A broker may not be a shepherd protecting a flock, but the broker's role is not merely to shear the sheep.

The responsibility of any salesperson can range from *caveat emptor* to paternalism. However, *caveat emptor* ("let the buyer beware") is not the rule of the modern marketplace because every seller is bound by a substantial body of law, including the Uniform Commercial Code, which requires "honesty in fact and the observance of reasonable commercial standards of fair dealing in trade." According to the Uniform Commercial Code, sellers also warrant that their products are of an acceptable level of quality and fit for the purpose for which they are ordinarily used. The underlying assumption is that a seller generally has superior knowledge, so that it is more cost effective to place the burden of consumer protection on sellers rather than buyers of products. If a sales clerk at a hardware store has a legal obligation to protect consumers in the sale of a wrench, then it is not unreasonable to expect at least as high a level of conduct from a broker selling limited partnerships.

However, the focus of a seller's obligations is on the product itself and on the way in which it is represented. The decision to buy is left to the buyer, and the typical seller has no obligation to ensure that the buyer makes a wise choice. An underlying assumption of the market system is that buyers are the best judge of their own interests and should be free to make their own decisions once they are fully informed. The alternative is *paternalism*, which is generally deplored as an unjustified limitation on people's freedom. However, a responsibility to protect clients—and hence some paternalism—is supported by two considerations. One is that the broker is more than a seller when he or she is serving as an adviser because an agency relation is thereby created by a kind of contract. The other consideration is that people are generally more vulnerable in making investment decisions than in making typical consumer purchases, so that a failure to protect their interests may be regarded as abuse or unfair advantage-taking. These two considerations raise the questions: What is the nature of the relation between a salesperson and a client or customer? And what constitutes abuse?

Unfortunately, these questions are difficult to answer without examining specific cases because each one is different. Aside from the responsibility of all sellers in a buyer–seller relation, some responsibilities are imposed as a matter of market efficiency or public policy. Thus, there is concern that pushing unprepared investors into stock mutual funds endangers the market if they are not prepared to withstand a long downturn. Perhaps the main basis of the responsibility of any seller of financial products and services is the "shingle theory." Under this theory, many different relations are possible, but any seller should be held to whatever level of responsibility he or she offers in "hanging out a shingle" and thereby opening up a business. Thus, to call oneself a broker is to create a certain expectation of competent and fair treatment.

For example, investment advisers represent themselves to clients as objective, independent consultants who will offer, for a fee, sound investment advice. Some advisers are "fee-only," which is to say that they seek to gain further client confidence by advertising that they do not accept commission or other compensation for investments made on behalf of clients. Whether investment advisers who are not "fee-only" have an obligation to reveal commissions and other compensation is more problematical. Another interesting example of a broker's obligation to clients is the case of soft-dollar brokerage.

Soft-dollar brokerage

Soft-dollar brokerage, or simply soft dollars, is an arrangement in which brokerage firms offer institutional investors products and services other than the execution of trades. Institutional investors, such as mutual funds and pension funds, pay a commission to brokerage firms to execute trades of securities. In addition to executing trades, brokerage firms offer some institutional investors noncash credits for other products and services, most commonly proprietary research. These products and services are typically provided by a third party, such as research firms, and are paid for in cash by the brokerage firm. The noncash credits for these products and service are called soft dollars.

This arrangement began in the 1950s with the growth of institutional investors during a period of fixed commissions for securities traded on the New York Stock Exchange. Barred from competing for volume customers by offering lower commissions, brokerage firms offered various nonprice benefits, including research services, in lieu of lower commission rates. After the system of fixed commissions was abolished in May 1975, the practice of soft dollars continued. Although commission rates declined after that date and customers could pay for only the execution of trades, soft-dollar arrangements continued to be an important form of competition among brokerage firms and a significant source of resources for institutional investment funds.

The legislation ending fixed commissions, the Securities Act Amendments of 1975, reiterated that fund managers have a fiduciary duty to secure the "best execution" of trades, which includes paying low commissions. However, Section 28(e) created a "safe harbor" that allows soft-dollar arrangements as long as the managers believe in good faith that a higher-than-market commission is "reasonable in relation to the value of the brokerage and research services provided."

For such a little-known practice, soft dollars has received a surprising amount of moral concern, with one observer claiming that it did not pass "the smell test."[7] Soft dollars was the subject of a 1998 report by the Securities and Exchange Commission,[8] and in the same year the Association for Investment Management Research issued extensive guidelines for soft-dollar arrangements.[9]

Moral criticism of soft dollars has two sources. First, soft dollars is a virtually invisible process that appears to depart from the ideal of arm's-length economic transactions. In soft-dollar arrangements, the managers of institutional investment funds seem to be paying brokers more than necessary for executing trades and receiving other benefits in return. The costs of execution and research are bundled together in ways that other parties (mutual fund investors, for example) may not be aware of and cannot easily evaluate. Expressed in the terms of agency theory, investors (the principals) have the task of monitoring fund managers (their agents). The lack of transparency and market forces makes the monitoring of fund managers by investors more difficult. As a result, investors either suffer the agency costs of inadequate monitoring or else are forced to incur additional monitoring costs. That transactions should be unbundled and made transparent are key elements not only of sound financial practice but of effective monitoring.

Second, investment fund managers, as fiduciaries, have a fiduciary duty to act in the best interests of a fund's investors. This includes obtaining "best execution" and using any soft dollars solely for the benefit of a fund's investors. However, soft dollars appears to create incentives for fund managers to advance their own interests or the interests of a fund's advisor to the detriment of investors. This would be not only a violation of fiduciary duty but an unacceptable conflict of interest. Fund managers might unjustly enrich themselves through soft-dollar arrangements by engaging in excessive trading or "churning" designed merely to generate more soft dollars. They might also use soft dollars for purposes other than research that benefits a fund's investors, and, finally, the benefit from soft dollars may make managers more careless about monitoring the quality of a brokerage firm's execution. All of these possibilities would violate the "safe harbor" provision of Section 28(e), but critics of soft dollars complain that the vagueness of this law leaves investors with inadequate protection.

Some defenders of soft dollars argue that these moral concerns are misplaced and that soft-dollar brokerage is not only morally justified but economically sound.[10] First, to the criticism that the practice tempts fund managers to violate their fiduciary duty to seek "best execution" and use any soft dollars in the investors' interest, defenders argue that the intense competition in institutional investing would punish fund managers who did not use all resources for the benefit of investors. Second, they argue that instead of increasing the monitoring costs of investors, soft dollars aligns the interests of investors and fund managers because fund managers are in a better position than investors to monitor the execution of trades by brokerage firms.

This agency argument is rather complex, but the debate between critics and defenders can be settled ultimately only by an empirical comparison of fund performance. If funds that use soft dollars produce superior returns to those that do not, then their practices, including soft dollars, would appear to be more efficient. The evidence to date is that soft dollars has a slightly positive correlation with fund performance, which suggests that the practice succeeds in solving investors' agency problem.[11]

Critics of soft dollars generally favor two measures: restricting the scope of Section 28(e), thus giving fund managers less of a "safe harbor," and mandating greater disclosure of soft dollar practices. Defenders of soft dollars would expand the scope of Section 28(e), thus giving fund managers greater discretion in making arrangements with brokerage firms. Although they are not opposed to greater disclosure in principle, some defenders question the usefulness of this information for investors and whether the cost would exceed the benefit.

Churning, Twisting, and Flipping

The variety of abuses in the financial services industry has spawned a colorful vocabulary that is more appropriate to con artists than dedicated professionals. No one in the industry defends these practices, and firms diligently guard against them. Nevertheless, rogue employees and occasionally whole organizations are guilty of these unsavory tactics, and the record of the industry in punishing the perpetrators and compensating the victims has not been exemplary. The offending individuals often switch jobs and continue their misconduct, and firms generally fight complaints vigorously rather than settle them justly. Churning, twisting, flipping, and other abusive practices stain the reputation of the financial services industry and undermine public confidence.

Given that these practices are unethical and usually illegal, the main ethical questions are what constitutes churning, twisting, and so on, and what ought to be done to prevent them. Churning is wrong by definition, but there may be honest differences of opinion on whether losses in a portfolio are due to churning by the broker or to the client's own mistakes or inattention. Brokers and their firms may be victimized by disgruntled investors who seek to recover their losses by falsely charging that their accounts were churned.[12] Similar problems attend twisting and flipping. What separates these unethical practices from aggressive but ethical selling of insurance policies or consumer loans?

The ethical issues

First, some definitions. *Churning* is defined as excessive or inappropriate trading for a client's account by a broker who has control over the account, with the intent to generate commission rather than to benefit the client. *Twisting* refers to the practice by insurance agents of persuading a policyholder to replace an older policy with a newer one that provides little if any additional benefit, but generates a commission for the agent. Typically, in twisting, the cash value of an old ordinary or straight life insurance policy is used to finance the new policy. The corresponding tactic in the consumer loan business is called *flipping*. A loan officer who "flips" a customer manages to replace an existing loan with a new one that usually provides the customer with some additional cash. Since new loans are accompanied by numerous fees, flipped loan customers may end up paying as much in fees as they receive in loan proceeds. In one case, an illiterate retiree with equity in a home was flipped ten times in a four-year period as an original $1,250 loan grew to $45,000.[13] The victim paid $19,000 in loan fees for the privilege of borrowing $23,000, so that fees constituted a whopping 83 percent of the loan proceeds.

The poor are frequent targets of other abuses by loan providers. In 1989, ITT Consumer Financial Corporation settled suits in many states for pressuring loan customers to add on various "options," including credit, property, and term life insurance and membership in the ITT Consumer Thrift Club.[14] In 1997, Sears, Roebuck & Co. was charged with unfair credit-card collection practices for persuading customers whose debts had been legally wiped out by personal bankruptcy to pay the outstanding balances anyway.[15] Sears admitted that it had used "flawed legal judgment" in not filing the documents (called "reaffirmation agreements") with the bankruptcy court, as required by law.

Although churning occurs, there is disagreement on the frequency or the rate of detection. The brokerage industry contends that churning is a rare occurrence and is easily detected by firms as well as clients. No statistics are kept on churning, but complaints to the SEC and various exchanges about unauthorized trading and other abuses have risen sharply in recent years. In 1995, SEC chairman Arthur Levitt, who has been especially critical of the compensation system in the securities industry, commissioned a report on compensation practices that concluded that churning was "at the heart of many of the concerns" that it heard over the past year.[16] The report identified some "best practices" in the industry that might prevent churning, including ending the practice of paying a higher commission for a company's own products, prohibiting sales contests for specific products, and tying a portion of compensation to the size of a client's account, regardless of the number of transactions. Some critics of the industry cite May 1, 1975, as a major turning point in the treatment of small investors because on that day (called "Mayday" by worried brokers) the industry changed from fixed commissions to variable, negotiated commissions. In 1995, an SEC panel concluded that the commission system "is too deeply rooted" to be significantly changed and recommended better training and oversight by brokerage firms.

The ethical objection to churning is straightforward: It is a breach of a fiduciary duty to trade in ways that are not in a client's best interests. Churning, as distinct from unauthorized trading, occurs only when a client turns over control of an account to a broker, and by taking control, a broker assumes a responsibility to serve the client's interests. An insurance agent or a loan officer, like a broker who merely recommends a trade, is not acting on behalf of a client or customer and is more akin to a traditional seller. The ethical fault with twisting and flipping, then, is that they violate the ethics of the buyer–seller relation. Typically, these practices involve deception or unfair advantage-taking or both, and they are often facilitated by building a relation of trust that is then abused. The courts have generally refused to enforce grossly one-sided contracts by employing a test of conscionableness. An unconscionable agreement may be defined loosely as one that no person in a right frame of mind would accept and no honest person would offer.

What is churning?

Despite clear-cut instances of churning, the concept is difficult to define. Some legal definitions offered in court decisions are: "excessive trading by a broker disproportionate to the size of the account involved, in order to generate commissions,"[17] and a situation in which "a brokers, exercising control over the frequency and volume of trading in the customer's account initiates transactions that are excessive in view of the character of the account."[18] Federal suits under Section 10(b) of the Securities Exchange Act of 1934 have raised the question of the need to establish that a broker traded with the intention of generating commission rather than benefiting the client. The legal term is *scienter*, which is "a mental state embracing intent to deceive, manipulate, or defraud."[19] In *Ernst & Ernst v. Hochfelder* (1976), the Supreme Court held that *scienter* is a necessary element of churning. The legal definition of churning contains three elements, then: (1) the broker controls the account; (2) the trading is excessive for the character of the account; and (3) the broker acted with intent *(scienter)*.

Whether a broker has control of an account or is trading at the direction of the client is often a source of dispute. A broker is not authorized to control an account and to trade without explicit directions unless the client has signed a statement giving approval. However, many brokers who have the authority to control an account still consult with the client and seek approval for specific trades. Thus, a broker may claim that the questionable trades were made with the knowledge and consent of the client. Some brokerage firms seek to cover themselves by sending "comfort" or "happiness" letters when a broker's manager notes unusual trading activity. These letters typically thank the client for doing business with the firm, express the hope that the client is satisfied, and specifically solicit suggestions for improvement. Although clients often discard these letters as junk mail, the firm may use them later to show that any excessive trading was approved by the client and that the broker did not have control.

The most difficult issue in the definition of churning is the meaning of "excessive trading." First, whether trading is excessive depends on the character of the account. A client who is a more speculative investor, willing to assume higher risk for a greater return, should expect a higher trading volume. Second, high volume is not the only factor; pointless trades might be considered churning even if the volume is relatively low. Examples are "in-and-out" trading or "switching," in which one stock is replaced by another with similar characteristics, and cross trading, in which blocks of stock are transferred between two similar accounts. In addition, a broker who does not cancel a customer's call at its expiration but exercises the option and then immediately sells the stock could garner two commissions while making no change in a client's portfolio. Third, churning might be indicated by a pattern of trading that consistently favors trades that yield higher commissions. Common to these three points is the question of whether the trades make sense from an investment point of view. High-volume trading that loses money might still be defended as an intelligent but unsuccessful investment strategy, whereas investments that represent no strategy beyond generating commission are objectionable, no matter the amount gained or lost.

Several attempts have been made to quantify excessive trading on the basis of the *annualized turnover ratio* (ATR) of a portfolio.[20] An often cited measure is the 2–4–6 rule, whereby a turnover during any period that is proportionate to buying and selling twice the value of a portfolio during a year (ATR = 2) is considered to be possible churning. When there is a fourfold annualized turnover ratio (ATR = 4), churning is presumed, and an ATR of 6 is conclusive proof of churning. The 2–4–6 rule takes no account of the variation in turnover that is due to the character of the account. An alternative that considers this factor is a measure based on the mean annualized turnover rate of mutual funds with investment objectives that match those of the investor.[21] Specifically, the proposal is that churning occurs when the ATR is equal to the mean for the appropriate category of mutual funds plus twice the standard deviation. If aggressive growth mutual funds have a mean ATR of 0.9 and a standard deviation of 1.3, then the ATR of the portfolio of a client who wants aggressive growth should not exceed 3.5 [ATR = 0.9 + (2 × 1.3)].

Neither of these quantitative measures serves to define churning.[22] First, the measures are arbitrary. Although 2–4–6 is plausible, why not 1–3–5, or any other similar sequence of numbers? Second, churning could conceivably occur when the turnover ratio is substantially less than any given figure, and not occur when the turnover ratio is substantially higher. In short, the reasonableness of the trades must be taken into account. Third, the use of any numerical measure is potentially dangerous because it might encourage commission-driven trading up to any permissible limit. At the same time, a rigid numerical measure might discourage legitimate, potentially profitable trading in a client's account for fear of being charged with churning. For these reasons, a court declared in one important case, "Churning cannot and need not be established by any one precise rule or formula."[23]

Suitability

Churning, twisting, flipping, and other abusive practices are not indicated merely by the volume of transactions but by their suitability. A brokerage account with a high volume of suitable trades might not be considered a case of churning, whereas an account with a lower volume of unsuitable trades might be. Of course, a single recommendation, in which churning is not alleged, can also be unsuitable. In general, brokers, insurance agents, and other salespeople have an obligation to recommend only suitable securities and financial products. However, suitability, like churning, is difficult to define precisely.

The rules of the NASD include the following:

> In recommending to a customer the purchase, sale, or exchange of any security, a member shall have reasonable grounds for believing that the recommendation is suitable for such customer upon the basis of the facts, if any, disclosed by such customer as to his other security holding and as to his financial situation and needs.[24]

A legal suit alleging unsuitability must meet three tests: (1) the broker has made a recommendation; (2) the security in question is unsuitable; and (3) the broker has acted knowingly (with *scienter*).

The NASD rule and the legal test it contains raise several difficulties. First, when has a broker made a recommendation? After discussing an investment with a customer, a broker may believe that the customer has made a choice, despite attempts by the broker to warn the customer of risks, while the customer may believe that he or she is acting at the urging of the broker. The conversation between a broker and customer is obviously subject to misunderstanding. Second, the rule expresses an obligation to seek information from the customer about his or her financial means and objectives. But how far should a broker probe? How can a broker be assured that the information is sufficient and accurate? The frequently offered refrain, "Know your customer," requires a broker to use due diligence in learning the essential facts about a customer. However, the standards for due diligence in this context are not always easy to determine. Third, *scienter* is difficult to prove, because it involves the broker's knowledge of both the customer's financial means and objectives and the nature of the security, and the broker can claim inadequate knowledge of one or both. The recommendation of an unsuitable security can be made out of incompetence or negligence rather than with fraudulent intent, and the distinction between the two types of cases may be difficult to draw. However, reckless conduct in which a competent broker should know that the security is unsuitable is often sufficient to establish *scienter*.

Of course, the most difficult question is: When is a security unsuitable? Rarely is a single security unsuitable except in the context of an investor's total portfolio. Investments are most often deemed to be unsuitable because they involve excessive risk, but a few risky investments may be appropriate in a well-balanced, generally conservative portfolio. Furthermore, even an aggressive, risk-taking portfolio may include unsuitable securities if the risk is not compensated by the expected return.

Modern portfolio theory provides a suitability test for portfolios by means of the concept of the *efficient frontier*.[25] The efficient frontier is a curve on a graph that plots portfolios with the maximum return for each level of risk, Possible portfolios far from the frontier consist of demonstrably unsuitable securities because an investor could gain a higher return for the same risk or assume less risk for the same return. A portfolio at or near the frontier contains unsuitable securities only if the degree of risk is not that desired by the investor. In that case, suitability can be achieved by moving up or down the curve that marks the efficient frontier. Securities are unsuitable, then, when the risk is excessive with respect either to the preferences of the investor or to the expected return.

The most common causes of unsuitability are: (1) *unsuitable types of securities*—recommending stocks, for example, when bonds would better fit the investor's objectives; (2) *unsuitable grades of securities*, such as selecting lower-rated bonds when higher-rated ones are more appropriate; (3) *unsuitable diversification*, which leaves the portfolio vulnerable to changes in the markets;

(4) *unsuitable trading techniques*, including the use of margin or options, which can leverage an account and create greater volatility and risk; and (5) *unsuitable liquidity*. Limited partnerships, for example, are not very marketable and are thus unsuitable for customers who may need to liquidate the investment. Ensuring that a recommended security is suitable for a given investor involves many factors, but people in the financial services industry offer to put their specialized knowledge and skills to work for us. We expect suitable recommendations from physicians, lawyers, and accountants. Why should we expect anything less from finance professionals?

Arbitration

The American humorist Alexander Woollcott once quipped that a broker is "a man who runs your fortune into a shoestring." Unfortunately, not a few investors have entrusted their life savings to a broker only to discover their once-large nest egg consumed by churning, unauthorized trading, or the failure of a broker to follow orders—or simply by a broker's incompetence. Justice requires that the victims of abusive or incompetent brokers be compensated for their losses and perhaps that the wrongdoers be punished. Of course, investors may attempt to blame brokers for their own failures and misfortunes, and so a method for settling disputes is required, lest an injustice be done to brokers and their firms. The court system is designed to handle disputes of this kind in a just manner, but costly and lengthy legal battles do not serve the interests of either party. Individual investors who have few resources or whose losses are minor would be deterred from seeking compensation if a court fight were their only recourse, while brokerage firms would face constant litigation if every disgruntled client were to sue.

Arbitration, instead of litigation, appears to be a quick, low-cost method of dispute resolution that serves the interests of all concerned. Most labor contracts, for example, provide for binding arbitration because of the advantages over court action. Similarly, in the securities industry, predispute arbitration agreements (PDAAs), which commit customers (and employees) to binding arbitration, are standard. Many investors are precluded, therefore, from suing their brokers in court and are forced to submit disputes to a panel of arbitrators. In addition, employees who might otherwise be able to sue for discrimination or other illegal treatment are often forced into arbitration, and, as noted in chapter 1, credit-card customers and other users of financial services are increasingly being required to arbitrate disputes.

Despite the virtues of arbitration, the process is open to abuse, and critics charge that many investors have been denied justice. Arbitration, they say, is heavily weighted in favor of the industry, so that investors who have been wronged once by a dishonest or incompetent broker are wronged yet again by a bullying brokerage firm. Some of the most elemental principles of due process are not observed by arbitration panels. In addition, the promise of quick, low-cost dispute resolution has not been realized because arbitration is sometimes as hard-fought as court battles. And the industry itself complains that unpredictable punitive damage awards expose firms to potentially heavy liability. All sides in the arbitration controversy recognize the need for thoroughgoing reform.

In 1994, the NASD, which handles 85 percent of all arbitration claims in the securities industry, appointed an eight-member Arbitration Policy Task Force under former SEC chairman David S. Ruder to make recommendations for an overhaul of the current system. The task force report, *Securities Arbitration Reform*, which was issued in January 1996, contains more than seventy recommendations that represent, according to a press release, "the most comprehensive revamping of securities industry arbitration since it was established to resolve investor disputes more than a century ago."[26] The so-called Ruder Commission investigated four main areas of concern: the requirement of compulsory arbitration through the use of PDAAs; the "hardball" legal tactics of securities firms; the competence and accountability of arbitrators; and the permissibility of punitive damages.

Compulsory arbitration

Investors who open accounts with a brokerage firm are usually asked to sign a PDAA. PDAAs are required for virtually all margin or option accounts and more than 60 percent of money management accounts, but not commonly for cash trading accounts. Customers who refuse to waive the right to sue will generally be told to go elsewhere, but they will find the same form awaiting them at any other firm. Can investors be said to agree voluntarily to compulsory arbitration if signing a PDAA is a condition of doing business with a brokerage firm? One congressional critic of arbitration describes "fair compulsion" as an oxymoron and contends, "Investors should not be forced to make the Faustian bargain of signing away rights to litigate in order to invest in our financial markets."[27]

The law for self-regulating organizations (SROs), under which NASD is organized, and the NASD code permit customers to insist that any dispute be arbitrated, regardless of whether a PDAA has been signed, but legally customers have a right to litigate—unless, of course, they waive that right. However, at least two questions must be asked about compulsory arbitration agreements. Should the law permit brokerage firms to require that investors sign a PDAA as a condition of opening an account? And, in particular, should a PDAA be legally enforceable if compulsory arbitration does not enable an investor to protect rights granted by law?

In 1987, the US Supreme Court addressed these questions in *Shearson/ American Express, Inc. v. McMahon.*[28] The court unanimously upheld the right of the securities industry to require customers to submit claims to arbitration, on the grounds that the law that provides the basis for arbitration creates a federal policy favoring arbitration by SROs. In short, it is the judgment of Congress that the American public is better served by arbitration, rather than litigation, in the securities industry. The right to require a PDAA does not apply to an agreement that results from fraud, but this exception aside, PDAAs are legally enforceable. Investors also have a right under securities law not to be defrauded by brokers. Do PDAAs require investors to forgo this legal protection? No, the court ruled in the *McMahon* decision, as long as arbitration is reasonably effective in enforcing investor rights in securities transactions. And whether arbitration provides sufficient protection is a matter for Congress, not the courts, to decide. The bottom line, however, is that PDAAs are fair to investors only if they effectively protect other investor rights.

Other ethical and legal issues are whether investors should be told that they are agreeing to compulsory arbitration by opening an account, and whether they should understand fully what signing a PDAA entails. Customers complain that the agreement provisions are expressed in impenetrable legal language buried deep inside the documents for opening an account. Many people do not realize that the rules for arbitration are different from those in the courts. The Ruder Commission report specifically recommends that the PDAA be highlighted and that investors be required to acknowledge the agreement in writing. Further, the following disclosures should be prominently displayed:

(1)   Arbitration is final and binding on the parties.
(2)   The parties are waiving their right to seek remedies in court, including the right to a jury trial.
(3)   Discovery is generally more limited and different from discovery in judicial proceedings.
(4)   The arbitrator's award is not required to include factual findings or legal reasoning and any party's right to appeal or to seek modification of the arbitrators' rulings is strictly limited.
(5)   The panel of arbitrators will typically include a minority of arbitrators who were, or are, affiliated with the securities industry.[29]

Some states, most notably New York, do not permit punitive damages in securities arbitration. Whether arbitration agreements involving customers and firms in other states can include waivers of any right to punitive damages is unclear, but in any event, some investors have signed PDAAs that preclude punitive damages without being aware of having done so. Prior to 1995, many brokerage firms inserted a clause in their PDAAs that specified that in arbitration the laws of New York State will prevail—without adding, of course, that these laws prohibit arbitrators from awarding punitive damages. A college professor in Chicago named Antonio C. Mastrobuono signed such an agreement with Shearson Lehmann Hutton, Inc., little realizing the implications, and when he won punitive damages from an arbitration panel, the brokerage firm filed suit to block the award, contending that Mastrobuono had waived the right to punitive damages. In a 1995 decision, the Supreme Court found in favor of Mastrobuono on the grounds that the contract was not sufficiently explicit, although the high court did not express an opinion on either the merit of awarding punitive damages or the ethics of hiding a waiver in non-revealing language. Professor Mastrobuono, a Dante scholar, was more forthcoming: "To allow Wall Street to steal from customers and then limit what they can recover in a forum of its choosing," he said, "would be institutional immorality worthy of punishment in Dante's fourth circle of hell."[30]

"Hardball" legal tactics

Although arbitration is intended to be less formal than a court trial, it has become a legal battleground in which platoons of lawyers from both sides fight tooth and nail over every aspect of the proceedings. Despite their professed commitment to arbitration, brokerage firms have eagerly gone to court to get their way in arbitration. Thus, investors who can seek justice only through arbitration face a foe who can fight in two arenas at once. The main points of contention in arbitration and litigation are: (1) the eligibility of a claim for arbitration, especially whether the time limit for making claims has expired; (2) the rules to be followed, especially those governing the admissibility of evidence and the applicable law; and (3) the documents that must be produced in discovery. Investors have accused brokerage firms of refusing to produce documents or delaying as long as possible, and although arbitration panels have subpoena power, they rarely exercise it or exact consequences for non-compliance. Many complaints are settled before they reach an arbitration panel, some no doubt on generous terms, but brokerage firms have been known to take advantage of investors' lack of resources and uncertain prospects to settle cheaply. Virtually all settlements contain confidentiality agreements that prevent unfavorable publicity about problem brokers and their firms. In general, customers who enter arbitration can expect a "hardball" legal approach from brokerage firms seeking to minimize legal liability, no matter the cost to the industry's reputation for fair treatment of customers.

The Ruder Commission report addresses these problems with three main recommendations.[31]

(1) *Bar collateral court litigation over procedural issues in arbitration until after the arbitration award.* The Commission recommends that the parties seek to resolve procedural issues in the arbitration forum and delay any court litigation until the arbitration panel has ruled.

(2) *Suspend the six-year eligibility rules and resolve issues of whether an arbitration claim is time barred by more vigorously applying applicable state and federal statutes of limitations.* Under the current rule, claims must be brought within six years of the alleged wrongdoing. Aside from the fact that some investors might not discover fraudulent activity within this period of time, the six-year rule is difficult to apply because of uncertainty over the date of the alleged offence. If churning occurs over a three-year period, does the clock begin ticking on the first day or the last? Much of the discovery process may be taken up with establishing the starting date of the six-year period, so that suspension of the six-year rule removes a major source of collateral litigation.

(3) *Simplify document production and other discovery, and require early resolution of any discovery dispute.* The Commission concluded from its study that the process of obtaining documents from the opposing side was a main obstacle to quick, low-cost arbitration and the source of much collateral litigation. Discovery is also abused by lawyers who use "vacuum-cleaner" tactics, common in civil litigation, that seek to gain all available evidence and at the same time burden the opposing side with heavy production requirements. By limiting the documents that each side must produce and by specifying those that must be produced early on, the process can be greatly expedited.

Problems with arbitrators

Critics of arbitration complain that some arbitrators are inattentive to the proceedings, ignorant of the relevant law and of arbitration procedures, capricious and inconsistent in their rulings, and biased in favor of the industry. Arbitrators, for their part, feel overburdened and undercompensated and lament the lack of time and resources for more training. Some of the complaints about arbitrators are compounded by the rules for arbitration. For example, at least one arbitrator on a panel must have ties to the industry, thus creating an impression of a stacked deck. The limited number of arbitrators and the limited opportunity of the parties to select among them reduces confidence in the system. Arbitration panels typically do not explain their reasoning, nor can their decisions be appealed. Thus, the parties are deprived of any basis for judging the soundness of the decision-making process or the competence of the decision makers.

The Ruder Commission report notes a tension between a traditional model of arbitrators as peers, who draw upon their knowledge and experience, and a more recent model of professional, full-time arbitrators, not unlike the judiciary.[32] The traditional model may have served the securities industry well in the past, but the report suggests that the time has come for the shift to the professional model that prevails in labor relations and large commercial disputes. In addition to making numerous recommendations for improvements in the training and compensation of arbitrators and an increase in their number, the Ruder Commission report also proposes that complaints involving smaller amounts be arbitrated using simplified procedures. Also, greater use should be made of mediation and "early neutral evaluation" (ENE).

Punitive damages

The Ruder Commission report observes, "No subject has generated more controversy or so polarized opinion between the investor community and the securities industry than the availability of punitive damages in securities arbitration."[33] The industry has made the elimination of punitive damages its main goal, while investors have sought to maintain the possibility of punitive damage awards.

The industry view is that arbitration is intended to compensate investors for actual losses, not to punish individuals and firms for past misconduct or to deter them from future misconduct. If arbitration panels were to aim at punishment and deterrence, then they would have to consider many factors besides the case at hand. Moreover, punishment and deterrence are the province of the state and ought to be left to regulators acting to protect the public, not to arbitrators who are settling private disputes. Because punitive damages can be enormous, it is unfair that they be imposed in proceedings that lack important procedural safeguards, such as the consideration of all relevant information and the right of appeal. Finally, the possibility of punitive damages raises the stakes for brokerage firms and induces them to take a "hardball" legal approach.

Investors argue that punitive damages protect against predatory behavior by brokerage firms. Since the *McMahon* decision permits brokerage firms to require PDAAs as a condition of opening an account and to force customers to settle disputes through arbitration, investors should not be further deprived of a remedy that would otherwise be available in civil litigation. In short, investors should have the same remedies in arbitration that they have in court—especially since they have little say in the choice of venues. This principle is expressed, moreover, in SEC and NASD rules that prohibit the placing of any restrictions on arbitrators with regard to the kind and amount of awards.

The right of brokerage firms to include a waiver of punitive damages in PDAAs is also brought into question by the *Mastrobuono* decision. Firms might get around this decision by stating explicitly that customers who sign a PDAA are waiving the right to seek punitive damages (instead of stating merely that the laws of New York State will prevail), but legal experts warn that this may not be possible because of the SEC and NASD rules. That is, states, such as New York, may prohibit punitive damages in securities arbitration, but brokerage firms themselves may not write a waiver into PDAAs nor stipulate arbitrarily the state laws that will prevail.

The Ruder Commission concedes the merits of both views and does not side with either one. Instead, the report offers a compromise position: that punitive damages be retained subject to a cap. Specifically, the proposed cap is the lesser of two times the compensatory damages, or $750,000. The main benefit of a cap, whatever the amount, is to alleviate industry concern with the unlimited exposure that exists under the present system. And the recommended amount is high enough that few investors would be affected.[34] In addition, the Ruder Commission report proposes that the availability of punitive damages in arbitration be determined by whether punitive damages would be available in court for the same claim under the laws of the investors state at the time that the claim was filed. "By this standard," the report notes, "investors will be no better or worse off than if they had brought their claim to a judicial forum."[35]

Disputes between investors and brokers are inevitable, and so some means of just resolution must be available. However, the securities industry should also aim to eliminate the causes of disputes, and not merely deal with the them as they arise. As a commentator in *BusinessWeek* observed, "The industry's proposals simply amount to a more efficient shovel brigade for the elephant parade. Instead, the industry should work on the front end to prevent abuses in the first place."[36]

Personal Trading

The explosive growth in mutual funds has brought Wall Street to Main Street. The stock market, which was once the province of the very rich, is now easily accessible to millions of ordinary investors. This revolutionary development has drawn attention to the men and women who manage billion-dollar portfolios and has even made celebrities of a few. When Jeffrey Vinik, the idolized manager of Fidelity's $54-billion Magellan Fund, touted Silicon Graphics in 1995, people took note and the share price rose—before it collapsed. The financial writer Michael Lewis, who bought 500 shares of Silicon Graphics on the way up, recalled, "As my money disappeared, my warm feelings toward Jeff Vinik went with it."[37] This fund manager's stock picks turned into an ethics case when, as Lewis reports, "Vinik was quoted by journalists singing the praises of two companies—Micron Technologies and Goodyear Tire and Rubber—at virtually the same time that he was selling his own stake in these companies."[38]

Cases like this remind us that mutual fund managers wear two hats: They manage money for others, but they often trade for their own account. Even though most fund managers toil in obscurity and refrain from giving stock tips, they still have immense opportunities to benefit personally from their privileged position. The potential for abuse was recognized in 1940 by the drafters of the Investment Company Act (ICA), which governs mutual funds. In 1970, Congress added Section 17(j) to the original legislation, which gave the SEC the power to set rules that require each investment company to adopt a code of ethics and develop procedures for detecting and preventing abuse, including the collection of information on employees' personal trading activities. Because of this long-standing regulation, personal trading in the mutual fund industry has led to very little abuse, and the occasional instances have drawn a vigorous response.

Recent concern about personal trading was sparked by the case of John Kaweske, mentioned in chapter 1. News stories about Kaweske's failure to disclose personal trades as required prompted Congress to ask the SEC to study the problem, and a report, *Personal Investment Activities of Investment Company Personnel*, was released in September 1994.[39] In anticipation of the SEC report, the Investment Company Institute (ICI), the trade association of the mutual fund industry, issued its own report by a special Advisory Group on Personal Investing on May 9, 1994.[40] The two reports reach similar conclusions: that personal trading should not be banned and that the current system of regulation works well but can be improved.

On the whole, there is very little controversy over personal trading, only the recognition of the potential for abuse and the need to prevent it. The main ethical issues, therefore, concern the rationale for regulation and the details of the appropriate regulatory system. The section examines, first, the potential for abuse and the current regulatory framework; second, the debate over whether personal trading should be banned; and, third, remaining questions that need a closer look.

The scope of the problem

Investment companies, of which mutual funds are the best-known type, invest their capital in other companies, usually by purchasing stock or other securities. Closed-end mutual funds have a fixed number of shares which are commonly traded on a market, while open-ended mutual funds sell new shares to the public and stand ready to redeem them at any time. Among the benefits of mutual funds over direct investments in securities are diversification, lower transaction costs, liquidity, and professional management. Like the managers of a corporation, mutual fund managers have a fiduciary duty to act in all matters solely in the interests of the shareholder-investors. Specifically, the managers of mutual funds have an obligation to avoid conflicts of interest that would lead them to put their own interests ahead of those they are duty bound to serve. In addition, mutual funds serve the role of an investment adviser, which also carries with it a fiduciary duty.

One aim of government regulation of investment companies is to ensure that managers fulfill their fiduciary duty. Investment companies also have a strong interest in maintaining investor confidence. The SEC report on personal trading notes:

> The success of the investment company industry is in no small measure the result of the industry's excellent record. . . . The industry's continued health, however, depends on its meeting the expectation of American investors, many of whom are new to the market. The industry will continue to be trusted by investors only if it demonstrates that it maintains the highest possible ethical standards and that it operates free from abusive and fraudulent practices.[41]

Hence the concern in Congress and the industry when the Kaweske case raised even the suggestion of improper personal trading by a fund manager.

Conflicts of interest from personal trading are possible for so-called "access people," that is, investment company personnel such as portfolio managers, analysts, and traders who have access to proprietary research and information about pending transactions.[42] Access people are in a position to use this information to trade ahead of a fund's purchase (called *frontrunning*) and benefit from any upward price movement. If frontrunning raises the price of a stock, then the fund pays more for a security than it would otherwise. Similarly, an access person with advance knowledge of a fund's sale of a stock could capitalize on the information by selling short. An access person might be in a position to influence transactions that serve primarily to protect or promote that person's investment in a security. Conflicts of interest also arise when a fund manager allocates a security that is in short supply, such as shares in a "hot" initial public offering, or distributes gains and losses between different funds in ways that benefit the manager at the expense of some investors. In addition, a fund manager who takes advantage of an opportunity, such as a special placement, for his or her own portfolio rather than investing for the fund is in a conflict of interest. Some of these practices are prohibited by the securities acts and would be illegal if performed by anyone, and so the focus of the ICA is on conflicts of interest among mutual fund personnel that are not addressed by other laws.

The SEC study, which examined data on personal and fund trading in 30 companies, found that relatively few managers actively buy and sell securities for their own account. In 1993, 56.5 percent of the fund managers in the groups studied engaged in any personal trading, and the median number of personal transactions was two. Fewer than 5 percent of the personal transactions took place in a ten-day period prior to a transaction in the same security held by another fund in the company, and only 2 percent of personal transactions were made within ten days before a transaction in a fund for which the manager selected securities. The data analyzed in the SEC study may understate or overstate the frequency of matching transactions. Trading in the shares of large corporations, for example, is unlikely to have any market-moving effect, whereas the price of thinly traded stock of small capitalization companies is easily moved. Of course, the amount of personal trading and the number of matching trades reflects close regulatory oversight. No one can predict the consequences if the current system of regulation were relaxed.

Several studies in the 1960s revealed substantial personal trading that posed conflicts of interest, and so in 1970 Congress added Section 17(j) to the 1940 ICA. This addition granted rule-making power to the SEC in order to prohibit any fraudulent, deceptive, or manipulative act by an access person in the purchase or sale of any security. Using its power, the SEC promulgated Rule 17j-1 in 1980. In brief, the rule:

(1) prohibits directors, officers, and employees of investment companies (and the investment advisers and principal underwriters) from engaging in fraudulent, manipulative or deceptive conduct in connection with their personal trading of securities held or to be acquired by the investment company;

(2) requires investment companies (and their investment advisers and principal underwriters) to adopt codes of ethics and procedures reasonably designed to prevent trading prohibited by the rule;

(3) requires every "access person" to file reports with the firm concerning his or her personal securities transactions, within ten days of the end of the quarter in which the transaction was effected; and

(4)   requires investment companies (and their investment advisers and principal underwriters) to maintain records related to the implementation of their procedures.[43]

Section 17(j) and Rule 17j-1 reflect three important points in the approach of Congress and the SEC toward personal trading.[44] First, the regulation of personal trading by investment company personnel is best done by the companies themselves. That is, an employee's own firm provides a strong first line of oversight. Second, every mutual fund is different, and they can provide better oversight if they are given flexibility to develop a code of ethics and specific procedures that fit their individual circumstances. Third, there is a recognition that not all personal trading poses a conflict of interest and that judgment is required for carefully evaluating each case. Thus, both a complete ban on personal trading and rigid rules are inappropriate forms of regulation.

Should personal trading be banned?

Both the SEC and ICI reports contain lengthy sections on the question of a complete ban on personal trading. This attention suggests that the issue is not closed, despite the firm rejection of a ban in each report.

Two points should be noted at the outset. First, the question addressed in both reports is whether personal trading by access people in mutual fund companies ought to be banned industrywide, not whether any given company should impose such a ban on its own employees. The reports reject a *mandatory* ban for the industry but leave the door open to a *voluntary* ban by individual mutual fund companies. Second, personal trading by access people is already subject to considerable restrictions, and a complete ban is merely one end of a long continuum. As a debate proposition, a complete ban is a red herring that diverts attention from the critical question, namely how restrictive should the regulation of personal trading be? Thus, the arguments for and against a complete ban are worth examining, even if a complete ban is rejected, because the same considerations enable us to determine the appropriate level of restrictiveness.

The arguments for a complete ban can be summarized as follows:

(1)   *The image of the industry.* Regardless of the seriousness of the actual problem (which may be slight), the success of the mutual fund industry depends on a "squeaky-clean" image that reassures investors, especially those new to the market. Personal trading creates a perception of conflict of interest that may be worse than the reality, and a unequivocal policy is the only effective means for countering this perception.

(2)   *The heavy responsibility of managing funds.* The sheer volume of assets currently under management by mutual funds and the importance of

mutual funds to the savings plans of Americans create a responsibility to adhere to the highest level of ethics, and to avoid even the remote possibility of harm to investors from mismanagement. Aside from any direct loss to investors due to personal trading, there is a possible indirect loss if fund managers devote their time and energies to their own portfolios rather than attending to the work at hand.

(3) *The (in)effectiveness of regulation.* Any regulation short of a complete ban creates too many opportunities to take advantage of loopholes and fuzzy lines. Fund managers, analysts, and other access people who are intent on benefiting from their positions may be tempted to skirt the edge of ethical and legal trading without overstepping the line. A simple complete ban can be better understood and more easily enforced than complicated rules and regulations.

(4) *Fairness to other investors.* Access people are insiders who are privy to information that other investors lack, so that personal trading may constitute insider trading and be objectionable for the same reasons. Like proprietary corporate information, information about pending transactions is provided to access people in order for them to perform a job. Trading on the basis of this information is thus a misappropriation of company property for personal use. Some argue that fund managers should trade on the same basis as their clients and invest in mutual funds themselves. That is, they should "eat their own cooking." One advocate asks whether you would buy your meat from a vegetarian butcher. If not, why would you hand your money over to "a manager who won't put his own cash into the fund he's pushing for you"?[45]

The arguments against a complete ban include the following:

(1) *The lack of need.* A complete ban is unnecessary for several reasons. First, a multitude of funds compete fiercely with each other on the basis of performance, and in this environment, no company can succeed if it does not put the interests of the customer first. In short, the market is a powerful force for motivating companies to protect investors against abuses from personal trading. Second, fund managers compete against each other and are judged by the returns that they achieve. As the ICI report observes:

> No firm is likely to tolerate a portfolio manager becoming preoccupied with personal investments at the expense of a fund and its shareholders. Nor is a portfolio manager, whose personal compensation is frequently linked to the performance of the fund, likely to be motivated to engage in trading activities that benefit him at the expense of fund performance.[46]

Third, personal trading is already stringently regulated, and the lack of apparent abuse indicates that the current regulatory system works well.

(2) *No benefit to investors.* A ban on personal trading would make it difficult for mutual fund companies to attract and retain the best analysts, traders, and fund managers. Competition for the most talented people is already stiff, and a complete ban would put investment companies at a disadvantage with pension plans, insurance companies, investment banking firms, commercial bank trust departments, and other financial institutions which permit personal trading. Mutual fund customers would lose the benefit that they now derive from the skills of top-performing professionals if a complete ban were imposed.

(3) *Unfairness to fund personnel.* The opportunity to invest is vital to people's economic well-being, and so a ban on personal trading that would limit people's freedom on such an important matter requires weighty justification. In general, people's freedom should not be restricted any more than is necessary to achieve the desired ends. If the current regulatory system works reasonably well, then would more stringent regulation compensate for the loss of freedom? Even trustees, who have a strong fiduciary duty, are not barred from whole classes of transactions that are unrelated to the administration of a trust. Moreover, the argument that fund managers should "eat their own cooking" overlooks the point that the fund may be inappropriate for that manager's investment objectives. Investment in one's own fund serves to align a manager's interests with those of customers, but the same end can be achieved by tying compensation to performance. Some funds attempt to gain the confidence of investors by advertising the personal stakes of their managers, as witness a headline in the *Wall Street Journal*, "Mutual Funds Boast: We Buy Our Own Stuff."[47] Although this claim provides investors with some useful information, this is scarcely a reason to require that managers invest along with their customers.

In evaluating these arguments, the SEC considers three factors: "the prevalence of abusive securities transactions by access persons; the potential harm to fund shareholders caused by access persons' personal investment activities; and the likelihood that a ban would curb abusive trading by access persons.[48] The available data suggest that abusive personal trading is not prevalent, that it is not harmful to investors, and that any gains to investors from a complete ban would be slight. The SEC also questions whether a complete ban would deter more determined wrongdoers, some of whom are not deterred by current regulation. Banning all personal trading in an attempt to prevent the last vestiges of abuse is a misguided enterprise. The SEC report concludes that even though an industrywide ban on personal trading is not warranted at this time, the directors of mutual funds have a responsibility to assess the benefits of personal trading for shareholders and adopt more restrictive rules and procedures, or even a complete ban, if such a step is in the shareholders' interests.

Remaining questions

The current regulatory system on personal trading allows mutual fund companies great flexibility, and the rules and regulations of individual companies vary widely. Any given question, therefore, may have already been answered by one company and be completely unaddressed by another. And the answers that different companies give to these questions by may be justifiably different. However, some questions are at the forefront of discussion and have yet to be firmly settled industrywide.

Codes of ethics
Although Rule 17j-1 requires investment companies to adopt a code of ethics, the content of these codes is not legally mandated. The ICI Advisory Group on Personal Investing recommends that every code of ethics incorporate certain general principles:

> These principles should, at a minimum, reflect the following: (1) the duty at all times to place the interests of shareholders first; (2) the requirement that all personal securities transactions be conducted consistent with the code of ethics and in such a manner as to avoid any actual or potential conflict of interest or any abuse of an individual's position of trust and responsibility; and (3) the fundamental standard that investment company personnel should not take inappropriate advantage of their positions.[49]

The implementation of these general principles in specific rules and procedures raises many questions, including who is covered, what transactions are prohibited, and what transactions must be reported. The term *access people* covers a range of personnel who may not be easily identified, and some distinctions among them may be appropriate. Some codes of ethics employ a tiered structure in which employees on different tiers are subject to different regulation. The securities in question may need to be distinguished. Generally, codes of ethics exempt money-market instruments, Treasury securities, shares of mutual funds or small blocks of stocks in large, actively traded corporations on the grounds that fund trading in these securities is unlikely to affect the price. Some argue that the definition of a security should be broadened because of the development of new financial instruments such as options, derivatives, and commodities futures.

Rule 17j-1 mandates that employees disclose all personal trading in quarterly reports. A loophole at the present time is that access people are not required to disclose their portfolio holdings when they begin employment. Thus, quarterly transactions may not reveal a conflict of interest that involves an undisclosed preemployment securities holding. Although mutual fund companies are legally required to adopt a code of ethics, there is no legal obligation to disclose it to the public. The SEC and ICI reports each recommend that mutual fund companies disclose their policy on personal trading and provide an overview of their rules and procedures in the prospectus for each fund.[50] The SEC proposes that investment companies be legally required to include the full text of the code of ethics as an attachment to the company's registration statement so that it will be publicly available, while the ICI Advisory Group's recommendation states only that a company may elect to include it at its discretion.

Trading practices

Generally, conflicts of interest are created by matching transactions in which an access person makes personal trades in conjunction with fund trades. Matching transactions can be addressed not only by disclosure—which enables a company to analyze the pattern of trades—but also by *blackout* periods which provide specific guidelines. Questions still arise, however, about the length of the blackout period, whether it applies before or after a fund transaction or both, and whether there are different blackout periods for different types of securities transactions. For example, some codes of ethics create a longer blackout period for transactions over which a fund manager has decision-making power. Other remaining questions about trading practices are: (1) the personal purchase of initial public offerings (IPOs) and private placements; (2) short-term trading; and (3) short-selling stocks that are held by a company's funds.

IPOs raise the possibility of a conflict of interest because the intense interest in certain "hot" new issues limits the number of investors who can participate. Fund shareholders may rightly ask why a fund manager who had the opportunity to purchase shares did so for his or her personal account and not for the fund. Private placements do not raise this concern because they generally do not involve securities that could be purchased by a fund. Still, the opportunity to participate in a private placement may be regarded by fund shareholders as a conflict of interest if, for example, it was offered by a start-up firm as an incentive for the manager to invest for the fund should the venture go public in an IPO. Both IPOs and special placements are potentially profitable opportunities that raise questions about the ability of a fund manger to exercise unbiased judgment in future transactions.

Short-term trading—which is generally interpreted as holding securities for less than 90 days—is prohibited by some mutual fund companies for the reason that quick profit-taking is more likely to utilize information about fund transactions: A rule against short-term trading is an especially effective precaution against frontrunning that, at the same time, does not prevent employees from realizing long-term gain in the stock market. Thus, the benefits to the company and its shareholders are likely to outweigh any small losses to fund managers and other access people.

Neither the SEC nor the ICI report addresses short-selling—which is the practice of borrowing a stock and selling it in the hopes of replacing it later at a lower price—although shorting might fall under the category of short-term trading. Short-selling is practiced by investors who believe that the price of a stock will decline, which raises the question of why a prudent fund manager does not reduce the fund's holdings. Shorting evades restrictions on matching transactions because there is no sale by the fund, and the conflict of interest arises when a fund manager makes a biased decision *not* to sell in order to short the stock for personal gain. Few companies have addressed the issue of short-selling, although some may do so after Fidelity Investments announced a ban on the shorting of stock held by its funds, saying that the practice could create an appearance of a conflict of interest.[51]

Mutual funds

Mutual funds, which manage about $7 trillion for more than 95 million Americans, are the domain of individual investors who do not want to actively manage a portfolio. Generally, sophisticated investors who trade frequently maintain accounts with brokerage firms or, increasingly, put their money into hedge funds. Mutual funds are certainly unlikely investment vehicles for large, aggressive, professionally managed investment funds. Yet, this picture of mutual funds as a quiet, safe place for patient, "buy-and-hold" individual investors was shattered in 2003 by reports that many mutual funds were allowing privileged access to a few favored clients, mostly investment funds, which were using mutual funds to engage in disruptive and, in some instances, illegal trading.

The main revelations concerned *market timing*, in which large investments are made for short periods of time in order to benefit from temporary changes in securities prices. Typically, market timing involves rapid "in-and-out" trades (also called "round trips") with purchases and redemptions within a few days of each other. Although market timing of individual stocks is common—indeed, it is the main tactic of so-called "day traders"—brokerage fees tend to limit the gain; and market timing of individual stocks is not suitable for capitalizing on broad market movements. Rapid in-and-out trading in mutual funds solves both of these problems: brokerage fees are avoided if the fund has no up-front or back-end fees, and diversified funds generally reflect the broader market. Market timing is especially attractive in international funds due to the time lag in distant markets. When an international fund closes for the day in New York, for example, the prices of Japanese stocks were set half a day earlier, and European stocks have been known for a few hours. The resulting "stale" prices create opportunities for market timing (also called "stale price arbitrage").

The other practice that came to light in 2003 is *late trading*, in which orders are placed after the close of trading in the United States, which is four o'clock New York time. Late trading, which is strictly illegal, enables investors to utilize information about the day's activities and announcements made after the markets' close. In some instances, offsetting trades are entered during the day, and then, after the markets close, one trade is cancelled, leaving the desired one to be effected. Whereas market timing still involves some judgment and risk, late trading is a sure bet, rather like betting on a horse race after the outcome is known.

In a 2003 SEC survey of the 88 largest mutual fund companies, more than half admitted that they allowed market timing, and 25 percent admitted to allowing late trading.[52] According to another estimate, between 2001 and 2003, over 90 percent of fund companies permitted market timing in at least one fund, and late trading was permitted by 30 percent of them.[53] During the same period, market timing is estimated to have cost investors $5 billion per year,[54] and late trading, $400 million, mostly in international funds.[55]

Unlike late trading, which violates established trading rules, market timing is legal as long it is permitted by the mutual fund sponsor. Market timing is ethically questionable, though, and possibly illegal when only a few favored clients are permitted to engage in the practice to the detriment of those who are discouraged or forbidden from trading on the same terms. Such disparate treatment of a majority of investors is arguably a violation a fund sponsor's fiduciary duty to serve the interests of all investors. The main ethical questions, then, are what, if anything, is wrong with these two mutual fund trading practices, and, if they are wrong, what should be done to prevent them. Before these questions are considered, more needs to be said about how market timing works.

How market timing works

The abuses in mutual fund trading first became public in 2003 with an investigation by Eliot Spitzer, the New York State attorney general, into the activities of Canary Capital, headed by Edward J. (Eddie) Stern, which had market-timing agreements with 30 mutual fund companies, including, most notoriously, Bank of America and its Nations Funds family.[56] Canary Capital managed the Stern family fortune, which was based on the Hartz Mountain pet food empire that was founded by the grandfather of Eddie Stern, who arrived in the United States in 1926 with 5,000 canaries to sell (hence the name Canary Capital). Founded in 1998, Canary engaged in market timing from the beginning, earning returns that greatly outpaced the market. In 1999, when the S&P 500 index rose 20 percent, Canary earned 110 percent, and the returns in 2000 and 2001 were 50 percent and almost 29 percent, respectively, when the market averages were down 9 percent and 13 percent, respectively.

During the 1990s, market timing, which was practiced on a large scale by perhaps a few hundred investors, was a mild irritant to mutual funds companies, which usually discouraged or, in some cases, banned the practice. The prospectuses for most funds emphasized that they were intended as long-term investment vehicles, and investors were restricted to a few rapid trades a year (most commonly four) and, in many cases, redemption fees were imposed for short-term trades. Most fund companies had "timing police," who identified market timers and enforced the rules. By 2000, market timers, who had previously managed to avoid detection by keeping a low profile and moving from one fund to another, now found it more difficult to operate without the cooperation of the mutual fund companies. Also, the increasingly large investments (often tens of millions of dollars) made it more difficult to operate undetected.

Although many mutual fund companies spurned the overtures of the market timers—Fidelity, for example, firmly declined to do business with any of them—others were receptive. This willingness of fund companies to permit market timing of their funds to the detriment of ordinary investors was prompted by the bear market that began in 2000, which reduced the assets under management and the management fees that these assets generated. Mutual fund companies were desperately looking for ways to maintain the income levels of better times. Thus, some companies were interested when market timers like Eddie Stern offered to share some of the gains to be made from rapid trading.

How did it work? As one writer explained:

Market-timing hedge funds—as well as brokers and other middlemen— negotiated secret "capacity" arrangements in which they gained the right to run a predetermined amount of money in and out of a fund and were exempted from short-term redemption fees. In return, the market timer handled over a second predetermined amount to the fund company—"sticky assets," which sat quietly and generated extra management fees for the fund complex. Often, the sticky assets were placed in low-risk money-market or government bond funds. But sometimes they'd end up in a hedge fund run by the fund managers, generating much juicier fees for both the portfolio managers and their firm.[57]

Canary Capital and some other market-timing funds also figured out how to engage in short-selling with mutual funds. (Short-selling is profiting from declining prices by selling borrowed shares and returning them later by buying them back in the market after the price has dropped.) The method consisted of developing a market instrument replicating holdings of a mutual fund that could be shorted. However, developing this instrument required knowledge of the holdings of the fund in question, which is information that is ordinarily released only twice a year. Canary was able to strike deals in which fund companies would provide a list of holdings at any given time, thus permitting market timers, but not other investors, to short their own funds.

Between 2000 and 2003, Canary Capital had market-timing agreements with some of the major mutual fund companies, including Strong Capital Management, Pimco Advisors, Janus Capital, Alliance Capital Management, Bank One (now part of JPMorganChase), and Invesco. The reputation of Putnam Investments was also badly tarnished for permitting other market timers to trade in its funds. However, no mutual fund company went to greater lengths to accommodate Canary than Bank of America, the sponsor of Nations Funds (now a part of Columbia Management). In 2001, Bank of America provided Canary with its own electronic trading terminal, installed in Canary's office, so that trades could be entered as late as 6:30 p.m. With direct access to Bank of America's trading system, Canary could disguise the origin of the trades by mixing them with the bank's own trading flow. Bank of America provided Canary with a $300 million credit line to finance market timing in its own funds, and the bank also revealed the portfolio holdings of funds so that Canary could engage in short selling.

Eventually, Bank of America settled all charges by agreeing to pay $125 million in penalties and $250 million in restitution to investors. Canary Capital paid a fine of $40 million, and Eddie Stern agreed to cooperate with prosecutors in providing information about the mutual fund companies with which he had market timing agreements. Most of the other offending mutual fund companies have entered into legal settlements and taken steps to compensate investors for their losses and restore their deeply tarnished reputations. In addition, a few individuals at the mutual fund companies have faced criminal charges for their involvement in this scandal.

One individual, in particular, provides a striking example of the abuse in mutual fund trading. Richard S. Strong was the founder, chairman, and chief investment officer of Strong Capital Management (SCM), as well as chairman of the board of directors of the 27 investment companies that managed the 71 SCM funds. When Richard S. Strong founded Strong Capital Management in 1974, he wanted it to be "the Nordstrom's of the financial industry," believing that this store provided the very best customer service. With this goal in mind, he built SCM into an investment company that by 2004 managed $33.8 billion in mutual fund and pension investments. In that year, though, SCM and Richard Strong came under scrutiny for market timing not only by an outside investor but by Mr Strong himself.

Despite the company's policy on market timing, Richard Strong engaged in market timing in SCM mutual funds, making 1,400 quick trades between 1998 and 2003, including 22 round trips in 1998 in a fund for which he was also a portfolio manager. In 2000, SCM's timing police detected the chairman's trading activity, and the general counsel spoke to him, noting that his trading was inconsistent with the company's stated position on market timing and its treatment of other market timers. After agreeing to quit, he increased his activity, making a record 510 trades in 2001. In total, he netted $1.8 million and obtained higher returns than ordinary investors in the same SCM funds.

Richard Strong's market timing was costly not only to SCM but also to Mr Strong personally. The company agreed to pay $40 million in fines and an additional $40 million in restitution, in addition to reducing the fees on SCM funds by a total of approximately $35 million of the next five years. Mr Strong personally agreed to pay $30 million in fines and the same amount in restitution, and to accept a lifetime ban from the financial services industry.[58]

It was SCM's involvement with Canary that eventually led to the downfall of both companies. In 2001 and 2002, Canary was making so much money and attracting so many new investors that it was finding it more difficult to obtain sufficient "capacity"; that is, mutual funds that would permit market-timing trades. In an effort to get the attention of Goldman Sachs, Canary hired a former employee, Noreen Harrington. Goldman Sachs was uninterested, and Harriman left in dismay when she discovered how Canary's money was made. She was not intending to blow the whistle until her sister complained about how much money she was losing in her mutual fund and how she would never be able to retire. "I didn't think about this from the bottom up until then," Harrington said.[59] A telephone call to the New York State Attorney General's office started the investigation that led not only to Canary but also to Richard Strong.

What is wrong with market timing?

Although market timing, unlike late trading, does not violate an explicit legal prohibition, it is morally objectionable and arguably illegal for several reasons.

First, it allows a few favored clients to trade under terms that are unavailable to the vast majority of ordinary investors. If a fund openly offers the opportunity to engage in rapid in-and-out trading with few if any restrictions so that all investors can take equal advantage of market-timing opportunities, then no one would be treated unfairly. Such a market-timing fund would have *transparency*—that is, all investors would know the rules—and it would provide *equal treatment*—that is, the same rules would apply to all. Market timing under these conditions would be morally unobjectionable and perfectly legal. However, very few funds openly permit market timing, although a few do. Most funds actively discourage short-term trading by advising against it, placing restrictions on the number of round trips, and imposing redemption fees on short-term investments. The objection to market timing in most mutual funds, then, is that that some investors are subject to different, more favorable rules (unequal treatment) of which other investors are not aware (transparency).

For example, Strong Capital Management, like most mutual fund companies, encouraged long-term holding of five years or more and advised that market timing does not work. Beginning in 1997, SCM warned shareholders that frequent traders could be banned: "Since an excessive number of exchanges may be detrimental to the Funds, each Fund reserves the right to discontinue the exchange privilege of any shareholder who makes more than five exchanges in a year or three exchanges in a calendar quarter." Like most other mutual fund companies, SCM also had timing police, who monitored trading activity for frequent activity, and from 1998 through 2003, hundreds of market timers were identified and barred from investing in Strong funds. When it was discovered that some SCM employees were market timing in their own accounts, the company issued a clear directive that the Strong funds were not to be used for short-term trading and that violators could have their trading privileges restricted. From these facts, a reasonable investor could assume that marketing timing does not take place in SCM mutual funds.

Second, allowing marketing timing hurts long-term mutual fund investors by increasing a fund's expense and reducing its returns. Large inflows and outflows in short periods of time add trading and other overhead costs. In addition, the manager of a fund with active market timers may have to keep a more liquid position in order to meet redemption orders or otherwise make different investment decisions. The result may be the adoption of trading strategies that are less than optimal for long-term investors. Also, frequent sales of securities to meet redemption orders by market timers may produce capital gains that result in higher taxes for all fund investors. Moreover, if the value of a fund rises after a market timer's investment was made, and if the trader cashes out quickly before the fund purchases any new securities, the effect is to dilute the earnings of a fund. Under such conditions, the earnings are due entirely to money provided by other investors, and yet the market timer shares in the returns. All of these possibilities involve losses to investors without any corresponding gains—except for the market timers. In short, market timers are able to impose costs on every fund investor for trading activity from which only they benefit.

Third, insofar as market timing is unfair and harmful to ordinary investors, it can be argued that the directors and executives of mutual fund companies are violating a fiduciary duty to serve investors' interests. Each mutual fund is, legally, an independent company with a board of directors and a chairman of the board (although the same persons may be directors and chairmen of dozens if not hundreds of funds offered by a single mutual fund company). The investors are the shareholders of a mutual fund, and the fund itself purchases and owns the securities that comprise the fund's assets. Although mutual funds are sponsored by a mutual fund company, such as Fidelity or Vanguard, legally the board of directors selects and contracts with the fund's sponsor. A mutual fund company is simply an agent hired by the directors of a fund to administer or advise the fund. Accordingly, the directors and executives of a mutual fund have the same kind of fiduciary duty to its investors as the directors and executives of a publicly held company have to its shareholders.

Indeed, all company personnel have an obligation to refrain from actions that would harm a fund's investors. In the SCM code of ethics, which was distributed to all employees, Richard Strong summed up the "three most important principles" for dealing with clients:

- You must deal with our clients fairly and in good faith;
- You must never put the interests of our firm ahead of the interests of our clients; and
- You must never compromise your personal ethics or integrity, or give the appearance that you may have done so.

Thus, because of the fiduciary duty imposed by law on the directors and executives of mutual funds, as well the codes of ethics that mutual fund companies adopt and publish, investors have a right to expect that their interests will not be harmed by capacity agreements with market timers, and especially not by market timing by a company's own personnel.

The wrongness of market timing, then, lies not in the practice itself, whether it is done by investors making frequent trades or by mutual fund companies in allowing such trading. No, the wrongness consists rather in the inconsistency of presenting mutual funds as safe, reliable investment vehicles for relatively unsophisticated investors and at the same time collecting additional revenue from market timers who are allowed to benefit at the expense of ordinary investors. By allowing market timers, mutual fund companies are professing to play by one set of rules while secretly playing by another. At bottom, mutual fund companies are betraying a trust that is the cornerstone of their industry, and market timers are inducing fund personnel to betray that trust.

What should be done?

If market timing is wrong, then the obvious remedy is for all parties to refrain from doing it. This solution overlooks the conditions that led to the scandal in the first place. The failure is not a simple lack of recognition about what is right and wrong but rather the result of a number of converging forces. When an unethical practice occurs simultaneously in such a large number of financial institutions, including some of the most respected and successful mutual fund companies, the underlying causes are likely to be complex.

In this case, the factors are easily recognized. The mutual fund industry is relatively young, coming into existence after the passage of the Investment Company Act of 1940. Only in recent years has institutional investing by mutual funds, as well as pension funds, exceeded individual stock ownership. The popularity of mutual funds increased significantly with the bull market of the 1990s. Because of the small size of the industry through much of its short history and its reputation for trust and integrity, it has been lightly regulated. Although mutual fund companies are not recognized as self-regulating organizations like the major exchanges, such as the New York Stock Exchange or NASDAQ, and are formally under the jurisdiction of the SEC, they operate with little oversight, and neither Congress nor the SEC has seen a need for extensive regulation. The mutual fund industry is supported by a large national trade association, the Investment Company Institute, founded in 1940, which aggressively advances the interest of its member companies and generally opposes proposed additional regulation.

The market-timing scandal occurred between 2000 and 2003, which was a difficult period of reduced returns due to the piercing of a bubble in the economy. The decade prior saw a bull market in which the mutual fund industry experienced tremendous growth and record-setting revenues. However, a few large mutual fund companies, including Fidelity and Vanguard, had captured a large market share, leaving a multitude of small firms to compete for the rest of the market. In 2001, the combination of too many mutual fund companies and fewer, more wary investors created great pressure on mutual fund companies to maintain the expected high earnings. In the words of one observer, the explanation of the scandal is as follows:

Put it all together—light regulation, a savvy trade association, a compliant Congress, a declining market, and frantic competition over a shrinking investment pie—and you get the witches' brew of unsavory business practices now being uncovered. It was a disaster waiting to happen.[60]

In the wake of the mutual fund scandal, many reforms have been proposed. However, one school of thought contends that no action is needed because the market has already worked to correct the problem. The loss of reputation, as well as the heavy financial penalties incurred, have sufficiently punished the offenders and provided a deterrent to others. Moreover, the conditions that gave rise to the scandal are unlikely to occur again soon. Among the proposed reforms are the following:

(1) *Governance.* Where were the directors of mutual funds when market timers were allowed to engage in rapid in-and-out trading? Ultimately, the board of directors of a fund is responsible for ensuring that investors' interests are served. However, directors typically serve on dozens, if not hundreds, of boards. In some mutual fund companies, every fund has the same directors and chairman. Many of the directors and chairmen are also company executives or else have close ties to the company, so that they are not truly independent. Thus, they face a conflict of interest: Is their first loyalty to the investors, whose interests they have a fiduciary duty to serve, or to the mutual fund company, which has selected them to serve on this board? Various proposals have been advanced to limit the number of boards on which directors serve, to increase the percentage of independent directors, and to require that the chairman of the board be an independent party who is not otherwise connected with the mutual fund company.

(2) *Disclosure.* If market timing harms investors, then the losses should be reflected in the form of reduced returns, which, if detected, would enable investors to avoid market-timing funds. In a market with perfect information, investors would be adequately protected. However, the lack of disclosure makes it difficult for investors to detect such losses or to assess the costs of a fund and compare the returns of competing funds. Mutual fund investors pay a management fee, which is typically around 1 percent. Whether any particular fee is high or low depends on the quantity and quality of the trading that takes place, which is difficult for an investor to determine. Generally, the compensation to fund managers is not broken out. The management fee does not include brokerage expenses, which are subtracted from the fund's returns. Any soft-dollar arrangements, which are rolled into brokerage fees, are also not disclosed. Many mutual funds impose separate 12(b)-1 fees, which

pay for marketing expenses. Proposals have been advanced to require the disclosure of information about a fund's expenses that would enable investors to determine whether they are receiving adequate value for the fees they pay and whether their return is being reduced by market timing and other abuses in mutual fund trading.

(3) *Pricing.* Market timing, especially in international funds, is possible because of the problem of stale prices. If the net value of a fund that is reported at four o'clock New York time does not accurately reflect the current prices of the securities in the fund's portfolio, then an opportunity for stale price arbitrage exists. Rather than prohibit or otherwise try to protect against this practice—by changes in governance or disclosure rules, for example—another strategy is to eliminate the opportunity. There have been various proposals for mutual funds to implement what is called "fair-value pricing," in which the net values of funds that are reported each day at the close of the market incorporate any market-moving developments. Fair-value pricing would affect principally international funds and would require that Asian and European securities be priced not at the close of local markets, which occurred many hours ago, but at the price they are likely to have when the local markets open. Some mutual fund companies already practice fair-value pricing when trading has halted in a stock or a thinly traded stock has no recent activity. Fair-value pricing is also practiced by some companies, and is endorsed by the SEC, when closing prices are affected by "significant events" that raise or lower stock prices by some threshold amount, usually around 3 percent. Some critics of fair-value pricing argue, though, that it gives too much discretion to fund managers and that uneven use could affect the reporting of fund returns.[61]

Whatever reforms are eventually made, the mutual fund industry, which had a relatively blemish-free reputation prior to 2003, has shown that it is not immune to scandal and that greater oversight of some form—whether it be industry self-regulation or government regulation—is necessary.

Notes

1. "Burned by Merrill," *BusinessWeek*, April 25, 1994, 122–5.
2. This condition for fairness in exchange is limited to the two parties to a transaction, but an exchange between two parties can also be unfair to a third party. Thus, further conditions for fairness must be developed to address the problem of fairness to third parties.
3. The concept of economic rationality is explained in most introductory textbooks in economics. For more detailed explanations, see John Harsanyi, *Rational*

Behavior and Bargaining Equilibrium in Games and Social Situations (Cambridge: Cambridge University Press, 1977); and Edward McClennen, *Rationality and Dynamic Choice: Fundational Explorations* (Cambridge: Cambridge University Press, 1990).

4. Penelope Wang, "Why Mutual Funds Investors Need a Truth-in-Labeling Law," *Money Magazine*, October 1995, 54; John S. Longstaff, "Has Your Mutual Fund Changed its Personality?" *Money Magazine*, January 1996, 47.

5. Ellen E. Schultz, "SEC Staff Supports Limited Disclosure of Variable-Annuity Fees in Ad Charts," *Wall Street Journal*, November 7, 1995, C25.

6. Schultz, "SEC Staff Supports Limited Disclosure of Variable-Annuity Fees in Ad Charts."

7. Remark by Peter Rawlins, then chairman of the London Stock Exchange, *Times Business News*, February 29, 1992, B1.

8. Office of Compliance, Inspections and Examinations, Securities and Exchange Commission, *Inspection Report on the Soft Dollar Practices of Broker–Dealers, Investment Advisers and Mutual Funds*, September 22, 1998.

9. Association for Investment Management and Research, *CFA Institute Soft Dollar Standards: Guidance for Ethical Practices Involving Client Brokerage*, 1998.

10. D. Bruce Johnsen, "Property Rights to Investment Research: The Agency Costs of Soft Dollar Brokerage," *Yale Law Journal on Regulation*," 11 (1994), 75–113.

11. D. Bruce Johnsen and Stephen M. Horan, *The Welfare Effects of Soft Dollar Brokerage: Law and Economics*, monograph from the Association for Investment Management and Research, 2000.

12. Stanley Luxenberg, "Who's Churning Whom?," *Forbes*, December 1985, 73.

13. Jeff Bailey, "A Man and His Loan: Why Bennie Roberts Refinanced 10 Times," *Wall Street Journal*, April 23, 1997, A1, A13.

14. Walt Bogdanish, "Irate Borrowers Accuse ITT's Loan Companies of Deceptive Practices," *Wall Street Journal*, February 26, 1985, A1. Charles McCoy, "ITT Unit Settles Fraud Charges in California," *Wall Street Journal*, September 22, 1989, A3.

15. Robert Berner, "U.S. Files Suit Against Sears Roebuck Charging Unfair Card-Debt Collection," *Wall Street Journal*, April 18, 1997, A10.

16. *Report of the Committee on Compensation Practices*, issued by the Securities and Exchange Commission, April 10, 1995.

17. *Marshak v. Blyth Eastman Dillon & Co. Inc.*, 413 F. Supp. 377, 379 (1975).

18. *Kaufman v. Merrill Lynch, Pierce, Fenner & Smith*, 464 F. Supp. 528, 534 (1978).

19. *Ernst & Ernst v. Hochfelder*, 425 U.S. 185, 193 (1976); 96 S. Ct. 1375, 1381 (1976).

20. The formula is $ATR = P/E \times 365/D$, where P = total cost of purchases made during a given period, E = average equity in the account during the same period, and D = the number of days during the period.

21. Marion V. Heacock, Kendall P. Hill, and Seth C. Anderson, "Churning: An Ethical Issue in Finance," *Business and Professional Ethics Journal*, 6 (1) (1987), 3–17.

22. For objections to these measures, see Robert F. Almeder and Milton Snoeyenbos, "Churning: Ethical and Legal Issues," *Business and Professional Ethics Journal*, 6 (1) (1987), 22—31.

23. *Hecht v. Harris, Upham & Co.*, 238 F. Supp. 417, 435 (1968).

24. *NASD Rules of Fair Practice*, art. III, sec. 2.

25. Harry M. Markowitz, "Portfolio Selection," *Journal of Finance*, 7 (1952), 77–91; and Harry M. Markowitz, *Portfolio Selection* (New Haven, CT: Yale University Press, 1959).

26. "Arbitration Task Force Issues 70 Recommendations in Largest Revamping of Securities Arbitration Since Its Start More than a Century Ago," NASD Press Release, January 22, 1996.

27. Rep. Edward I. Markey of Massachusetts, quoted in Shirley Hobbs Scheibla, "See You in Court," *Barron's*, June 5, 1989, 13.

28. 482 U.S. 220 (1987), cert. denied 483 U.S. 1056 (1987).

29. *Securities Arbitration Reform: Report of the Arbitration Policy Task Force*, January 1996, 15.

30. Margaret A. Jacobs and Michael Siconolfi, "Investors Fare Poorly Fighting Wall Street—And May Do Worse," *Wall Street Journal*, February 8, 1995, A8. The quotation from the *Wall Street Journal* is a paraphrase of the speaker's words.

31. NASD Press Release, January 22, 1996.

32. *Securities Arbitration Reform*, 88.

33. *Securities Arbitration Reform*, 10.

34. The Ruder Commission estimated that a limit of two times compensatory damages would have reduced the punitive damage award in 20 percent of the approximately 200 cases in which punitive damages were assessed between 1991 and 1995, and would have affected approximately 0.2 percent of all NASD arbitration cases. During the same period, a $750,000 cap would have reduced the punitive damage award in 11 of the 200 cases. *Securities Arbitration Reform*, 44.

35. *Securities Arbitration Reform*, 45.

36. Michael Schroeder, "Wall Street Should Stop Playing the Bully," *BusinessWeek*, December 20, 1993, 92.

37. Michael Lewis, "Fidelities Revisited," *New York Times Magazine*, January 21, 1996, 18.

38. See also Robert McGough and Jeffrey Taylor, "SEC Boosts Its Scrutiny of Magellan Fund," *Wall Street Journal*, December 11, 1995, Cl; Jeffrey Taylor, "SEC Has Array of Tools in Magellan Probe," *Wall Street Journal*, December 26, 1995, C19; and Jeffrey Taylor, "SEC Action Is Unlikely on Vinik," *Wall Street Journal*, May 9, 1996, Cl.

39. *Personal Investment Activities of Investment Company Personnel*, Report of the Division of Investment Management, United States Securities and Exchange Commission, September 1994.

40. *Report of the Advisory Group on Personal Investing*, Investment Company Institute, May 9, 1994. For a discussion of the ICI report, see Ronald F. Duska, "Should Mutual Fund Managers Be Banned From Personal Trading?" in W. Michael Hoffman, Judith Brown Kamm, Robert E. Frederick, and Edward S. Petry, eds., *The Ethics of Accounting and Finance: Trust, Responsibility, and Control* (Westport, CT: Quorum Books, 1996), 18–27.
41. *Personal Investment Activities of Investment Company Personnel*, 1.
42. For convenience, the terms *fund manager* and *access people* will be used interchangeably, and both apply to portfolio managers, analysts, traders, and all others for whom personal trading is an issue.
43. This summary is taken from *Report of the Advisory Group on Personal Investing*, 10.
44. These points are developed in *Personal Investment Activities of Investment Company Personnel*, 4.
45. Roger M. Klein, "Inspire Them to Own That Which They Tout," *New York Times*, October 29, 1995, sec. 3, p. 12.
46. *Report of the Advisory Group on Personal Investing*, 21–2.
47. Karen Damato, "Mutual Funds Boast: We Buy Our Own Stuff," *Wall Street Journal*, March 15, 1997, Cl.
48. *Personal Investment Activities of Investment Company Personnel*, 28.
49. *Report of the Advisory Group on Personal Investing*, 27.
50. *Personal Investment Activities of Investment Company Personnel*, 33; *Report of the Advisory Group on Personal Investing*, 50.
51. Robert McGough, "Few Mutual Funds Ban Personal Shorting," *Wall Street Journal*, June 24, 1996, C21.
52. Paula Dwyer and Amy Borrus, "The Coming Reforms," *BusinessWeek*, November 10, 2003, 116.
53. Testimony of Eric W. Zitzewitz before the United States House of Representatives, Committee on Financial Services, Subcommittee on Capital Markets, Insurance, and Government-Sponsored Enterprises, November 6, 2003.
54. Eric W. Zitzewitz, "Who Cares about Shareholder? Arbitrage-proofing Mutual Funds," *Journal of Law, Economics, and Organization*, 19 (2006), 245–80.
55. Eric W. Zitzewitz, "How Widespread Was Late Trading in Mutual Funds," *AEA Papers and Proceedings*, May 2006.
56. Peter Elkind, "The Secrets of Eddie Stern," *Fortune*, April 19, 2004, 106. Much of the information in this section is taken from this article.
57. Ibid.
58. Riva D. Atlas, "Fund Executive Accepts Life Ban in Trading Case," *New York Times*, May 21, 2004, sec. A, p. 1.
59. Elkind, "The Secrets of Eddie Stern."
60. Paul Dwyer, "Breach of Trust,' *BusinessWeek*, December 15, 2003, 98.
61. Andrew Caffrey, "Critics Decry Uneven Use of 'Fair-value Pricing'," *Boston Globe*, September 12, 2003, D1.

Chapter Four

Ethical Issues in Investment Decisions

The importance of financial institutions for our personal economic well-being is obvious, but investment decisions by large holders of capital profoundly affect the quality of life in our communities and the nation. Investment decisions are critical to society because they select from the opportunities that are available and determine the direction that we will take as a people. However, investment decisions are supposed to be based on objective calculations of risk and reward, not on considerations of the public good or social welfare. According to Adam Smith's famous metaphor, though, an "invisible hand" hovers over the marketplace and promotes an end that is not a part of anyone's intention. The marketplace is prone to many well-known failures, however, and the market mechanism is not intended to promote some ends, such as equality in society. Correcting for market failures and managing the equity/efficiency trade-off are accepted tasks of government. Such a neat separation of roles is not always possible or desirable, and it is questionable whether a viable economy can permit investment decisions to be made without some attention to their social impact.

This chapter is concerned with the ethical aspects of investment decisions. Whereas the previous chapter addresses the financial services industry, in which institutions serve primarily as intermediaries; the focus of this one is on major economic actors, that is, on institutions that actively invest. Commercial banks are included in this group because they have traditionally invested in the communities where they are located, providing loans for homeowners and businesspeople. In the pursuit of profits, some banks have allegedly ignored community needs and contributed to urban decay by figuratively marking off areas on city maps in a process known as *redlining*. Some individuals are "investing with their heart" and are seeking with their investment dollars to support corporations that have a beneficial impact on society. This phenomenon, known as *socially responsible investing*, raises some important ethical issues. Finally, institutional investors, especially the managers of large pension funds, face peculiar problems in exercising the responsibilities of shareholders on behalf of the people whose pension funds they manage. The rise of large institutional investors thus raises questions about their role in corporate governance, and one response to these questions has been the development of *relationship investing*. This chapter concludes with an examination of the ethical implications of the so-called "new finance" for investment decision making.

Bank Lending Practices

In the classic 1946 film "It's a Wonderful Life," the kind-hearted banker George Bailey, played by James Stewart, considers a person's character in assessing creditworthiness, while Mr Potter, a stingy, suspicious banker, routinely denies mortgages to poor but creditworthy citizens. The climactic scenes of the film feature an angel who deters George Bailey from committing suicide after the failure of his bank, by showing what would have happened to the community had he never existed. The film vividly illustrates the importance of bank loans for ordinary people and the difference between the lending policies of a George Bailey and a Mr Potter.

The banking industry has changed dramatically since 1946, but some issues have remained constant.[1] The responsibility of banks to serve the people in their community is at issue today in the charge that lending practices discriminate against the residents of decaying urban areas, especially racial minorities.[2] In 1990, Comerica, a Detroit-based bank, rejected 13 percent of mortgage applications from white applicants, while the rejection rate for blacks was 43 percent. Across the country black applicants are turned down at a rate that is 2.4 times higher than the rate for whites, and rates of rejection are also high for Hispanic applicants.[3]

The discrepancy might be explained by differences in the creditworthiness of white and nonwhite applicants. However, a study conducted by the Federal Reserve Bank of Boston in 1992 applied a formula for creditworthiness based on 19 factors, and discovered that nonwhite applicants were still rejected at higher rates than the formula predicted.[4] Use of the formula reduced the difference between the rejection rate for white and nonwhite applicants from 18 percentage points to 8. Thus, differences in creditworthiness between white and nonwhite applicants might account for 10 percentage points, but the remaining 8 percentage points are due, apparently, to discrimination. Despite objections to the statistical interpretation of the data (which is discussed below), the Boston Federal Reserve Bank study has galvanized critics of bank lending practices and increased the calls for reform.

Whether racial discrimination occurs in bank lending is important for two reasons. One is its bearing on the fight against racial discrimination in employment, housing, education, and other areas of life. The issue is one of civil rights. The second reason is the impact of discriminatory lending patterns on urban development. If banks engage in redlining in the belief that certain neighborhoods are in decline, then their predictions become self-fulfilling and condemn these areas to further deterioration. The banks argue that they are merely responding to market forces, but others question whether they correctly understand urban trends or recognize the economic opportunities. As one writer observed, "neighborhood residents and small business owners began to discern a red pen in the invisible hand of the market."[5]

The redlining controversy has arisen in a complex set of circumstances that includes the decay of America's inner cities and the deregulation of the banking industry. The competition to increase the volume of high-interest loans fueled both the reckless extension of credit to less-developed countries (LDCs) in the 1970s and the savings-and-loan (S&L) crisis of the 1980s. These developments raise many ethical issues that cannot be examined here. A complete discussion of ethics in banking would also include the operation of rogue banks, such as the Bank of Credit and Commerce International (BCCI), the laundering of drug money and the movement of capital for international organized crime, and bank secrecy. For example, Swiss banks, which are famed for their secrecy, have been accused of hiding Nazi gold and the deposits of Holocaust victims for more than 50 years.

The redlining controversy

In testimony before Congress in 1992, a member of the Board of Governors of the Federal Reserve System declared:

> Let me be absolutely clear about the position of the Board of Governors. Discrimination based on race, gender, or ethnic background is not only illegal, it is morally repugnant. Indeed, there is only one legitimate criterion on which to base loan decisions: the expectation that repayment will be made according to the terms stipulated in the loan agreement. Our efforts must be directed at ensuring that only this criterion is used to make home mortgage or other loan decisions.[6]

That the law prohibits discrimination in home mortgage lending is clear. In addition to the 1964 Civil Rights Act, which addresses discrimination in many areas, Congress has passed the 1968 Fair Housing Act (amended in 1988), the 1974 Equal Opportunity Credit Act, the Home Mortgage Disclosure Act of 1975 (HMDA, pronounced "hum-da"), the Community Reinvestment Act of 1977 (CRA), and the 1989 Financial Institutions Reform, Recovery, and Enforcement Act (FIRREA). The CRA imposes a legal obligation on regulated lending institutions to meet the legitimate credit needs of the residents in their service area, and the HMDA further requires lenders to report by census tract the location of their mortgage and home improvement loans. The FIRREA expanded the reporting requirements of lending institutions and mandated public disclosure of the CRA ratings on each bank's performance.

Although creditworthiness is commonly accepted as the only legally and ethically acceptable criterion for making loan decisions, considerable controversy still surrounds the interpretation of this criterion and the means for enforcing it. The problem in a nutshell is how regulators and community activists can determine whether the loan practices of a bank are nondiscriminatory. Alternatively, what can banks do to show that they are in compliance with the law? The CRA has not been vigorously enforced, in part because of the difficulty of interpreting the available evidence. This lack of enforcement harms the people and communities that the CRA is intended to help. On the other hand, banks are placed at undue risk if they are unable to assess their own performance and correct any deficiencies.

Prior to the Clinton administration, enforcement of the CRA was based largely on process rather than performance. Banks documented their compliance by detailing their efforts to serve their communities. Critics charge that this emphasis on process encourages lending institutions to engage in highly visible but not always productive activities. For many banks, CRA compliance has been an exercise in public relations. Examiners also check for compliance by targeting files for further review. Typically, this process consists of comparing the loan applications of marginally qualified white applicants which were approved and the loan applications of marginally qualified nonwhite applicants which were not approved, in order to determine whether the deciding differences are related to race. Unfortunately, there is no uniform, objective methodology for comparing the selected files. An examiner is in the position of second-guessing the judgment of the original loan officer, and banks can never be sure that their method of selection will match that of an examiner.

Federal regulators and academic investigators have come to rely increasingly on the statistical analysis of large bodies of data Such a numbers-driven approach—which is represented by the Boston Federal Reserve Bank study—has been welcomed by critics of bank lending practices and by the banking industry itself. Although objective quantitative measurement enables critics to back up their charges more effectively, it also gives banks better guidance on how to comply with the law. The stumbling block is the interpretation of the data. Despite abundant HMDA data, researchers disagree on whether discrimination is occurring and, if so, what is the cause and what can be done to counter it.

The Boston Fed study

In 1992, the Federal Reserve Bank of Boston released a study which concluded that racial discrimination is widely practiced in the banking industry. The study was based on detailed information on black and Hispanic applicants from 131 home mortgage lenders in the Boston area. In comparing this data with a random sample of white applicants, the researchers found that non-white applicants were 2.7 times more likely to be rejected than white applicants. Many of the applications were rejected for legitimate reasons, but after adjusting the data for creditworthiness, the rejection of nonwhite applicants was still 1.6 times that of whites. The release of the Boston Fed study strengthened the hand of community activists nationwide and increased the pressure on banks to redouble their efforts. Boston area lenders agreed to provide $200 million in financing for subsidized housing and another $30 million for below-market-rate mortgages.[7] Shawmut National Corporation, the third largest bank in New England, settled a lending-discrimination suit with the Justice Department by paying $960,000 to black and Hispanic residents who were denied loans.[8]

Soon after the release of the Boston Fed study, academic critics questioned the soundness of the results.[9] Some critics charged that the data omitted important variables that loan officers consider, such as the ability to confirm information that applicants have provided and the availability of cash for closing costs. Others found anomalies in the data, such as five applicants who were turned down for government-subsidized mortgages because they earned too much to qualify for them.[10] Much of the debate over the Boston Fed study focuses on the statistical techniques that the researchers used.

One widely reported objection, supported by economist Gary S. Becker in a *BusinessWeek* column, is the lack of an expected difference in default rates between white and nonwhite mortgage holders.[11] If discrimination occurs in home mortgage lending, then presumably some marginally qualified nonwhite applicants are rejected while white applicants with the same qualifications are extended loans. As a consequence, successful nonwhite applicants would be, on average, more qualified than successful white applicants and hence less likely to default on their loans. The default rate for nonwhites, therefore, should be lower than for whites if discrimination occurs, but no such difference can be found. Indeed, critics argue that identical default rates for all races actually show that lenders are adept at evaluating risk without regard for race.[12]

The Boston Fed researchers rebut the default-rate argument by noting, first, that the argument assumes that discrimination operates by excluding marginally qualified nonwhite applicants, so that successful nonwhite applicants must be more creditworthy than their white counterparts. However, if some lenders discriminate against all nonwhite applicants or practice discrimination in a random or arbitrary manner, then the same lack of difference in default rates could still be observed. Second, the critics' argument assumes that if there were no discrimination, then creditworthy applicants of all races would default at the same rate. However, factors other than discrimination could lead to differences in the rate of default. Hypothetically, white mortgage-holders could be less creditworthy as a group but default no more often than nonwhite mortgage-holders because of, say, a higher income.[13]

Despite some contrary voices, the Boston Fed study is widely respected by experts.[14] The dispute turns primarily on technical points in statistical analysis, which are scarcely matters of ethics. Some important questions of ethics are still at issue. In particular, whether there is discrimination in mortgage lending is vitally important to bank regulation. Because regulators have enormous discretion in approving applications to open and close branches, expand into new fields, and so on, banks are eager to take steps to avoid charges of discrimination. If these steps involve unwise lending practices, then the higher cost of mortgage lending is passed along to all bank customers. Even if investment in low- and moderate-income neighborhoods is a worthy social goal in its own right, it is better, as a matter of public policy, to appropriate the funds for that purpose than to mandate community investment under the guise of enforcing antidiscrimination laws.[15]

Tests of discrimination

Regardless of whether discrimination is widespread, statistical tests are needed in order to determine whether any given lender is discriminating.[16] The tests that have been proposed are not wholly satisfactory, and the appropriateness of any given test depends on problematical assumptions about the causes of discrimination.

One alleged cause of home-mortgage discrimination is *systematic disinvestment*, whereby banks receive deposits from the residents of an area but do not return a proportionate amount in loans. One test for systematic disinvestment is the *ratio of loans to deposits* for any given, community—60 percent is commonly used by federal regulators—and possible solutions include steps to increase the loan-to-deposit ratio to some specified level. However, if systematic disinvestment is not the cause—that is, if banks are making loans to all creditworthy residents who need credit—then regulatory pressure to increase the proportion of loans could lead banks to make unsound loans to racial minorities or to push loans onto people who do not need them. Both results would harm rather than help the residents of poor communities.

Another possible cause of discrimination is that banks do not exploit poor communities but, rather, neglect them. Banks may serve their defined service area well, providing loans in a uniformly high ratio to deposits, but if the boundaries include well-to-do neighborhoods and exclude the less well-to-do, then discrimination may still occur. A proposed remedy for this kind of neglect is the *market share test.* This test is applied by comparing a bank's loans in low- and moderate-income areas with other lenders in the larger community. Thus, a bank with a 15 percent market share of business in the greater Chicago area should make approximately 15 percent of the total loans that are made by all lending institutions in poorer communities. The market share test has been urged by several influential members of Congress and was proposed by the Clinton administration in December 1993, but it has not yet been adopted by federal regulators because of vigorous opposition by the banking industry.

The market share test addresses the problem that loan applicants in poorer communities are generally less creditworthy. The underlying assumption is that if a bank employs standard criteria for evaluating loan applications *and* serves a representative service area, then the proportion of that bank's loans to low- and moderate-income areas should be equal to or greater than the proportion of similar loans for all local lending institutions. If adopted, the market share test would not force a bank to serve the whole of a major metropolitan area—some geographical specialization would still be permitted—but it would virtually prevent a bank from serving only select, affluent areas. Moreover, the market share test relies on the effectiveness of market competition because of the further assumption that enterprising lenders will seek out creditworthy but underserved inner-city residents. As a result, the overall proportion of loans in poorer areas will increase, and all local lending institutions will be forced to follow suit. In short, the leaders in the inner-city market will set the standard for other lenders to follow.

Opponents of the market share test argue that its adoption would skew market share percentages in favor of small banks that specialize in loans to poorer communities, and large multipurpose banks that can easily expand their service area and perhaps afford riskier loans.[17] Even so, the market share test would prevent a bank from expanding in an affluent area without also expanding in poorer neighborhoods, where more banking outlets may not be needed. Small, community-based mortgage lenders which cannot expand beyond a core service area would be handicapped. This objection might be met by setting different standards or providing a "streamlined" review procedure for smaller lending institutions which demonstrate that they meet local community needs.

The loan-to-deposit test and the market share test bypass the question of the causes of discrimination and focus attention on an outcome of a nondiscriminatory mortgage loan system. Their effectiveness as statistical measures depends, however, on some assumptions about causes, such as systematic disinvestment and selective service areas, and their implementation could possibly have unforeseen adverse consequences. Still, the ethical debate over the remedies for discrimination in the mortgage loan market revolves around issues of fairness, not only to mortgage loan customers but between lending institutions.

The redlining controversy shows us that agreement on an ethical imperative—in this case the abolition of all discrimination in home mortgage lending—is not always the end of a debate but sometimes merely the beginning. The debate is primarily factual. Does discrimination occur? How can banks demonstrate that they are not discriminating? What could they do to prevent discrimination? However, the use of statistical studies to settle public policy questions itself raises some ethical difficulties, and the use of tests of discrimination, such as loan-to-deposit ratios or the market share test, must be decided, in part, on ethical grounds.

Socially Responsible Investing

In picking stocks, some individuals consider values to be as important as P/E ratios. These virtuous souls want to make sure that their dollars do not support objectionable business activities. Similarly, charities, foundations, religious groups, universities, and other nonprofit organizations have long sought stocks that are compatible with their institutional values. By contrast, some investors avidly pursue so-called "sin stocks." Morgan Funshares, for example, specializes in alcohol, tobacco, and gambling companies and finds support among folks who take delight in profiting from the folly of others.[18] The only trouble with tainted profits, they say, is "there 'taint enough of them." For most people, however, the stock market is merely a place to invest with no thought to the uses that others make of their money. The advice of financial experts is that if you care about the environment, civil rights, or public health, contribute your gains to worthy causes or engage in political activity—but don't mix money and morals.[19]

In recent years, investors who care about where their money goes have been aided by mutual funds and pension funds that screen for social responsibility factors, and a number of organizations now provide research for socially responsible investing (SRI).[20] A study by the Social Investment Forum in 1995 found that $162 billion is currently being managed by socially screened funds and an additional $474 billion by institutional investors that actively support socially responsible change. SRI is a rapidly growing movement in the United States and a few other countries, most notably the United Kingdom.

Despite the admirable intent of socially responsible investors, some troubling questions surround the movement. In addition to the practical difficulty of identifying socially responsible and irresponsible companies, critics challenge whether the effort makes any difference. Investors engage in SRI for different reasons—some to feel good about making money in stocks, others to bring about changes in corporate America—and whether SRI makes any difference depends on the aim. Individual investors are free to buy stocks for any reason they please and to pay the price if SRI produces lower returns. Likewise, mutual fund and pension companies are at liberty to attract investors by offering to screen their holdings, as long as the commitment to SRI is clearly stated and investment is voluntary. More debatable, however, is whether portfolio managers who have a fiduciary duty to seek the highest return for investors have a right to consider nonfinancial factors in the selection of stocks—especially if SRI reduces overall results.

What is socially responsible investing?

SRI takes many forms. It can be as simple as a policy to avoid "sin stocks" or companies engaged in unpopular causes. During the 1970s, many individuals and institutions shunned the stocks of companies that were linked with South Africa or the war in Vietnam, and today many investors still reject stocks that are associated with military weapons or nuclear energy. More commonly, specialty mutual funds and pension funds promise to select stocks that meet certain standards of social responsibility. Other forms of SRI activity include sponsoring shareholder resolutions on social issues, engaging in a dialogue with corporations on matters of concern, and investing in specific, socially responsible ventures. The latter are commonly called Program Related Investment (PRI) and Economically Targeted Investment (ETI).

Screened funds employ negative screens to exclude the stock of companies which are engaged in particular businesses or which have objectionable records of performance. Some also use positive screens that identify companies with notable achievements in such areas as environmental protection, the promotion of women and minorities, family-friendly programs, charitable giving, community outreach, customer and supplier relations, product quality and safety, political activity, and responsiveness to public concerns. Many mainstream mutual fund and pension fund companies offer one or more SRI funds. Support for SRI is provided by socially responsible investment advisory and portfolio management companies and by organizations, most notably the Social Investment Forum.

Proponents of SRI have diverse aims. Some investors apparently feel a personal responsibility for the use that is made of their money. Many would no doubt refuse to invest in a brothel in Nevada (where prostitution is legal) on the grounds that they would be participating in an immoral activity, enabling others to act immorally, or profiting from the immorality of others. However, it is not evident that a shareholder in a brothel enterprise would actually be participating in this activity or enabling others to do so. Obviously, the responsibility of investors for the activities of the firms in which they invest is a perplexing ethical issue.[23] Much depends on whether investors' decisions have any substantial impact on corporate behavior, a question that is discussed below.

Many active members of the SRI movement are not motivated by "feel-good" impulses but by a desire to change the world. Historically, the movement developed in the l960s as part of the struggle against apartheid in South Africa and the war in Vietnam. Frustrated activists used protests at annual meetings, shareholder resolutions, and pressure on institutional investors, such as university endowment funds, to advance their cause. In 1969, the Council on Economic Priorities was formed, and their work resulted in a series of guides for investors and consumers with such titles as *Rating America's Corporate Conscience: a Provocative Guide to the Companies behind the Products You Buy Everyday*[22] and *The Better World Investment Guide*.

Today, most SRI proponents believe that screened funds serve primarily to provide competitive returns, with the achievement of some beneficial results as a secondary aim. SRI, they claim, is a viable investment approach that takes advantage of the superior long-term performance of socially responsible corporations. Corporations that pass SRI screens are generally well run and unlikely to face major crises and scandals. SRI may also contribute to improved performance by increasing communication between corporations and investors about social issues, and prompting corporations to undertake socially responsible initiatives.

The research to date has failed to find any statistically significant difference in the returns of SRI funds.[23] Their performance is, on the whole, no better and no worse than comparable stock portfolios. However, these studies cover a relatively brief time-period in which the stock market has risen steadily. The returns must be adjusted for risk, and some researchers suggest that SRI funds may be riskier, on the whole, because of less diversification and greater holdings of small capitalization stocks.[24] In addition, successful firms are able to invest more in social responsibility, so that SRI screens may introduce a bias in favor of corporations with strong past earnings records. Such a bias would explain competitive short-term results but would be a poor predictor of performance in the long run.

Can SRI make a difference?

Is socially responsible investing capable of producing superior results while making the world a better place? If so, then the case for SRI could not be stronger. Even if the returns are competitive or only slightly lower, then the beneficial consequences would still make SRI an attractive alternative for investors who want to do good as they do well. Unfortunately, the prospects for making the world a better place and making a profit at the same time are not very bright. First, finance theory and, in particular, the efficient market hypothesis challenge the claim that SRI can produce superior returns. Second, the claim that SRI can change corporate investment policy lacks a basis in finance theory.

SRI and fund performance

Finance theory suggests that screened funds should have a lower return because of a lack of diversification and higher transaction costs. That is, reducing the universe of available stocks and adding the cost of screening are self-imposed restrictions that should hamper rather than enhance a fund's performance. The greatest theoretical challenge to the claimed benefits of SRI is posed by the Efficient Market Hypothesis.[25] The semi-strong form of the hypothesis holds that all publicly available information is already reflected in the price of stocks. As a result, the stock market is efficiently priced, and no investor can expect to beat the market on a risk-adjusted basis. That is, investors can achieve superior returns only if they assume more risk (in which case their risk-adjusted returns are the same), or else they must possess information that has not yet been registered in stock prices (which requires that the market be inefficient). The Efficient Market Hypothesis suggests further that actively evaluating individual stocks by any criteria, financial or social, is a waste of resources and that investors should passively select a balanced portfolio that mirrors the broader market.

The stock market is not perfectly efficient, however, and research can yield some gains.[26] But this state of affairs provides little support for SRI, unless the information that is not reflected in prices involves a firm's *social* performance. The case for SRI, then, must be based on the claims that the market is inefficient and that the source of this inefficiency is a failure to recognize the significance of socially responsible activity in the evaluation of stock price. The argument, in short, is that there is a link between social performance and financial performance that is generally ignored in the market, and so SRI funds can beat the market by taking advantage of information that other investors ignore.

That social and financial performance are linked is a reasonable claim that has received some empirical support.[27] That the market ignores information about social responsibility is a more dubious proposition. A firm that has a strong record on the environment, for example, may outperform less environmentally responsible firms because they are more likely to avoid the costs of meeting new regulation and settling legal claims for environmental damage. The reason for this superior performance, however, may be due to a rational calculation that an ounce of prevention is worth a pound of cure. If so, then a higher stock price reflects the fact that the company has made an investment in order to avoid future liabilities, and the lower stock price of a less responsible rival results from the lack of such an investment and a greater potential for future liabilities.

The vulnerability of a corporation to adversity of any kind is information that is ordinarily registered in the market and is not detected solely by social responsibility screens. SRI funds avoid tobacco stocks for ethical reasons, but these stocks are already discounted in the market because of uncertainty over the industry's potential liability. If American tobacco companies were ever to collapse from catastrophic liability judgments, then SRI firms would appear to be vindicated in their exclusion of such a "sin" stock, but the long-term returns of balanced portfolios that include tobacco stocks might be the same as the returns of SRI funds because of the discounting. That is, tobacco stocks now produce superior earnings relative to their (discounted) price, and so the losses to possible future holders of worthless tobacco stocks would be offset by these superior earnings.

The challenge of the Efficient Market Hypothesis, therefore, is that if the market is efficient, then any information about socially responsible practices that is relevant to financial performance will already be registered in the market. SRI funds act on this information by excluding (negative screens) or including (positive screens) the stock. By contrast, the market operates by discounting the price of a stock on the basis of negative information and placing a premium on a stock in the case of positive information. The difference between SRI and ordinary investing is the manner in which each responds to information. SRI funds can produce superior returns, then, only if their screens consistently reflect information that the market has somehow missed, which is unlikely, but still possible.

SRI and investment policy

Whether socially responsible investing is capable of making a better world depends on the ability of investors to change corporate behavior by their investment decisions. The law of supply and demand suggests that if the demand for a stock is increased by socially concerned investors, then the price of a stock in fixed supply will rise. Thus, socially responsible companies will be rewarded by SRI investors with a higher stock price. However, if the price of a stock rises above a level that is supported by its fundamentals, then other investors will sell stock that they own or else cease their demand for the stock. As a result, supply and demand will return to an equilibrium state and the price of the stock will fall to its market value. In the long run, the price of the stock will be unaffected. The only difference will be that the stock of socially responsible companies will be in the hands of socially concerned investors.

This argument assumes that supply and demand are perfectly elastic, which is true for larger, heavily traded corporations. SRI investors are more likely to affect the stock price of smaller, relatively unknown firms, for whose stock the demand is somewhat inelastic. But can the willingness of SRI investors to bid up the price of a stock influence the investment policy of a company? Theoretically, the answer is yes.[28] If a firm makes investment decisions by selecting the opportunity with the highest net present value (NPV), then the increased stock price that results from socially responsible investments would lower the cost of equity for the firm and increase the expected rate of return. In practical terms, however, the shareholders are subsidizing socially responsible activities through their willingness to pay a higher price for the company's stock and accept lower financial performance, which runs counter to the claim that SRI can produce superior returns.

Alternatively, SRI provides an opportunity for smaller companies to compete in the crowded, noisy market for equity. Firms that wish to operate in a socially responsible manner or that merely want ready access to capital may make themselves attractive to SRI funds. Much socially responsible activity is cost-free, and a reputation for social responsibility can be an asset, especially in marketing. Smaller companies that market products like soaps and lotions (The Body Shop), toothpaste (Tom's of Maine), and ice cream (Ben & Jerry's) are able to compete in the mass market with industry giants by offering natural, environmentally friendly products to socially concerned consumers. Such socially responsible companies are usually founded and led by value-driven entrepreneurs who want to do business in a different way. Although they might successfully raise capital in the general market on the basis of their balance sheets, the existence of supportive, understanding SRI investors facilitates the task.

The conclusion to be drawn, then, is that SRI is unlikely to have any impact on larger, heavily traded corporations. It can alter the investment policy of a firm only by raising the price of the firm's stock significantly over a long period of time, but the resulting increase in stock price represents a willingness of investors to subsidize investment in social responsibility. Perhaps the most enduring contribution of SRI is to provide a ready capital market for socially responsible companies that would have difficulty raising capital otherwise. These companies are often highly profitable, so that SRI investors need not necessarily pay a price. But investors need to understand these companies and seek them out in the first place. Socially responsible companies have an impact on American business by pioneering practices that are later adopted by mainstream corporations. Because of this impact, then, socially concerned investors can, in the end, make a difference.

Relationship Investing

Within two decades, a profound shift occurred in the ownership of stock in American corporations. In 1970, individuals held more than 72 percent of shares, while institutional investors (pensions, mutual funds, insurance companies, and private trusts and endowments) accounted for about 16 percent.[29] By 1990, the holdings of institutions had risen to more than 53 percent, with private and public pension funds owning approximately 28 percent of the equities of US firms. By 2003, the percentage of institutional ownership of American equities was 59.2 percent.[30] This transformation has implications not only for the responsibilities of institutional investors toward their beneficiaries but also for the role of institutional investors as shareholders in the American system of corporate governance. In this changed environment, the concept of *relationship investing* (RI) has emerged as one answer to the many questions that institutional investors now face.

Because of the size of their holdings, institutional investors cannot behave like individuals. They cannot easily sell an underperforming stock, for example, but are generally locked into their investments. Instead of active portfolio management that seeks out undervalued stocks, institutional investors passively manage a large portion of their portfolios by indexing them to broad market measures, such as the S&P 500. Institutions also have some opportunities that individual investors lack. In particular, they are in a position to pressure managers of corporations for changes, and some argue that fund managers are not fulfilling their fiduciary duties if they do not exert this power. Individual investors have not taken an active role in corporate governance, with the result that some corporate managers have gotten by with lackluster performance. The rise of institutional investors has been hailed by many as a restoration of strong shareholder control.

Relationship investing is undertaken by institutional investors for diverse reasons. Broadly speaking, the advocates of relationship investing cite three grounds for engaging in it. First, relationship investing is an effective investment strategy that prudent investors may choose to adopt. Indeed, some individual investors, most notably Warren Buffet, have used relationship investing with great success. Second, the fiduciary duties of fund managers may require them to take advantage of the opportunities offered by relationship investing. Third, relationship investing is a solution to a number of critical problems in corporate governance, so that this approach ought to be encouraged. Each of these reasons is examined in turn.

RI as an effective investment strategy

Relationship investing may be defined as a situation in which an investor takes an active interest in a corporation and attempts to influence the corporation's operations. As such, RI is not a new idea. It harks back to an earlier time when stockholding was more concentrated and a few large investors exercised close oversight. Today, venture capitalists and lenders to small businesses, who watch their investments closely, could be called relationship investors. Similarly, the concept of relationship investing has been used to describe the close working relation in Germany and Japan between corporations and large banks, which are the major holders of corporate equity in those countries. Among individual investors, Warren Buffet is known for his strategy of taking large stakes in a few, well-chosen firms and working with them to increase earnings. Other individual investors seek out troubled firms with weak management and seek to increase the value of their investment by pressing for changes in leadership or strategic direction. In some instances, the investors believe that they have expertise that can increase the value of the firm.

Large institutional investors do not have the resources to establish a relation with every corporation in their portfolio. For many years, CalPERS, the pension fund for California state employees, has compiled an annual "hit list" of companies which have underperformed over the previous five-year period.[31] CalPERS executives meet with the CEOs of these companies in order to analyze the causes of low returns and to develop strategic plans for improving performance. In situations where these efforts have failed, CalPERS has resorted to shareholder resolutions and even litigation. CalPERS's efforts have borne fruit. One study reported that 42 companies that CalPERS targeted for aggressive action between 1987 and 1994 lagged the S&P 500 by an average of 66 percent Afterwards, the returns of these companies averaged more than 41 percent *above* the S&P 500.[32]

The ability of institutional investors to influence corporate managers is enhanced when they can combine forces. In the past, SEC proxy rules have made such concerted action difficult by requiring shareholders to file cumbersome statements, but in 1992 the SEC relaxed these rules, thereby increasing the ease of communication among institutional investors. Traditional proxy fights have required dissidents to educate large numbers of relatively unsophisticated shareholders about the issues, whereas today a handful of highly sophisticated institutional investors are able to confer and agree on changes quickly. Activist investors have formed several organizations—most notably the Council of Institutional Investors—in order to exert joint pressure more effectively.

Generally, institutional investors have focused on major issues in corporate governance and strategic direction and have avoided social issues. This choice has been dictated both by a fiduciary duty to increase bottom-line value for the funds' beneficiaries and by the difficulty of articulating a position on social issues that reflects the interests of all beneficiaries. In recent years, concerted action by institutional investors has forced CEO changes at Chrysler, American Express, and Borden, and resulted in major restructurings at USX, Westinghouse, Sears, and Eastman Kodak. Institutional investors have pressured corporations to include more outside directors on boards, establish independent compensations committees, separate the roles of CEO and chair of the board of directors, and avoid poison pills and other defences against takeovers. In addition, institutional investors have supported regulatory reform, such as the changes in SEC proxy rules that facilitate communication.

As an investment strategy, RI is forced upon institutional investors by the size of their holdings. Institutional investors are not like traditional investors, who can move in and out of the market freely; they are more like owners, who are stuck with a stock. CalPERS CEO Dale M. Hanson uses the analogy: "If we buy an office building and the property manager isn't properly maintaining it, we don't sell the building—we change the property manager."[33] The largest pension and mutual funds, such as CalPERS and Fidelity, hold between 1 and 3 percent of the largest American corporations. Positions of that size cannot be sold in the open market without depressing prices, and the only buyers are other institutional investors, who are apt to hold a similar evaluation of a stock.

Although the costs of relationship investing are high, they are typically less than the expense involved in selling one stock and buying another. Albert O. Hirschman, in his book *Exit, Voice, and Loyalty*, observes that dissatisfied members of an organization who can easily leave (exit) do not attempt to speak up for change (voice), but that members who cannot use the exit option have no choice but to use voice.[34] Thus, RI is a rational choice for institutional investors who are locked in and have only the voice option to express their dissatisfaction.

Many advocates of RI argue that not only shareholders but managers themselves benefit from more active, informed involvement. Institutional investors provide patient capital, which is cited as a feature of the German and Japanese systems that enables firms to develop long-term plans. Outsiders also provide specialized skills and fresh perspectives that can help solve problems and prevent costly mistakes. Corporate managers are advised to view relationship investors as a valuable resource. On the downside, more cautious critics argue that relationship investing can lead to meddling by outsiders that distracts managers and diffuses their focus. Institutional shareholders may be pursuing agendas that run counter to the interests of the corporation and other shareholders. In particular, the change in the SEC rules that permits greater communication among institutional investors has been criticized for shifting the balance of power away from individual shareholders.[35]

RI and fiduciary duties

Individual shareholders are responsible to no one. Hence, they can pursue investment strategies and exercise their shareholder rights as they choose. The fact that institutional investors are typically both shareholders and fiduciaries creates possibilities for conflicts between these two roles.

First, if RI is an effective investment strategy that is suited to the special circumstances of institutional investors, then they may fail as fiduciaries if they do not take advantage of the opportunity. Some have argued that the decision to index a fund creates a fiduciary duty of active involvement with management, given the commitment not to sell an underperforming stock.[36] As fiduciaries, institutional investors may also face conflicts of interest. For example, investment management companies, which manage portions of portfolios for large pension plans, are reluctant to offend corporations on whom they depend for other business. Similarly, the managers of corporate pension funds face numerous conflicts of interest. Should they invest heavily in the company's own stock or seek better diversification? How should they vote when a management-sponsored proxy proposal is not in the employees' interests? Managers of company pension funds often refrain from pressuring the management of other corporations for fear of reciprocal action.[37] In order to avoid conflicts of interest, the managers of corporate pension funds must be given greater independence to serve the interests of the employees exclusively, which might include the use of RI. Other reforms might include index-ing of corporate pension funds to increase diversification or switching from defined benefit to defined contribution plans, which would increase account-ability of fund managers to employees.

Second, since shareholders have a role to play in corporate governance, institutional investors must decide how they will serve in this role. In par-ticular, they are called upon to take positions on proxy proposals in every corporation in their portfolio. To do nothing or to vote routinely with management is still to take a position. In the interpretation of the Employee Retirement Income Security Act (ERISA) of 1974, which covers private pension plans, the right to vote proxies is considered to be a plan asset and thus is subject to the same strict fiduciary duties that apply to any other asset. Accordingly, pension funds subject to ERISA are legally obligated to develop policies on the voting of proxies. A number of proxy voting services provide analyses and recommendations on proxy proposals and handle the mechanics of submitting proxy votes.

Third, the interests of the beneficiaries of pension funds and other institu-tional investments depend on the performance of the total portfolio. Because these portfolios contain a cross-section of corporations and are heavily indexed, their performance depends more on the health of the American economy than on the success of any particular company. Consequently, a fund manager with a fiduciary duty to serve the beneficiaries' interests has a broader perspective than an individual investor. For example, a merger or acquisition that benefits the shareholders of one company but harms those of another, or that benefits shareholders but harms bondholders, may be opposed by an institutional investor which holds stocks and bonds in both companies.

Furthermore, a pension fund manager might best provide for the secure retirement of a fund's beneficiaries by making investments that create good jobs, affordable housing, and an improved infrastructure. In 1989, the New York State Pension Investment Task Force recommended than the state pension funds use their assets to promote long-term economic growth rather than strict maximization. State pension funds are being urged by the Clinton administration to engage in economically targeted investment (ETI) on the grounds that retirement security depends on the health of the state's economy.[38]

If ETI leads to reduced rates of return, then it violates the fiduciary duties of private pension fund managers under ERISA. The Clinton administration has held that ETI is permissible under ERISA if it meets "the traditional scru-tiny but also create[s] collateral benefits."[39] However, ETI almost always offers a lesser return adjusted for risk, because otherwise the investment would be made without the need for special consideration. So the question becomes how much return can rightly be sacrificed for the collateral benefits, especially when the value of the collateral benefits is difficult to judge.

Public pension funds, which are not subject to ERISA, are especially vulnerable to political influence, and so managers must exercise considerable care to resist unwise uses of fund assets. Experience shows that the managers of public pension funds do not always make wise choices. For example, the Connecticut state pension fund lost $25 million in an unsuccessful attempt to save the jobs provided by Colt Industries, a manufacturer of firearms that eventually declared bankruptcy.[40] The Kansas pension fund invested in a local steel mill and a savings and loan association in order to save jobs and lost more than $100 million when both went bankrupt.[41] Some consider any use of public pension fund money for ETIs to be unsound public policy. If a project benefits the people of a state, then it is worth supporting through the political system with tax dollars that everyone provides. If the investments lower the returns for retirees, then they have been, in effect, taxed to provide a benefit for others.[42]

Improving corporate governance

The shareholders' role in corporate governance is to exercise oversight and ensure accountability. In short, shareholders are the *monitors* of corporations. Before the separation of ownership and control, shareholders were often the managers of an enterprise or else actively involved owners. The rise of the large, publicly held corporation with a mass shareholder base diluted the power of individual shareholders and decreased their incentives to take any action. The result has been the imperial CEO, backed by a complacent board of directors. Without effective monitoring, corporations have engaged in unwise expansion, avoided difficult but necessary changes, and provided lavish compensation. Some companies languish because of operational problems or mistaken strategic plans. The hostile takeover wave of the 1980s was a financial remedy for excesses that were permitted by inadequate monitoring. Relationship investing has been hailed by some advocates as a political alternative that will replace hostile takeovers in the 1990s. John Pound proclaims, "This new form of governance based on politics rather than finance will provide a means of oversight that is both far more effective and far less expensive than the takeovers of the 1980s."[43]

Traditionally, shareholders have monitored corporations by electing the board of directors and voting on proposals for major changes that have been submitted by either shareholders or management. For companies in distress, the main corrective has been the board of directors, which has the authority to replace the top officers and set a new strategic direction. When boards do their job, this form of corporate governance can be very effective. Shareholders have little recourse, however, against an inattentive or incompetent board of directors; board elections and proxy battles are generally too slow and unwieldy to bring about the needed changes. In the 1980s, hostile takeovers provided a quick, albeit ruthless, method for bringing about change. This form of corporate governance involves high transaction costs, however, because of the enormous fees to investment bankers and lawyers, and it also imposes social costs as a result of the dislocation that typically follows in takeovers. (The consequences of hostile takeovers are examined in the next chapter.)

Relationship investing enables present shareholders to bring about the same kind of changes that a raider would make. Nell Minow calls relationship investing a "nontakeover takeover." She explains, "Like the raiders, we [relationship investors] hope to realize value that's buried there. We've found a better, easier way to do it."[44] A number of factors have limited the use of hostile takeovers in the 1990s, including a lack of ready financing and the advent of state antitakeover laws. At the same time, developments have been favorable to concerted action by institutional investors. John Pound cites the further advantage that corporate governance through relationship investing is politically acceptable and consonant with basic American values. He writes:

> Americans have always had a deep distrust and political intolerance for pure finance, and the transactions of the 1980s stirred the populist pot of suspicions to an unprecedented degree. LBOs [leveraged buyouts] and other takeover transactions were based on secrecy, speed, and surprise. They eschewed due process and public debate. . . . The new politics of corporate governance stands in sharp contrast to the old ways of doing business. At the core of the new movement is a substantive discussion and debate over corporate policies. The new initiatives embrace due process and demand public debate. . . . [T]hey create a system that holds corporate management accountable to the same kinds of rules to which Americans hold their public officials accountable.[45]

As a form of corporate governance, RI raises some fears. Critics predict that institutional investor demands for quarterly performance will lead to more short-term emphasis instead of the patient capital that some predict. Others warn that in a politicized environment every corporate decision will become a matter of public debate and that segments of the public will attempt to influence corporate decision making. In addition, the relentless effort to satisfy institutional investors has already led to restructuring and reengineering that have caused dislocation in the workforce, and some contend that employees and other constituencies will lose additional power to institutional investors as corporations continue to become "mean and lean." The danger is that greater accountability might be achieved by reducing the responsiveness of corporations to social concerns. Thus, the question of whether relationship investing is merely a passing attempt to reform corporate governance or an enduring legacy of the 1990s remains to be decided.

Investment and the New Finance

The purpose of finance theory is to guide decisions about the allocation of resources in a market system in which the price of assets includes an element of risk. Before the late 1950s, the knowledge that guided such decisions was limited largely to descriptions of standard financial practices. In this respect, financial decision makers were like farmers who grow crops based on a knowledge of what has worked in the past but without the benefit of the science of agronomy that provides an explanation. During the second half of the twentieth century, finance has developed into a science, which is to say that it has become a theoretical body of knowledge that is capable of explaining and predicting, and not merely describing.

Doctrines of the New Finance

The theoretical foundation for a science of finance is microeconomics, and especially price theory, with an emphasis on the effects of risk and time on the valuation of assets. From macroeconomics, finance theory has also taken the analytical tools of utility functions and partial and general equilibrium. On this foundation, finance has developed several theoretical doctrines that together constitute modern finance theory or the New Finance. These are: the Irrelevance Theorem, the Efficient Market Hypothesis, the Capital Asset Pricing Model (CAPM), and Option Pricing Theory.[46] Agency theory, which is also regarded as part of the New Finance, is discussed separately in chapter 2.

The Irrelevance Theorem
Developed mainly by Franco Modigliani and Merton Miller, this theorem holds that under ideal market conditions a firm's financial policy is irrelevant to the evaluation of the firm.[47] In particular, decisions about capital structure (that is, the ratio of debt to equity and the choice of methods for raising capital) and dividend policy are irrelevant because investors in an ideal market,

who (by definition) can make the same transactions as the firm at the same cost, will make changes in their own portfolios to achieve any desired outcome. Thus, an investor who would prefer that a corporation have a different debt-to-equity ratio or a different level of dividends can make other investments that offset the financial policy of the corporation in question. As a practical matter, managers who accept the Irrelevance Theorem should focus on non-financial decisions that can affect the firm's valuation and investors should attend to the characteristics of their own portfolio and ignore those of individual firms.[48]

The Efficient Market Hypothesis

A capital market is said to be efficient if the prices of securities accurately reflect all relevant information. Depending on which information is regarded as relevant, three forms of the hypothesis are possible. The weak form, which considers only information about past historical performance, has received substantial empirical confirmation. The semi-strong and strong forms assume, respectively, that all publicly available information and all information known by anyone are reflected in security prices. The semi-strong form is well confirmed, although the strong form is not.

The practical effect of the Efficient Market Hypothesis for managers is that little can be gained by controlling the release of information or by attempting to falsify information, because an efficient market will correct for any such efforts by managers. The main lesson for investors is that they are unlikely to "beat" the market by seeking out superior information, unless they are the first to trade on market-moving news (which is rare) or they are trading on nonpublic information (which may be illegal).

The Capital Asset Pricing Model (CAPM)

The CAPM, which is used to select risky assets for a portfolio, asserts that investors will demand a certain premium for assuming any given level of risk. The model enables investors to determine whether they are receiving a sufficient risk premium by comparing the expected return of a risk-adjusted portfolio to the return of riskless investments. An important consequence of the CAPM is that because the risk resulting from factors specific to a firm (called "unique risk") can be eliminated in a diversified portfolio, the only risk that matters to an investor is the risk inherent in the market (called "systemic risk"), which cannot be eliminated by diversification. The practical lesson for investors is that they should diversify so that they are affected only by systemic risk. For managers, the main result is that they cannot change the value of a firm by managing unique risks, because well-diversified investors will not reward them for doing so.

Option Pricing Theory
The theory for pricing options can be applied not only to standard options but to corporate equities of all kinds. Thus, shares of stock in a firm are functionally equivalent to an option to buy an asset of the firm from the bondholders. The exercise price of the option is the face value of the bond and the exercise date is the maturity date of the bond. The limited liability of shareholders can be analyzed as an option to sell the assets of a firm to the bondholders and other creditors and thereby avoid any loss beyond their equity investment. As a method for pricing equities and various shareholder rights, Option Pricing Theory raises no ethical concerns. However, modeling the role of shareholders and their relations with other corporate constituencies in terms of options to buy and sell provides a very narrow basis for corporate decision making, one that excludes any moral considerations. One writer contends that Option Pricing Theory yields "a thoroughly immoral view of finance."[49] In order to determine whether such criticism of Option Pricing Theory or any other doctrine of the New Finance is warranted, we need to examine further the ethical implications of these doctrines.

Ethical implications

Insofar as the New Finance has turned finance theory into a science that tells us what *is* instead of what *ought to be*, it is beyond ethical criticism. We can no more find moral fault with the New Finance than we can blame our knowledge of physics for enabling us to develop the atomic bomb, for example. Both finance theory and atomic physics provide knowledge of means and leave the choice of ends to us. However, if managers, investors, and others think only in terms of the New Finance and allow it alone to guide their decisions, certain ethically objectionable consequences could follow. It is important to recognize these potential results in order to understand that ethics is also essential for financial decision making.

The root problem of the New Finance, according to critics, is that it focuses managers' attention on certain aspects of their jobs and labels others as irrelevant.[50] Taken to its logical conclusion, the New Finance entails a kind of "managerial nihilism," in which much of what managers *do* simply does not matter. This nihilism could result in harm to shareholders, other investors, and the securities markets generally, and it also has the potential to adversely affect employees and other corporate constituencies.

Investors
Critics charge that some parts of the New Finance could lead to a neglect of important shareholder interests. Shareholders have an interest in the overall

return on their investments, and managers have an obligation to serve the shareholders' interests by maximizing this return as measured by share price. Beyond maximizing the price of a firm's shares, however, do managers have any obligation to consider the preferences of shareholders in other matters that affect their financial interest? In particular, should shareholder preferences play any role in the choice of capital structure or dividend policy?

The Irrelevance Theorem suggests that such a concern is unnecessary, because shareholders can pursue individualized investment strategies that satisfy their own preferences. This overlooks the fact that in actual markets individual investors are not always able to invest under the same terms as corporations, and hence they may incur a greater cost in satisfying their own risk and return preferences. A potential consequence of the Irrelevance Theorem, therefore, is a neglect of all shareholders' interests other than those concerned narrowly with share price. As James O. Horrigan observes, "If all corporate managers presume that capital structure and dividend decisions are irrelevant, the entire burden of determining optimal strategies is thrust upon the investors."[51]

While some critics charge that the Irrelevance Theorem leads to a neglect of shareholders' interests in the way just described, another part of the New Finance may induce shareholders to gain unfairly at the expense of other corporate constituencies. If shares in a corporation are viewed as options to buy or sell, as Option Pricing Theory suggests, then the value of the shareholders' option to "buy" the assets of the corporation from bondholders can be raised by increasing the riskiness of the firm's operations. Any increased risk to the firm works to the disadvantage of bondholders because options are essentially a zero-sum game.[52] Whether shareholders are taking unfair advantage of bondholders by increasing the risks to a firm is a question for debate, but Horrigan argues that deliberate strategies by shareholders to benefit from direct losses to bondholders are unethical. "The only gains to stockholders that can be ethically justified," he contends, "are those arising out of the creation of real value, through the production of goods and services."[53]

In the event of default from the increased risk, the limited liability of shareholders serves as an option to "sell" the corporation to the bondholders and other creditors, which enables them to walk away from a firm and leave its problems in the hands of others.[54] When a firm is already in distress, shareholders are especially tempted to pursue high-risk strategies with a big payoff to themselves in the event of success, because the losses of failure will be borne mainly by bondholders and other creditors. Critics object that shareholders who adopt such strategies treat bankruptcy as an acceptable risk and thereby place little or no value on the firm as a going concern. Bankruptcy losses to bondholders and other creditors cannot be blamed directly on

Option Pricing Theory—the theory is, after all, purely technical—but because the theory is silent about the ethics of any financial strategy, it gives no ethical guidance to those who employ it. Therefore, exclusive reliance on Option Pricing Theory is apt to encourage shareholders and managers to adopt unethical strategies that force bondholders and other creditors to assume an increased risk of loss.

Employees

High-risk strategies that flirt with bankruptcy also affect employees, along with customers, suppliers, and the community at large. When a company goes bankrupt, shareholders lose some or all of their investment, but employees and other groups often suffer more from the loss of jobs. Such a situation, in which the benefits of a private decision flow mainly to the decision maker while the costs are borne largely by society, is known as *moral hazard*, which is discussed in chapter 2. Insofar as Option Pricing Theory leads managers and shareholders to regard bankruptcy as an acceptable risk and to place little value on the firm as a going concern, employees are liable to suffer great loss as a consequence of the moral hazard that is present.

Bankruptcy aside, employees are at great risk in a firm because, unlike investors, they are unable to diversify. Their welfare is closely tied to the fortunes of the employing firm. The conventional view is that employees are not investors; rather, they are suppliers who "sell" their labor for wages. Consequently, laid-off employees who find new jobs may be relatively unaffected by a firm's problems, while shareholders of a troubled firm may suffer a permanent loss. This view overlooks the fact that some of an employee's assets— namely the knowledge and skills that an employee develops for a particular employer—are *firm-specific* and cannot be easily transferred to another firm. Employees with firm-specific assets receive higher wages than they would otherwise, but they may, for the same reason, lose income when they are forced to move to another employer. Because the value of firm-specific assets can be realised only in an employee's current employment, employees also make an investment in a firm that puts them at risk. In the same way, suppliers who invest in equipment to make goods that can be used only by one firm assume risk. Customers, too, are at risk if they become dependent on one firm to supply some needed good, and communities assume risk when they make investments that benefit particular firms.

The inability of employees to diversify their investment in a firm makes them vulnerable not only to the implications of Option Pricing Theory, which may lead shareholders to devalue the firm as an ongoing concern, but also to the conclusion of the CAPM that unique risk does not matter. Although well-diversified investors may be affected only by the systemic risk inherent in the market, employees who make firm-specific investments are vulnerable to all of the unique risks of a firm. Because the livelihood of employees is threatened by unique risk, Horrigan argues that "managers choosing to be unconcerned about those threats are simply acting unethically."[55] Not only employees but all corporate constituencies would be affected if managers followed the implications of the CAPM and made no attempt to manage unique risk. As Richard A. Bettis observes, managing unique risk is at the heart of strategic management, which is critical to the success of individual firms.[56] Investors have an interest in the collective success of the firms that comprise their portfolio, but the CAPM tells investors not to reward the managers of any individual firm for successful strategic management that concerns itself with unique risks.

The market
Finally, the doctrines of the New Finance are potentially disruptive of the stock market because of a tendency toward increased *volatility*, which is the sensitivity of the price of a firm's shares to changes in the overall market. A tendency toward increased volatility is possible, first, if managers, following the CAPM, do not seek to limit the unique risks of a firm because they believe that they will not be rewarded by investors for doing so. Option Pricing Theory, for reasons already noted, would encourage shareholders to favor an increase in the volatility of a firm's shares in order to raise the value of the options that their shares represent. The presence of moral hazard would further encourage high-risk strategies that increase the volatility of a firm's shares. In addition, the Efficient Market Hypothesis could increase volatility if investors, who believe that costly analysis cannot enable them to "beat" the market, turn instead to long-shot gambles.[57]

The ethical implications of the New Finance are merely dangers to be avoided and not inevitable consequences. However, they reveal the incompleteness of the New Finance and finance theory generally. A world in which financial decision makers pursue their own interests guided only by the doctrines of the New Finance would be, in the words of one critic, "not a nice place ethically."[58] If finance theory is purely technical, however, and concerned only with means and not ends, then perhaps we should look elsewhere for the guidance that would make the world ethically a better place.

Notes

1. For convenience of expression, the term *bank* is used in this section to cover all regulated lending institutions, including commercial banks, savings banks, savings and loan associations, and credit unions.

2. For a comprehensive overview, see Gregory D. Squires, ed., *From Redlining to Reinvestment: Community Responses to Urban Reinvestment* (Philadelphia: Temple University Press, 1992).
3. Jeffrey Zack, "Banks Caught Red-handed on Redlining," *Business and Society Review,* Winter 1992, 54–75.
4. Alicia H. Munnell, Lynn E. Browne, James McEneaney, and Geoffrey M. B. Tootell, "Mortgage Lending in Boston: Interpreting the HMDA Data," Federal Reserve Bank of Boston, Working Paper No. 92–7, 1992. Geoffrey M. B. Tootell, "Redlining in Boston: Do Mortgage Lenders Discriminate against Neighborhoods?," *Quarterly Journal of Economics,* 8 (1996), 1049–79.
5. Peter Dreier, "Redlining Cities: How Banks Color Community Development," *Challenge,* November–December 1991, 16.
6. Statement by Lawrence B. Lindsey, member, Board of Governors of the Federal Reserve System, before the Subcommittee on Housing and Community Development and Subcommittee on Consumer Affairs and Coinage of the Committee on Banking, Finance and Urban Affairs, US House of Representatives, May 14, 1992.
7. Dreier, "Redlining Cities," 21.
8. Peter Passell, "Race, Mortgages and Statistics," *New York Times,* May 10, 1996, Cl.
9. Peter Brimelow and Leslie Spencer, "The Hidden Clue," *Forbes,* January 4, 1993, 48; David K. Home, "Evaluating the Role of Race in Mortgage Lending," *FDIC Banking Review,* Spring/Summer 1994, 1–15; Stan J. Liebowitz, "A Study that Deserves No Credit," *Wall Street Journal,* September 1, 1993, A14; and Peter Passell, "Redlining Under Attack," *New York Times,* August 30, 1994, D1. For a response by the Boston Fed study researchers, see Lynn Elaine Brown and Geoffrey M. B. Tootell, "Mortgage Lending in Boston – A Response to the Critics," *New England Economic Review,* September–October 1995, 54–78.
10. Home, "Evaluating the Role of Race in Mortgage Lending."
11. Gary S. Becker, "The Evidence against Banks Doesn't Prove Bias," *BusinessWeek,* April 19, 1993, 18; Brimelow and Spencer, "The Hidden Clue."
12. Brimelow and Spencer, "The Hidden Clue."
13. For further criticism of the default argument, see George C. Galster, "The Facts of Lending Discrimination Cannot Be Argued Away by Examining Default Rates," *Housing Policy Debate,* 4(1) (1993), 141–6; and Geoffrey M. B. Tootell, "Defaults, Denials, and Discrimination," *New England Economic Review,* September–October 1993, 45–51.
14. John Yinger, "Economists Know About Bias in Lending," *New York Times,* September 4, 1994, sec. 4, p. 10.
15. These points are made in Passell, "Redlining Under Attack."
16. Kevin T. Kane, "Measuring Commitment," *Mortgage Banking,* 54(12) (1994), 34–44.
17. Saul Hansell, "Stretching the Borders," *New York Times,* August 25, 1994, C1.

18. Michele Galen, "Sin Does a Number on Saintliness," *BusinessWeek*, December 26, 1994, 8; and John Rothchild, "Why I Invest with Sinners," *Fortune*, May 13, 1996, 197.

19. Ritchie P. Lowry, *Good Money: A Guide to Profitable Social Investing in the '90s* (New York: W. W. Norton, 1991), 19.

20. For a short history of social investing, see The Council on Economic Priorities, Mayra Alperson, Alice Tepper Marlin, Jonathan Schorsch, and Rosalyn Will, *The Better World Investment Guide* (New York: Prentice Hall, 1991). See also Elizabeth Judd, *Investing with a Conscience* (New York: Pharos Books, 1990); Peter D. Kinder, Steven D. Lydenberg, and Amy L. Domini, *The Social Investment Almanac: A Comprehensive Guide to Socially Responsible Investing* (New York: Henry Holt, 1992); and Jack A. Brill and Alan Reder, *Investing from the Heart* (New York: Crown, 1992).

21. For an attempt to address this issue, see William B. Irvine, "The Ethics of Investing," *Journal of Business Ethics*, 6 (1987), 233–42; and Robert Larmer, The Ethics of Investing: A Reply to William Irvine," *Journal of Business Ethics*, 16 (1997), 397–400.

22. Steven D. Lydenberg, Alice Tepper Marlin, Sean O'Brien Strub, and the Council on Economic Priorities, *Rating America's Corporate Conscience: A Provocative Guide to the Companies behind the Products You Buy Everyday* (Reading, MA: Addison-Wesley, 1986).

23. Sally Hamilton, Hoje Jo, and Meir Statman, "Doing Well While Doing Good?" *Financial Analysts Journal*, November–December 1993, 62–6; J. David Diltz, "The Private Cost of Socially Responsible Investing," *Applied Financial Economics*, 5 (1995), 69–77; and C. Mallin, B. Saadouni, and R. J. Briston, "The Financial Performance of Ethical Investment Funds," *Journal of Business Finance & Accounting*, 22 (1995), 483–96.

24. D. J. Ashton, "A Problem in the Detection of Superior Investment Performance," *Journal of Business Finance & Accounting*, 17 (1990), 337–50; and John H. Langbein and Richard A. Posner, "Social Investing and the Law of Trusts, *Michigan Law Review*, 79 (1980), 72–112.

25. For a discussion of the implications of finance theory for social investing, see Larry D. Wall, "Some Lessons from Basic Finance for Effective Socially Responsible Investing," *Economic Review*, 8 (1995), 1–12.

26. Maria O'Brien Hylton, " 'Socially Responsible' Investing: Doing Good versus Doing Well in an Inefficient Market," *American University Law Review*, 42 (1992), 1–52.

27. Attempts to measure the relation between social and financial performance have been marred by problems of definition and measurement, and the results of the many studies have been contradictory and inconclusive. For a brief overview, see Archie B. Carroll, *Business and Society: Ethics and Stakeholder Management*, 3rd edn. (Cincinnati: South-Western, 1996), 58–61.

28. Wall, "Some Lessons from Basic Finance for Effective Socially Responsible Investing," 4.

29.   *The Brancato Report on Institutional Investment* (Fairfax, VA: The Victoria Group), 1993, 1994.

30.   Carolyn Kay Brancato and Stephan Rabimov, *The 2005 Institutional Investment Report* (New York: The Conference Board, 2005).

31.   Dale M. Hanson, "Much, Much More than Investors," *Financial Executive,* March–April 1993, 48–51.

32.   The study by Stephen Nesbitt of Wilshire Associates is reported in Ed McCarthy, "Pension Funds Flex Shareholder Muscle," *Pension Management,* January 1996, 16–19.

33.   Hanson, "Much, Much More than Investors," 48.

34.   Albert O. Hirschman, *Exit, Voice, and Loyalty* (Cambridg, MA: Harvard University Press, 1970).

35.   See Nell Minow, "Proxy Reform: The Case for Increased Shareholder Communication," *Journal of Corporation Law,* 17 (1991), 149–62.

36.   "Indexing Fingered," *The Economist,* April 30, 1994, 84.

37.   John Brook, "Corporate Pension Fund Asset Management," in *Abuse on Wall Street: Conflicts of Interest in the Securities Industry* (Westport, CT: Quorum Books 1980), 224–66.

38.   "The Politically Correct Pension Fund," *BusinessWeek,* March 21, 1994, 108; and "Clinton Administration Official Advocates Relationship Investing," *Pension World,* July 1994, 6.

39.   Diane E. Burkley and Shari A. Wynne, "The Clinton Administration Is Attempting to Persuade Pension Plans to Invest Their Vast Resources in Projects that Offer Benefits to Low-Income Communities," *National Law Journal,* September 5, 1994, B5.

40.   Adam Bryant, "Colt's in Bankruptcy Court Filing," *New York Times,* March 20, 1992, D1.

41.   Richard W. Stevenson, "Pension Funds Becoming a Tool for Growth," *New York Times,* March 17, 1992, D1.

42.   See Roberta Romano, "Public Pension Fund Activism in Corporate Governance Reconsidered," *Columbia Law Review,* 93 (1993), 812. Romano notes that the alternative is to make up the shortfall by taking tax dollars away from some other state services.

43.   John Pound, "Beyond Takeovers: Politics Comes to Corporate Control," *Harvard Business Review,* March–April 1992, 83.

44.   Quoted in Judith H. Dobrzynski, *BusinessWeek,* March 15, 1993, 68.

45.   Pound, "Beyond Takeovers," 88.

46.   The term *irrelevance theorem* is used in James O. Horrigan, "The Ethics of the New Finance," *Journal of Business Ethics,* 6 (1987), 97–110. The term *irrelevance proposition* occurs in Michael C. Jensen and Clifford W. Smith, Jr, "The Theory of Corporate Finance: An Historical Overview," in *The Modern Theory of Corporate Finance* (New York: McGrawHill, 1984), 2–20.

47.   Franco Modigliani and Merton H. Miller, "The Cost of Capital, Corporation Finance, and the Theory of Investment," *American Economic Review,* 48 (1958),

261–97; and Merton H. Miller and Franco Modigliani, "Dividend Policy, Growth, and the Valuation of Shares," *Journal of Business*, 34 (1961), 411–33.

48. Modigliani and Miller formulated the irrelevance theorem for decisions of financial policy by managers. For the implications for investors, see Joseph Stiglitz, "A Re-examination of the Modigliani–Miller Theorem," *American Economic Review*, 59 (1969), 784–93.

49. Horrigan, "The Ethics of the New Finance," 105.

50. Much of the discussion of the ethical implications of the New Finance is taken from Horrigan, "The Ethics of the New Finance." Other critics include M. C. Findlay and E. E. Williams, "A Positivist Evaluation of the New Finance," *Financial Management*, 9 (Summer 1980), 7–17; Richard Brealey and Stewart Myers, *Principles of Corporate Finance* (New York: McGraw-Hill, 1981); and Richard A. Bettis, "Modern Financial Theory, Corporate Strategy, and Public Policy: Three Conundrums," *Academy of Management Review*, 8 (1983), 406–15.

51. Horrigan, "The Ethics of the New Finance," 100.

52. Ibid., 104.

53. Ibid., 105. Horrigan credits this view to William E. Fruhan, Jr, *Financial Strategy: Studies in the Creation, Transfer, and Destruction of Shareholder Value* (Homewood, IL: Richard D. Irwin, 1979).

54. This point is made in Brealey and Myers, *Principles of Corporate Finance*, 211–12.

55. Horrigan, "The Ethics of the New Finance," 103.

56. Bettis, "Modern Financial Theory, Corporate Strategy and Public Policy," 408–9.

57. Horrigan, "The Ethics of the New Finance," 101.

58. Ibid., 107.

Chapter Five

Ethics in Financial Markets

Anything that can be owned can be traded, and if trading in something is frequent, a market probably exists for that purpose. This holds true not only for commodities and valuable objects such as pork bellies and French Impressionist paintings, but for financial instruments of all kinds. However, unlike pork bellies, which can be carved up and packaged only in limited ways, financial instruments can take an unlimited variety of forms for trade in a market. With puts and calls, swaps and strips, and a host of other colorfully named techniques, the possibilities for trading in financial markets are limited only by human imagination and the reach of the law.

The broad aim of financial market regulation is to secure "fair and orderly markets" or "just and equitable principles of trade." These expressions combine the economic value of efficiency with an ethical concern for fairness or equity, thereby giving rise to the familiar equity/efficiency trade-off. The concept of fairness in financial markets is explained in chapter 2 by listing the ways in which people can be treated unfairly, and indeed most financial regulation has developed in response to abuses or breakdowns in the market. The main forms of unfair treatment—fraud and manipulation, unequal information and bargaining power, and inefficient pricing—result either in *harm* to particular individuals and to the market system as a whole or in a violation of *rights*.

In order to understand the ethical principles of market regulation and to observe them in practice, this chapter examines four specific areas of market activity which raise substantial ethical issues. These are insider trading, program trading, bankruptcy protection, and hostile takeovers. Although the legal prohibition of insider trading is vigilantly enforced, the ethical case against the practice is surprisingly difficult to make, and some economists and legal theorists object to laws against insider trading. Similarly, opinion on the benefits and dangers of program trading is sharply divided. Bankruptcy and hostile takeovers use financial markets for strategic ends, often to promote—

or, in the case of bankruptcy, to protect—the interests of various groups. All of these practices raise difficult questions of fairness in the treatment of other groups, including creditors, employees, suppliers, customers, and the public at large.

Insider and Program Trading

Insider trading is commonly defined as trading in the stock of publicly held corporations on the basis of material, nonpublic information. In a landmark 1968 decision, executives of Texas Gulf Sulphur Company were found guilty of insider trading for investing heavily in their own company's stock after learning of the discovery of rich copper-ore deposits in Canada.[1] The principle established in the *Texas Gulf Sulphur* case is that corporate insiders must refrain from trading on information that significantly affects stock price until it becomes public knowledge. The rule for corporate insiders is: Reveal or refrain!

Much of the uncertainty in the law on insider trading revolves around the relation of the trader to the source of the information. Corporate executives are definitely "insiders," but some "outsiders" have also been charged with insider trading. Among such outsiders have been a printer who was able to identify the targets of several takeovers from legal documents that were being prepared; a financial analyst who uncovered a huge fraud at a high-flying firm and advised his clients to sell; a stockbroker who was tipped off by a client who was a relative of the president of a company and who learned about the sale of the business through a chain of family gossip; a psychiatrist who was treating the wife of a financier who was attempting to take over a major bank; and a lawyer whose firm was advising another firm which was planning a hostile takeover.[2] The first two traders were eventually found innocent of insider trading; the latter three were found guilty (although the stockbroker case was later reversed in part). From these cases a legal definition of insider trading is slowly emerging.

The key points are that a person who trades on material, nonpublic information is engaging in insider trading when: (1) the trader has violated some legal duty to a corporation and its shareholders; or (2) the source of the information has such a legal duty and the trader knows that the source is violating that duty. Thus, the printer and the stock analyst had no relation to the corporations in question and so had no duty to refrain from using the information that they had acquired. The stockbroker and the psychiatrist, however, knew or should have known that they were obtaining inside information indirectly from high-level executives who had a duty to keep the information confidential. The corresponding rule for outsiders is: Don't trade on information that is revealed in violation of a trust. Both rules are imprecise, however, and leave many cases unresolved.

Arguments against insider trading

The difficulty in defining insider trading is due to disagreement over the moral wrong involved. Two main rationales are used in support of a law against insider trading. One is based on *property rights* and holds that those who trade on material, nonpublic information are essentially stealing property that belongs to the corporation. The second rationale is based on *fairness* and holds that traders who use inside information have an unfair advantage over other investors and that, as a result, the stock market is not a level playing field. These two rationales lead to different definitions, one narrow, the other broad. On the property rights or "misappropriation" theory, only corporate insiders or outsiders who bribe, steal, or otherwise wrongfully acquire corporate secrets can be guilty of insider trading. The fairness argument is broader and applies to anyone who trades on material, nonpublic information, no matter how it is acquired.

Inside information as property

One difficulty in using the property rights or misappropriation argument is determining who owns the information in question. The main basis for recognizing a property right in trade secrets and confidential business information is the investment that companies make in acquiring information and the competitive value that some information has. Not all insider information fits this description, however. Advance knowledge of better-than-expected earnings would be an example. Such information still has value in stock trading, even if the corporation does not use it for that purpose. For this reason, many employers prohibit the personal use of any information that an employee gains in the course of his or her work. This position is too broad, however, since an employee is unlikely to be accused of stealing company property by using knowledge of the next day's earning report for any purpose other than stock trading.

A second difficulty with the property rights argument is that if companies own certain information, then they could give their own employees permission to use it, or they could sell the information to favored investors or even trade on it themselves to buy back stock. Giving employees permission to trade on insider information could be an inexpensive form of extra compensation that further encourages employees to develop valuable information for the firm. Such an arrangement would also have some drawbacks; for example, investors might be less willing to buy the stock of a company that allowed insider trading because of the disadvantage to outsiders. What is morally objectionable about insider trading, according to its critics, though, is not the misappropriation of a company's information but the harm done to the investing public. So the violation of property rights in insider trading cannot be the sole reason for prohibiting it. Let us turn, then, to the second argument against insider trading, namely the argument from fairness.

The fairness argument
Fairness in the stock market does not require that all traders have the same information. Indeed, trades will take place only if the buyers and sellers of a stock have different information that leads them to different conclusions about the stock's worth. It is only fair, moreover, that a shrewd investor who has spent a great deal of time and money studying the prospects of a company should be able to exploit that advantage. Otherwise there would be no incentive to seek out new information. What is objectionable about using inside information is that other traders are barred from obtaining it, no matter how diligent they may be. The information is unavailable not for lack of *effort* but for lack of *access*. Poker also pits card players with unequal skill and knowledge without being unfair, but a game played with a marked deck gives some players an unfair advantage over others. By analogy, then, insider trading is like playing poker with a marked deck.

The analogy may be flawed, however. Perhaps a more appropriate analogy is the seller of a home who fails to reveal hidden structural damage. One principle of stock-market regulation is that both buyers and sellers of stock should have sufficient information to make rational choices. Thus, companies must publish annual reports and disclose important developments in a timely manner. A CEO who hides bad news from the investing public, for example, can be sued for fraud. Good news, such as an oil find, need not be announced until a company has time to buy the drilling rights, and so on; but to trade on that information before it is public knowledge might also be described as a kind of fraud.

Insider trading is generally prosecuted under SEC Rule 10b-5, which merely prohibits fraud in securities transactions. In fraudulent transactions, one party, such as the buyer of the house with structural damage, is wrongfully harmed for lack of knowledge that the other party concealed. So too—according to the fairness argument—are the ignorant parties to insider-trading transactions wrongfully harmed when material facts, such as the discovery of copper-ore deposits in the *Texas Gulf Sulphur* case, are not revealed.

The main weakness of the fairness argument is determining what information ought to be revealed in a transaction. The reason for requiring a homeowner to disclose hidden structural damage is that doing so makes for a more efficient housing market. In the absence of such a requirement, potential homebuyers would pay less because they would not be sure what they were getting, or they would invest in costly home inspections. Similarly—the argument goes—requiring insiders to reveal before trading makes the stock market more efficient.

The trouble with such a claim is that some economists argue that the stock market would be more efficient *without* a law against insider trading.[3] If insider trading were permitted, they claim, information would be registered in the market more quickly and at less cost than the alternative of leaving the task to research by stock analysts. The main beneficiaries of a law against insider trading, critics continue, are not individual investors but market professionals who can pick up news "on the street" and act on it quickly. Some economists argue further that a law against insider trading preserves the illusion that there is a level playing field, and that individual investors have a chance against market professionals.

Economic arguments about market efficiency look only at the cost of registering information in the market and not at possible adverse consequences of legalized insider trading, which are many. Investors who perceive the stock market as an unlevel playing field may be less inclined to participate or will be forced to adopt costly defensive measures. Legalized insider trading would have an effect on the treatment of information in a firm. Employees whose interest is in information that they can use in the stock market may be less concerned with information that is useful to the employer; and the company itself might attempt to tailor its release of information for maximum benefit to insiders. More importantly, the opportunity to engage in insider trading might undermine the relation of trust that is essential for business organizations.[4] A prohibition on insider trading frees employees of a corporation to do what they are supposed to be doing—namely, working for the interests of the shareholders—not seeking ways to advance their own interests.

The harm that legalized insider trading could do to organizations suggests that the strongest argument against legalization might be the breach of fiduciary duty that would result. Virtually everyone who could be called an "insider" has a fiduciary duty to serve the interests of the corporation and its shareholders, and the use of information that is acquired while serving as a fiduciary for personal gain is a violation of this duty. It would be a breach of professional ethics for a lawyer or an accountant to benefit personally from the use of information acquired in confidence from a client, and it is similarly unethical for a corporate executive to make personal use of confidential business information.

The argument that insider trading constitutes a breach of fiduciary duty accords with recent court decisions that have limited the prosecution of insider trading to true insiders who have a fiduciary duty. One drawback of the argument is that "outsiders," whom federal prosecutors have sought to convict of insider trading, would be free of any restrictions. A second drawback is that insider trading, on this argument, is no longer an offense against the market but the violation of a duty to another party. And the duty not to use information that is acquired while serving as a fiduciary prohibits more than insider trading. The same duty would be violated by a fiduciary who buys or sells property or undertakes some other business dealing on the basis of confidential information. That such breaches of fiduciary duty are wrong is evident, but the authority of the SEC to prosecute them under a mandate to prevent fraud in the market is less clear.

The O'Hagan *decision*

In 1997, the US Supreme Court ended a decade of uncertainty over the legal definition of insider trading. The SEC has long prosecuted insider trading using the misappropriation theory, according to which an inside trader breaches a fiduciary duty by misappropriating confidential information for personal trading. In 1987, the high court split four-to-four on an insider trading case involving a reporter for *The Wall Street Journal*, and thus left standing a lower-court decision that found the reporter guilty of misappropriating information.[5] However, the decision did not create a precedent for lack of a majority. Subsequently, lower courts rejected the misappropriation theory in a series of cases in which the alleged inside trader did not have a fiduciary duty to the corporation whose stock was traded. The principle applied was that the trading must itself constitute a breach of fiduciary duty. This principle was rejected in *U.S. v. O'Hagan*.

James H. O'Hagan was a partner in a Minneapolis law firm that was advising the British firm Grand Metropolitan in a hostile takeover of the Minneapolis-based Pillsbury Company. O'Hagan did not work on Grand Met business but allegedly tricked a fellow partner into revealing the takeover bid. O'Hagan then reaped $4.3 million by trading in Pillsbury stock and stock options. An appellate court ruled that O'Hagan did not engage in illegal insider trading because he had no fiduciary duty to Pillsbury, the company in whose stock he traded. Although O'Hagan misappropriated confidential information from his own law firm—to which he owed a fiduciary duty— trading on this information did not constitute a fraud against the law firm or against Grand Met. Presumably, O'Hagan would have been guilty of insider trading only if he were an insider of Pillsbury.

In a six-to-three decision, the Supreme Court reinstated the conviction of Mr O'Hagan and affirmed the misappropriation theory. According to the decision, a person commits securities fraud when he or she "misappropriates confidential information for securities trading purposes, in breach of a fiduciary duty owed to the source of the information." Thus, an inside trader need not be an insider (or a temporary insider, like a lawyer) of the corporation whose stock is traded. Being an insider in Grand Met is sufficient in this case to hold that insider trading occurred. The majority opinion observed that "it makes scant sense" to hold a lawyer like O'Hagan to have violated the law "if he works for a law firm representing the target of a tender offer, but not if he works for a law firm representing the bidder." The crucial point is that O'Hagan was a fiduciary who misused information that had been entrusted to him. This decision would also apply to a person who receives information from an insider and who knows that the insider source is violating a duty of confidentiality. However, a person with no fiduciary ties who receives information innocently (by overhearing a conversation, for example) would still be free to trade.

Program trading

Whereas insider trading strikes many as unfair because of the uneven playing field, program trading is criticized for involving another source of unfairness, namely inefficient pricing. The idea of profiting from market volatility is not itself objectionable, except when volatility is created solely for the purposes of benefiting from differences in pricing. The criticism of program trading is largely directed, then, not to the use of computers to make trading decisions but to a stock-trading strategy known as *index arbitrage*.

Index arbitrage is a practice in which a trader attempts to profit from a price difference between a basket of stocks and a futures contract based on the same stocks. By simultaneously buying the stocks or the futures contract and selling the other, usually in a different market, a trader can pocket the difference between the two prices. The report of the Presidential Task Force that investigated the causes of the October 1987 stock-market crash concluded that index arbitrage accelerated the decline, when the confusion from the record-breaking volume of trading opened up price differences between stocks and futures.[6]

Volatility from any source creates opportunities for index arbitrage, and critics of the practice charge that some traders produce artificial volatility solely for the purpose of exploiting the opportunities. For example, with the advent of index arbitrage, frontrunning—the (illegal) practice of executing trades with advance knowledge of a customer's market-moving order—can now take place in two different markets. In such "intermarket frontrunning," which is more difficult to detect than frontrunning in the same market, a trader who knows that a customer has placed a large order to buy or sell a stock in the stock market can issue a call or put option for the same stock in a futures market.

Instead of running in front of a customer's order, a trader can engage in "self-frontrunning" by trading in one market with the sole purpose of profiting from the volatility created by trading in another market. So-called "intermarket self-frontrunning"—which is loudly condemned as unethical but not as yet made illegal—is difficult to regulate, in part because the transactions may closely resemble legitimate hedging by the use of futures contracts. The separate transactions of a legitimate hedge do not always take place simultaneously, and any delay in the completion of the second "leg" of a two-legged transaction—a practice known as "legging"—creates the opportunity to speculate on market trends. Increased market volatility, which a trader can induce by market-moving trades, makes legging potentially more profitable.

Volatility for its own sake has no economic value beyond the enrichment of a few traders and is generally regarded as an unfair trading practice. Insofar as a series of transactions is made solely to move the market, the creation of volatility might be regarded as a form of manipulation. However, the aim is not to deceive other investors but to benefit from the possibilities for arbitrage that volatility creates, and the harm does not result from any deception but from the volatility itself and its effect on prices.

At least two remedies for the volatility of program trading are available, namely trading rules and trading halts. Program trading is subject to slightly differing rules: Traders are not bound by the uptick rule (which permits selling short only when a stock is rising, not when it is falling), and they are allowed to buy and sell on a 5 percent margin, when the margin for other investors is 50 percent. In addition, stocks are traded on a stock market with one set of rules, while futures are traded on a commodities market with a different set of rules. Some critics maintain that index arbitrage exploits the difference between the *rules* of different markets, and not differences between the *value* of the financial instruments. Accordingly, more uniform rules would reduce volatility as well as create a more level playing field.

Trading halts (also known as circuit-breakers and collars), which change the rules or stop trading entirely when the market rises or falls by certain amounts, introduce some inefficiency into markets insofar as they interfere with or delay price corrections by market forces. The benefit, supporters argue, is that they prevent inefficient pricing in the first place by restricting volatility. Any loss of efficiency in the short run is more than made up, according to supporters, by long-term efficiency gains.

The Ethics of Bankruptcy

Bankruptcy occurs when individuals and corporations that have insufficient assets to pay their debt obligations are subject to laws that provide some protection from creditors and permit an orderly distribution of assets to satisfy creditors' claims. Personal bankruptcy absolves individuals of many debt obligations and enables them to secure a "fresh start." For corporations, bankruptcy provides temporary relief from debt obligations while they seek to reorganize, or else it produces a liquidation of assets in which, ideally, all creditors are treated fairly.

Bankruptcy of an individual or a firm is commonly thought to constitute a failure. The only ethical issue, in the minds of many people, is the broken promise to pay one's debts or else the faulty character that leads people to accumulate unpayable debts. Prior to 1893—the year in which the United States enacted the first federal bankruptcy law—individual debtors could lose all their worldly goods and even be sent to prison, and firms were usually liquidated by creditors in a mad scramble for salvageable assets. This harsh treatment was generally regarded as just punishment for the bankrupt's profligacy, and an injustice was thought to occur only when creditors were not made whole.

In economics and finance, by contrast, bankruptcy is typically regarded as a natural event in an impersonal and unforgiving marketplace. Firms that cannot compete are eventually forced out of existence. Nothing of value is lost as long as the assets of the bankrupt firm are redeployed by someone. No moral opprobrium is attached to bankruptcy; in fact, bankruptcies should be welcomed, because this ruthless Darwinian struggle for survival strengthens the economy. There is no need to consider moral matters in bankruptcy proceedings because these proceedings are concerned primarily with enforcing, to whatever extent is possible, commitments made by a firm before it became insolvent. The main concern from an economic point of view is efficiency: The reorganization or liquidation of firms should be done at the lowest cost and in a way that puts assets to their most productive use.

Contrary to the common view of bankruptcy as a moral failing and the nonjudgmental view in economics and finance, bankruptcy raises many difficult and important ethical issues. These issues arise primarily from the use—or, some would say, the *abuse*—of bankruptcy protection.[7] In recent years, solvent firms have filed for bankruptcy for many reasons: to defer or avoid payments, renege on contracts, stop litigation, evade legal liability, break unions, and get rid of pension plans. Instead of being a last resort in a fight for survival, bankruptcy has become, in the view of its critics, just another management strategy for maximizing profits.[8] In the book *Strategic Bankruptcy: How Corporations and Creditors Use Chapter 11 to Their Advantage*, Kevin I. Delaney coins the term "strategic bankruptcy" and argues that bankruptcy is often a choice that companies make to achieve strategic ends.[9]

The discussion of bankruptcy that follows is concerned with the ethical justification of the bankruptcy system and, in particular, with what might constitute an ethically objectionable *abuse* of the bankruptcy process, especially by means of strategic bankruptcy. The ethical questions are concerned, at bottom, with the legal framework of the bankruptcy system, and as such they must be answered primarily by Congress in the drafting of bankruptcy legislation. However, the decisions of managers to engage in strategic bankruptcy can be criticized from a moral point of view. Indeed, moral concern about abuses and unfair treatment has prompted heated debate and calls for reform.

The ethical basis of bankruptcy law

The use of bankruptcy as a management strategy has been facilitated by a system that enables, indeed encourages, distressed or insolvent firms to reorganize instead of liquidating. The 1893 Bankruptcy Act required firms filing for bankruptcy to liquidate, and it was not until 1938, during the Great Depression, that a law was enacted to protect insolvent firms from their creditors and permit reorganization. A major overhaul of the federal Bankruptcy Code in 1978 (with further revisions in 1994) restructured the 1893 Act and created Chapter 11, under which corporate bankruptcy petitions are now filed. The 1978 Act eased the conditions for declaring bankruptcy (a company need not be insolvent, but must demonstrate merely that it faces insolvency without protection from creditors), and the Code removed the stigma from bankruptcy by eliminating pejorative terms (bankrupts are now called debtors, for example).

Once a firm files for bankruptcy under Chapter 11, creditors are prevented from enforcing their claims. The managers of the firm are left in control (unless a court finds dishonesty, mismanagement or incompetence), and they are allowed a period of time (initially 120 days, with extensions possible) to develop a reorganization plan. A plan generally reduces the claims of creditors and specifies how these reduced claims will be met. The plan offered by management must be accepted by most of the creditors whose claims are reduced. The plan must be approved by the shareholders as well.[10] In the event that no management plan is accepted within the time allowed, creditors are permitted to submit their own plans, subject to the same rules for acceptance.

The economic argument for this system of bankruptcy is that it maximizes a firm's assets.[11] The underlying assumption is that insolvency usually results from uncontrollable outside forces or from management mistakes that can be corrected. If insolvent but financially viable firms are given the opportunity to reorganize, then they can return to profitability and repay their creditors. Such an outcome is preferable, from an economic point of view, if reorganization instead of liquidation leads to more productive deployment of a firm's assets. This is often the case, because assets generally have greater value when they continue to be held by an ongoing entity than when they are broken up and sold off piecemeal. However, a bankrupt firm cannot be operated as an ongoing entity if diverse creditors are still allowed to press their conflicting claims. The solution, which is provided by bankruptcy law, is to force creditors to act collectively and to create incentives for them to make wealth-maximizing decisions.[12] In short, bankruptcy law forces creditors, who have control during the bankruptcy process, to act like a group of shareholders instead of acting as individual claimants.

The ethical argument follows directly from the economic argument. Called the "creditors' bargain," this argument employs a hypothetical contract approach and asks, What bankruptcy system would all creditors agree to in advance of any bankruptcy proceedings?[13] That is, suppose that creditors, both secured and unsecured, could write the Bankruptcy Code. What provisions would the law contain? The answer, it is assumed, is that creditors would favor a system that maximizes a firm's assets and that this can be best achieved by the current bankruptcy system. Although individual creditors, especially those with secured claims, might collect more of what they are owed in particular cases by liquidation or by litigation, the cost and uncertainty of these alternatives make them less attractive as a universal system. In addition, liquidation eliminates jobs and has an impact on customers, suppliers, communities, and other stakeholder groups. Thus, easy access to bankruptcy protection not only deploys assets more productively—which benefits creditors—but enhances the welfare of society.

The use and abuse of bankruptcy

Easy access to bankruptcy protection has resulted in a number of controversial uses of the law that were not envisioned by Congress in creating the modern bankruptcy system. Consider the following.

Product liability suits

In August 1982, Manville Corporation, a Fortune 500 company with annual earnings of $60 million and a net worth in excess of $1 billion, declared bankruptcy. Manville's business was healthy, but many users of its main product, asbestos, were not, and the sick and dying were threatening to bury Manville in a flurry of lawsuits. Manville had already settled 3,500 suits at a cost of $50 million; 16,500 were still pending; and new suits were being filed as the rate of 500 per month. In the bankruptcy petition, the company claimed that future suits against the company would eventually total between $2 billion and $5 billion dollars. In 1985, A. H. Robins filed for bankruptcy protection after agreeing to settle the claims of women who suffered injuries from the Dalkon Shield intrauterine birth-control device, and Dow Corning Corporation sought bankruptcy protection in 1995 in the face of heavy liability from suits over silicone breast-implants that women blamed for a variety of disorders.

Collective bargaining agreements
In 1983, two solvent companies, Wilson Foods and Continental Airlines filed for bankruptcy protection on the grounds that generous labor contracts placed the companies at a competitive disadvantage. Bankruptcy enabled each company to void collective bargaining agreements currently in force and to slash wages virtually in half. Continental also laid off about 65 percent of its workforce and resumed operation as a low-fare, nonunion carrier. Wilson Foods and Continental were following in the footsteps of Bildisco, a New Jersey building supply firm, that successfully broke a labor contract with the Teamsters Union by filing for bankruptcy. In the *Bildisco* decision, the US Supreme Court held in 1984 that collective-bargaining agreements are no different from any other contracts and can be unilaterally rewritten or terminated if the long-term solvency of the firm is at stake.[14] Congress has since revised the Bankruptcy Code to limit the ability of companies to act in this manner.[15]

Liabilities and contractual obligations
Bankruptcy has enabled many companies to reduce or avoid substantial liabilities and contractual obligations. LTV Steel used Chapter 11 in an attempt to dump $2.3 billion in underfunded pension liabilities onto the federal Pension Benefit Guaranty Corporation, and in the ensuing court fight, thousands of retirees found their pension benefits jeopardized. Texaco was ordered by a court to pay Pennzoil damages of $10.5 billion for "stealing" Getty Oil during merger negotiations between Pennzoil and Getty. Despite $35 billion in assets, Texaco declared bankruptcy and managed to reduce the payment for damages to $3 billion. The 1983 bankruptcy of HRT Industries, the operator of a chain of discount stores, achieved several ends.[16] Despite holding net assets of $50 million, the company declared bankruptcy because of a "very

recent" cash-flow problem after receiving the bulk of its merchandise for the Christmas season. Afterwards, HRT closed more than thirty unprofitable stores. The company's short sojourn in Chapter 11 thus enabled HRT to get an interest-free loan on all of its debt and to terminate a number of onerous long-term leases.

What is really wrong with bankruptcy?

The charge that companies such as Manville, Dow Corning, Continental, LTV, and Texaco are *abusing* the bankruptcy system suggests some moral wrong, but it is difficult to identify that wrong precisely. One charge is that these companies are using the bankruptcy law for purposes other than that for which it was enacted, but to use a law for an unintended end is not itself morally objectionable. Once a law is on the books, its use is limited solely by the wording of the law, not by the intent of the legislature in passing it. (For example, the use of SEC Rule 10b-5 to prosecute insider trading represents a novel application of law beyond its original scope.)

A second charge is that bankruptcy is being used in these instances to avoid ethical and legal obligations that result from contractual agreements or court judgments. However, bankruptcy law is designed, in part, to enable a firm to fulfill its obligations to the maximum extent possible (consistent with efficiency and fairness) when the firm is unable to fulfill these obligations fully. That is, Congress, in creating the bankruptcy system, has already taken into account the fact that a firm seeking bankruptcy protection will be avoiding some ethical and legal obligations, and Congress has determined that, all things considered, it is better to permit a firm to fulfill its obligations only in part and to continue as an ongoing entity than to require an immediate liquidation in which creditors will still not be made whole.

Furthermore, by seeking bankruptcy protection, firms do not avoid their obligations entirely but negotiate the terms under which they will be filled, and in the end, the claimants are often well served. When Manville emerged from bankruptcy in 1986, the majority of stock was transferred to two trusts, one to pay claims for health-related injuries and the second to pay for property damages. The victims of Manville thus became the owners, and the ability of these new owners to be compensated depends on the continued profitability of the company. Similarly, LTV emerged from bankruptcy after seven years of protracted negotiations with the Pension Benefit Guaranty Corporation and other creditors by agreeing to contribute $1.6 billion to the company's underfunded pension plans. The success of asbestos victims and pensioners in securing their claims did not come easily. They had to fight for their rights. But in the end, these claimants gained more than they might have done without the opportunity for the company to seek bankruptcy protection.

Bankruptcy as a strategic choice

A third and more promising objection to the conduct of Manville, Dow Corning, Continental, LTV, Texaco, and other companies that seek bankruptcy protection is not that claimants do not receive what they are owed but that claimants who receive their claims under one set of rules are forced to fight for them again under another set of rules. Victims of defective products who succeed in court suits must now win their case all over again in bankruptcy proceedings. Workers who negotiate a labor contract in good faith can find themselves back at the bargaining table, this time before a bankruptcy judge. And Texaco, which was ordered by a judge in a jury trial to pay Pennzoil $10.5 billion, gained another opportunity to dispute the case in an entirely different setting. Thus, bankruptcy provides a company with onerous obligations the opportunity to renegotiate or relitigate them under a different set of rules.

However, this charge—that bankruptcy provides a second chance under different rules—carries no weight if companies are genuinely insolvent. No claimant can seize assets that are not there, and every claim includes provisions for default. Thus, a creditor must expect to go to court if a debtor cannot or will not pay, and commercial law provides the means for resolving such disputes. The critical question is whether a company that seeks bankruptcy protection, and thereby changes the rules on claimants, is actually insolvent or would face insolvency without the protection of bankruptcy law. If an otherwise healthy company with heavy liabilities is able to use bankruptcy law to force creditors to renegotiate or relitigate their claims under different conditions, then arguably the system has been abused.

Critics of the bankruptcy system argue that bankruptcy is not always a condition that afflicts companies but is sometimes a deliberate *choice* that companies make for strategic ends.[17] Virtually any company could make itself "bankrupt" by amassing unpayable debt, but short of that step, a company with massive liabilities can easily arrange the balance sheets, shift assets, or even induce a crisis event so as to become insolvent. A company is held to be insolvent when its liabilities exceed its assets, as though liabilities and assets are objective, precisely measurable quantities. Not only do assets and liabilities reflect prior decisions made by a company, but the valuation of assets and liabilities is subject to manipulation. As a result, the bottom line is not a hard fact that everyone can observe in the same way but an artificial construct that is created by a firm's managers (within accepted accounting principles, of course).

For example, one critic contends that Manville chose not to include its liabilities for asbestos-related injuries on the company books prior to filing for bankruptcy.[18] Prior to 1982 the company claimed that it was not legally required to do so because the liabilities could not be accurately estimated. When Manville decided to "go bankrupt" in 1982, $2 billion in liabilities suddenly appeared on the company's balance sheets. Both Continental (90 percent of which was owned by Texas Air) and Texaco carefully defined the part of the company that was declared to be the "bankrupt unit," and Continental, according to some observers, provoked a union strike rather than negotiate in order to qualify for bankruptcy. Bankrupt Dow Corning is owned 50–50 by (solvent) Dow Chemical and (solvent) Corning Incorporated. Complex ownership structures permit a movement of assets from a "bankrupt unit" to a "nonbankrupt unit" prior to filing a bankruptcy petition.[19]

Such strategic use of bankruptcy law strikes us as unfair because the accepted rules for economic activity are suddenly changed. Strategic bankruptcy might be compared to a game of poker in which a dealer with bad cards is allowed to stop the game, rearrange some of the hands, perhaps take some money off the table, and resume play with different rules. However, the poker game just described is not unfair if the dealer's option is understood at the beginning of play. Under such conditions, the game is merely one of many possible forms of poker, albeit with rather complicated rules, and players can play their hands with the possibility of a rules change in mind. Similarly, a bankruptcy system that permits companies to seek bankruptcy protection for strategic reasons is not unfair merely because of the possibility of a change in the rules. The first few strategic bankruptcies might be considered unfair because the affected parties, such as the asbestos victims of Manville and the employees of Continental, had not anticipated this use of the Bankruptcy Code. After these well-publicized events, however, creditors and other groups should be aware of this possibility and play their hands accordingly.

The fairness and efficiency of Chapter 11

In order to understand what is really wrong with a bankruptcy system that permits bankruptcy as a strategic choice, we need to look at the impact of this system on the functioning of the economic system, in which considerations of both fairness and efficiency play a role.

One argument for the current Chapter 11 is that it is the bankruptcy system that would be selected by creditors themselves if they were to choose a system in advance of any bankruptcy filing. According to this argument—which is called *the creditors' bargain*—a bankruptcy system that permits reorganization rather than forced liquidation is preferable because it will maximize a firm's assets through an orderly adjudication of creditors' claims. However, the creditors' bargain argument does not provide clear answers to more specific questions. In particular, strategic bankruptcy is greatly facilitated by the 1978 revision of the Bankruptcy Code that gives distressed companies easier access to bankruptcy protection. If creditors could write the law on bankruptcy, what conditions would they include for filing for bankruptcy protection? And would creditors agree to the conditions in the current Chapter 11?

The answers to these questions are disputable, but some evidence suggests that creditors as well as shareholders have suffered losses from the 1978 revision of the Bankruptcy Code and that the winners are the managers of firms—and the legion of lawyers, accountants, and financial advisers who assist them. Two researchers, who studied 326 firms that filed bankruptcy petitions between 1964 and 1989, found that losses suffered by bondholders after 1978 was 67 percent greater than the losses suffered before the 1978 revision.[20] Shareholders have fared even worse. Before 1978, shareholders of bankrupt firms lost on average slightly more than one-half of the value of their investments, and after 1978, the losses were almost 100 percent. The researchers concluded: "Chapter 11, in other words, may be seen as a kind of management defensive tactic against corporate debtholders which, like certain antitakeover defensive measures, enhances management's wealth at the expense of corporate security holders."[21] If this result is correct, the current system of bankruptcy law would not be much of a bargain for creditors and would not be justified, therefore, by the "creditors' bargain" argument.

If the purpose of the Bankruptcy Code is debt collection—that is, enforcing the rights of creditors before a firm becomes insolvent—then there is no justification for creating any new rights unless doing so enforces creditors' preexisting rights.[22] Chapter 11 creates some new rights for managers: They are permitted under current law to control the process of filing the bankruptcy petition, to remain in their positions during the bankruptcy process, and to develop the first reorganization plan. The rationale for these rights is the assumption that creditors will be better served, but this assumption is not always well founded.

For example, bankruptcy protection allows mangers to "play games" at the creditors' expense. Both shareholders and managers have little to lose from continued operation of a troubled firm and might prefer a long-shot, "bet-the-farm" strategy that would leave creditors with little should the strategy fail. (This is the problem of moral hazard, which is discussed in chapter 2.) Furthermore, if bankruptcy is an acceptable risk, firms may be encouraged to court bankruptcy by pursuing exceptionally risky strategies. This is especially true when shareholders stand to gain the benefit while bondholders and other creditors assume the risk (again, the moral hazard problem). Thus, bankruptcy law—which is intended to protect creditors of distressed firms—may have the unintended effect of generating greater risk-taking that further endangers creditors.[23]

Easy access to bankruptcy protection has far-reaching and unpredictable implications for rights in market transactions and some areas of law. The effect is to complicate ordinary commercial relations and alter such diverse matters as labor relations and product safety.

One principle of market transactions is that investors and those who extend credit should have sufficient information to make reasonable judgments about risk and return. Thus, suppliers have access to the balance sheets of a retailer who is seeking merchandise on credit in order to negotiate terms. If the risk of extending credit to a retailer like HRT Industries includes the possibility of a bankruptcy filing for strategic reasons, then reasonable judgments of risk become more difficult to make. And the sources of risk are expanded from ordinary market conditions (such as the fact the HRT had a number of unprofitable stores) to include a firm's strategy (to seek bankruptcy protection in order to close unprofitable stores). Furthermore, if HRT was planning to file a bankruptcy petition at the same time that it was seeking credit, then (arguably) this is material information that ought to be disclosed to creditors. In any event, easy access to bankruptcy protection complicates such a fundamental matter as the extending of credit in ways that might be better avoided.

Both labor law and product liability law are premised on certain rights, namely the right of workers to organize and bargain collectively and the right of people who are injured by defective products to be compensated. The law in these areas is carefully constructed to balance the various competing rights and interests. Insofar as strategic bankruptcy enables firms to renege on labor contracts or avoid product-liability claims, then other rights may be denied, and the carefully constructed balance may be upset. At a minimum, union members and victims of defective products have lost ground as a result of bankruptcy reform because of the greater risk in collective-bargaining agreements and product-liability judgments.

In addition, liberal access to bankruptcy protection might encourage business firms and labor unions to bargain differently, knowing that agreements can be more easily broken, or it might encourage manufacturers to design and produce less safe products, knowing that liability suits are more easily evaded. Easy access to bankruptcy also has an impact on strategic planning. Some companies, such as airlines, operate for years with bankruptcy protection. As a result, their nonbankrupt competitors, which must meet all of their current obligations, complain that they are placed at an unfair competitive disadvantage.[24] Even the knowledge that a major competitor could engage in strategic bankruptcy at any time is an unsettling factor in a company's own strategic planning.

In conclusion, the American bankruptcy system is ethically justified on the grounds of both efficiency and fairness. The creditors' bargain assumes that because the system serves to maximize the assets of an insolvent firm—which is a consideration of efficiency—creditors would prefer such a system; hence it is fair. At bottom, the charge that strategic bankruptcies are morally wrong rests on the view that one or another corporate constituency is being treated unfairly. However, an evaluation of this charge depends on a complex analysis of the actual consequences of strategic bankruptcies, which are not clearly known.

Personal bankruptcy
The standard justification for personal bankruptcy, which allows individuals to discharge their debts and have a "fresh start," is based on welfare and justice. At one time, when individuals were unable to pay their debts, they were cast into prison. Even without the threat of imprisonment, people with heavy debts might spend a lifetime of economic struggle, with consequences not only for themselves but the whole of society. Everyone, debtors and creditors alike, are better off in a society that allows personal bankruptcy, because even creditors might find themselves with debts they cannot pay. Although there is an obligation to pay one's debts, the benefit of fulfilling this obligation may be outweighed by the loss that results when people are unable to live full, productive lives. In addition, it is unfair for people to suffer crushing debt loads that are caused, in many cases, by adversities beyond their control.

However, a liberal system of personal bankruptcy creates opportunities for abuse. Easy access to bankruptcy protection with little stigma or inconvenience might lead individuals to be less restrained in incurring debts. When facing bankruptcy, individuals might incur all the debt they can, knowing that it will soon be discharged, and seek to shield other assets from creditors by improper means (such as transferring the title for property to a relative). In the United States, creditors, most notably bank lenders and credit card issuers, whom critics accuse of enticing customers into unmanageable debt loads, have protested these abuses and sought changes in the law to prevent them.

The main issues in the debate over changes in the law of personal bankruptcy are: (1) Should individuals above a certain income level as determined by a "means test" be required to repay a certain portion of their debts instead of having them discharged completely? (2) Should some assets (such as a home or pension savings) be shielded from creditors during bankruptcy proceedings? (3) Should certain debts be nondischargable (for example, for luxury goods or large cash advances obtained just prior to seeking bankruptcy protection)?

In 2005, Congress passed and the president signed a sweeping overhaul of the Bankruptcy Code for individuals. The new law, long sought by the banking industry, utilizes a means test to limit access to a complete discharge of debts under Chapter 7 and forces more applicants to develop a five-year partial repayment plant under Chapter 13. In most cases, a debtor with income above the state median income may not file under Chapter 7. Other provisions of the new law include mandatory credit counseling and debtor education and limits on the amount of debt that can be discharged for purchases of luxury goods (over $500 within 90 days of filing) and cash advances ($750 within 70 days). In general, pension funds are exempt, as are assets in a home within limits set by state laws.

Opponents of more stringent personal bankruptcy laws argue that abuse is committed by only a small portion of those seeking protection and that the vast majority of personal bankruptcies are caused by job-loss, divorce, disability due to illness or injury, and business failure. For such people, a "fresh start" will often enable them to resume successful lives, whereas requirements to pay off a portion of their debts will mire them in a cycle of indebtedness. Opponents also claim that bankruptcy due to the failure of a business is more common than is generally recognized and that more stringent laws will strongly deter individuals from starting new businesses, thus damaging a vital engine of economic growth.

Hostile Takeovers

Since its founding in the nineteenth century, Pacific Lumber Company had been a model employer and a good corporate citizen. As a logger of giant redwoods in northern California, this family-managed company had long followed a policy of perpetual sustainable yield. Cutting was limited to selected mature trees, which were removed without disturbing the forests, so that younger trees could grow to the same size. Employees—many from families that had worked at Pacific Lumber for several generations—received generous benefits, including an overfunded company-sponsored pension plan. With strong earnings and virtually no debt, Pacific Lumber seemed well positioned to survive any challenge.

However, the company fell prey to a hostile takeover. In 1986, financier Charles Hurwitz and his Houston-based firm Maxxam, Inc., mounted a successful $900 million leveraged buyout of Pacific Lumber. By offering $40 per share for stock that had been trading at $29, Hurwitz gained majority control. The takeover was financed with junk bonds issued by Drexel Burnham Lambert under the direction of Michael Milken. Hurwitz expected to pare down the debt by aggressive clear-cutting of the ancient stands of redwoods that Pacific Lumber had protected and by raiding the company's overfunded pension plan.

Using $37.3 million of $97 million that Pacific Lumber had set aside for its pension obligations, Maxxam purchased annuities for all employees and retirees and applied more than $55 million of the remainder toward reducing the company's new debt. The annuities were purchased from First Executive Corporation, a company that Hurwitz controlled. First Executive was also Drexel's biggest junk-bond customer, and the company purchased one-third of the debt incurred in the takeover of Pacific Lumber. After the collapse of the junk-bond market, First Executive failed in 1991 and was taken over by the State of California in a move that halted pension payments to Pacific Lumber retirees. Today, Charles Hurwitz and Maxxam are mired in lawsuits by former stockholders, retirees, and environmentalists.

A hostile takeover—which is an acquisition that is opposed by the management of the target corporation—is merely one kind of restructuring; other kinds include friendly mergers and acquisitions, leveraged buyouts, breakups into two or more corporations, divestitures of whole divisions, sales of assets, and liquidations. These restructurings raise few ethical problems because the managers and shareholders of the firms in question come to a mutual agreement. Hostile takeovers, by contrast, typically involve sharp disagreements between managers, shareholders, and other corporate constituencies. In addition, hostile takeovers appear to violate the accepted rules for corporate change. Peter Drucker observed that the hostile takeover "deeply offends the sense of justice of a great many Americans."[25] An oil industry CEO charged that such activity "is in total disregard of those inherent foundations which are the heart and soul of the American free enterprise system."[26] Many economists—most notably Michael C. Jensen—defend hostile takeovers on the grounds that they bring about needed changes that cannot be achieved by the usual means.[27]

The ethical issues in hostile takeovers are threefold. First, should hostile takeovers be permitted at all? Insofar as hostile takeovers are conducted in a market through the buying and selling of stocks, there exists a "market for corporate control." So the question can be expressed in the form, Should there be a market for corporate control? Or should change of control decisions be made in some other fashion? Second, ethical issues arise in the various tactics that have been used by raiders in launching attacks, as well as by target corporations in defending themselves. Some of these tactics are criticized on the grounds that they unfairly favor the raiders or incumbent management, often at the expense of shareholders. Third, hostile takeovers raise important issues about the fiduciary duties of officers and directors in their responses to take-over bids. In particular, what should directors do when an offer that share-holders want to accept is not in the best interests of the corporation itself? Do they have a right, indeed, a responsibility, to prevent a change of control?

Fairness and the market for corporate control

Defenders of hostile takeovers contend that corporations become takeover targets when incumbent management is unable or unwilling to take steps that increase shareholder value. The raiders' willingness to pay a premium for the stock reflects a belief that the company is not achieving its full potential under the current management "Let us take over," the raiders say, "and the company will be worth what we are offering." Because shareholders often find it difficult to replace the current managers through traditional proxy contests, hostile takeovers are an important means for shareholders to realize the value of their investment. Although restructurings of all kinds cause some hardships to employees, communities, and other groups, society as a whole benefits from the increased wealth and productivity.

Just the threat of a takeover serves as an important check on management, and without this constant spur, defenders argue, managers would have less incentive to secure full value for the shareholders. With regard to the market for corporate control, defenders hold that shareholders are, and ought to be, the ultimate arbiters of who manages the corporation. If the shareholders have a right to replace the CEO, why should it matter when or how shareholders bought the stock? A raider who bought the stock yesterday in a tender offer has the same rights as a shareholder of long standing. Any steps to restrict hostile takeovers, the defenders argue, would entail an unjustified reduction of shareholders' rights.

Critics of hostile takeovers challenge the benefits and emphasize the harms. Targets of successful raids are sometimes broken up and sold off piecemeal, or downsized and folded into the acquiring company. In the process, people are thrown out of work and communities lose their economic base. Takeovers generally saddle companies with debt loads that limit their options and expose them to greater risk in the event of a downturn. Critics also charge that com-panies are forced to defend themselves by managing for immediate results and adopting costly defensive measures. Although takeovers and the threat of takeovers may force some beneficial changes on corporations, this flurry of activity serves primarily to enrich investment bankers and lawyers. The benefit to the shareholders of the companies involved comes at the expense of other constituencies. Not all takeovers result from sound financial decision making, and in any event, change-of-control decisions are too important to be made solely on the basis of financial considerations. The market for corporate control should be broadened to include more than the interests of shareholders, and perhaps government should play some role.

The debate over hostile takeovers revolves largely around the question of whether they are good or bad for the American economy. This is a question for economic analysis, and the evidence, on the whole, is that takeovers generally increase the value of both the acquired and the acquiring corporation.[28] These results must be viewed with some caution, however.

First, not all takeover targets are underperforming businesses with poor management. Other factors can make a company a takeover target. The "bust-up" takeover operates on the premise that a company is worth more sold off in parts than retained as a whole. Large cash reserves, expensive research programs, and other sources of savings enable raiders to finance a takeover with the company's own assets. The availability of junk-bond financing during the 1980s permitted highly leveraged buyouts with levels of debt that many considered to be unhealthy for the economy. Finally, costly commitments to stakeholder groups can be tapped to finance a takeover. Thus, Pacific Lumber's pension plan and cutting policy constituted commitments to employees and environmentalists respectively. Both commitments were implicit contracts that had arguably benefited shareholders in the past but which could now be broken with impunity.

Second, some of the apparent wealth that takeovers create may result from accounting and tax rules that benefit shareholders but create no new wealth. For example, the tax code favors debt over equity by allowing a deduction for interest payments on debt while taxing corporate profits. Rules on depreciation and capital gains may result in tax savings from asset sales following a takeover. Thus, taxpayers provide an indirect subsidy in the financing of takeovers. Some takeovers result in direct losses to other parties. Among the losers in hostile takeovers are bondholders, whose formerly secure, investment-grade bonds are sometimes downgraded to speculative, junk-bond status.

Third, there is little evidence that newly merged or acquired firms outperform industry averages in the long run.[29] This result counts against the claim that takeovers are cures for underperforming managers. The immediate boost to the stock's price may be due to one-time savings from tax and accounting rules, or it may reflect an upward adjustment by a market that had previously undervalued a company. The difference between short-term and long-term stock-market performance does not necessarily mean that the market is imperfect; it may result from financial judgments based on different time horizons. Thus, during a period of high interest rates, the market may apply a relatively high discount rate to investments, whereas managers may regard current interest rates as an aberration and apply a lower discount rate in making investment decisions. The justification of takeovers, then, depends on whether the economy is strengthened by investment decisions that take a long-term view of discount rates or by decisions that readjust with each short-term change in capital markets.[30]

Takeover tactics

In a typical hostile takeover, an insurgent group—often called a "raider"—makes a *tender offer* to buy a controlling block of stock in a target corporation from its present shareholders.[31] The offered price generally involves a premium, which is an amount in excess of the current trading price. If enough shareholders tender their shares in response to the offer, the insurgents gain control. In the usual course of events, the raiders replace the incumbent management team and proceed to make substantial changes in the company. In some instances, a tender offer is made directly to the shareholders, but in others, the cooperation of management is required.

The officers and directors of firms have a fiduciary duty to consider a tender offer in good faith. If they believe that a takeover is not in the best interests of the shareholders, then they have a right, even a duty, to fight the offer with all available means. Corporations have many resources for defending against hostile takeovers. These tactics—collectively called "shark repellents"—include poison pills, white knights, lockups, crown-jewel options, the Pac-Man defense, golden parachutes, and greenmail (see Table 5.1). Some of the defensive measures (such as poison pills and golden parachutes) are usually adopted in advance of any takeover bid, while others (white knights and greenmail) are customarily employed in the course of fighting an unwelcome offer. Many states have adopted so-called antitakeover statutes that further protect incumbent management against raiders. Because of shark repellents and antitakeover statutes, a merger or acquisition is virtually impossible to conduct today without the cooperation of the board of directors of the target corporation.

All takeover tactics raise important ethical issues, but three, in particular, have elicited great concern. These are unregulated tender offers, golden parachutes, and greenmail.

Tender offers
Ethical concern about the tactics of takeovers has focused primarily on the defences of target companies, but unregulated tender offers are also poten-

Table 5.1   Takeover defenses

Crown-jewel option   A form of lockup in which an option on a target's most valuable assets (crown jewels) is offered to a friendly firm in the event of a hostile takeover.

Golden parachute   A part of the employment contract with a top executive that provides for additional compensation in the event that the executive departs voluntarily or involuntarily after a takeover.

Greenmail   The repurchase by a target of an unwelcome suitor's stock at a premium in order to end an attempted hostile takeover.

Lockup option   An option given to a friendly firm to acquire certain assets in the event of a hostile takeover. Usually, the assets are crucial for the financing of a takeover.

Pac-Man defense   A defense (named after the popular video game) in which the target makes a counteroffer to acquire the unwelcome suitor.

Poison pill   A general term for any device that lowers the price of a target's stock in the event of a takeover. A common form of poison pill is the issuance of a new class of preferred stock that shareholders have a right to redeem at a premium after a takeover.

Shark repellent   A general term for all takeover defenses.

White knight   A friendly suitor which makes an offer for a target in order to avoid a takeover by an unwelcome suitor.

---

tially abusive. Before 1968, takeovers were sometimes attempted by a so-called "Saturday-night special," in which a tender offer was made after the close of the market on Friday and set to expire on Monday morning. The "Saturday-night special" was considered to be coercive because shareholders had to decide quickly whether to tender their shares with little information.[32] Shareholders would generally welcome an opportunity to sell stock that trades at $10 a share on a Friday afternoon for, say, $15. If, on Monday morning, however, the stock sells for $20 a share, then the shareholders who tendered over the weekend gained $5 but lost the opportunity to gain $10. With more information, shareholders might conclude that $15 or even $20 was an inadequate price and that they would be better off holding onto their shares— perhaps in anticipation of an even better offer.

Partial offers for only a certain number or percentage of shares and two-tier offers can also be coercive. In a two-tier offer, one price is offered for, say, 51 percent of the shares and a lower price is offered for the remainder. Both offers force shareholders to make a decision without knowing which price they will receive for their shares or, indeed, whether their shares will even be bought. Thus, tender offers can be structured in such a way that shareholders are stampeded into tendering quickly, lest they lose the opportunity. The payment that is offered may include securities—such as shares of the acquiring corporation or a new merged entity—and the value of these securities may be difficult to determine. Without adequate information, shareholders may not be able to judge whether a $15-per-share noncash offer, for example, is fairly priced.

Congress addressed these problems with tender offers in 1968 with the passage of the Williams Act. The guiding principle of the Williams Act is that shareholders have a right to make important investment decisions in an orderly manner and with adequate information. They should not be stampeded into tendering for fear of losing the opportunity or forced to decide in ignorance. Under section 14(d) of the Williams Act, a tender offer must be accompanied by a statement detailing the bidder's identity, the nature of the funding, and plans for restructuring the takeover target.[33] A tender offer must be open for 20 working days, in order to allow shareholders sufficient time to make a decision, and tendering shareholders have 15 days in which to change their minds—thereby permitting them to accept a better offer, should one be made. The Williams Act deals with partial and two-tier offers by requiring proration. Thus, if more shares are tendered than the bidder has offered to buy, then the same percentage of each shareholder's tendered stock must be purchased. Proration ensures the equal treatment of shareholders and removes the pressure on shareholders to tender early.

Golden parachutes
At the height of takeover activities in the 1980s, between one-quarter and one-half of major American corporations provided their top executives with an unusual form of protection—golden parachutes.[34] A golden parachute is a provision in a manager's employment contract for compensation—usually, a cash settlement equal to several years' salary—for the loss of a job following a takeover. In general, golden parachutes are distinct from severance packages because they become effective only in the event of a change of control and apply to both voluntary and involuntary termination. Thus, a golden parachute-equipped executive who is assigned to a lesser position after a takeover may be able to resign voluntarily and collect the compensation. Golden parachutes are usually limited to the CEO and a small number of other officers.[35]

The most common argument for golden parachutes is that they reduce a potential conflict of interest. Managers who might lose their jobs in the event of a takeover cannot be expected to evaluate a takeover bid objectively. Michael C. Jensen observes, "It makes no sense to hire a realtor to sell your house and then penalize your agent for doing so."[36] A golden parachute protects managers' futures, no matter the outcome, and thus frees them to consider only the best interests of the shareholders. In addition, golden parachutes enable corporations to attract and retain desirable executives because they provide protection against events that are largely beyond managers' control. Without this protection, a recruit may be reluctant to accept a position at a potential takeover target, or a manager might leave a threatened company in anticipation of a takeover bid.

Critics argue, first, that golden parachutes merely entrench incumbent managers by raising the price that raiders would have to pay. In this respect, golden parachutes are like poison pills; they create costly new obligations in the event of a change of control. All such defensive measures are legitimate if they are approved by the shareholders, but golden parachutes, critics complain, are often secured by executives from compliant boards of directors that they control. If golden parachutes are in the shareholders' interests, then executives should be willing to obtain shareholder approval.[37] Otherwise, they appear to be self-serving defensive measures that violate a duty to serve the shareholders.

Second, some critics object to the idea of providing additional incentives to do what they are being paid to do anyway.[38] Philip L. Cochran and Steven L. Wartick observe that managers are already paid to maximize shareholder wealth: "To provide additional compensation in order to get managers to objectively evaluate takeover offers is tantamount to management extortion of the shareholders."[39] One experienced director finds it "outrageous" that executives should be paid *after* they leave a company. Peter G. Scotese writes: "Why reward an executive so generously at the moment his or her contribution to the company ceases? The approach flies in the face of the American work ethic, which is based on raises or increments related to the buildup of seniority and merit."[40] These arguments suggest that even if golden parachutes can be justified economically, the perception that executives are abusing their power undermines public confidence in business and leads to demands for government action.

The principle for justifying golden parachutes is clear, even if its application is not. The justification for all forms of executive compensation is to provide incentives for acting in the shareholders' interests. If golden parachutes are too generous, then they entrench management by making the price of a takeover prohibitive—or else they motivate managers to support a takeover against the interests of shareholders. In either case, the managers enrich themselves at the shareholders' expense. The key is to develop a compensation package with just the right incentives, which, as Michael Jensen notes, will depend on the particular case.[41] Jensen recommends that golden parachutes be extended beyond the CEO to those who will play an important role in the negotiation and implementation of a takeover, and that the compensation provided by the parachute be tied in some way to the payoff of a takeover for shareholders.

Greenmail

Unsuccessful raiders do not always go away empty-handed. Because of the price rise that follows an announced takeover bid, raiders are often able to sell their holdings at a tidy profit. In some instances, target corporations have repelled unwelcome assaults by buying back the raiders' shares at a premium. After the financier Saul Steinberg accumulated more than 11 percent of Walt Disney Productions in 1984, the Disney board agreed to pay $77.50 per share, a total of $325.3 million, for stock that Steinberg had purchased at an average price of $63.25. As a reward for ending his run at Disney, Steinberg pocketed nearly $60 million. This episode and many like it have been widely criticized as *greenmail*.

The play on the word "blackmail" suggests that there is something corrupt about offering or accepting greenmail. A more precise term that avoids this bias is *control repurchase*. A control repurchase may be defined as a "privately negotiated stock repurchase from an outside shareholder, at a premium over the market price, made for the purpose of avoiding a battle for control of the company making the repurchase."[42] Control repurchases are legal; there is nothing in the Securities Exchange Act, which governs the sale of stock, or the Williams Act, which regulates takeovers, to prohibit them. Congress has conducted hearings on proposals to ban control repurchases in response to recommendations by the SEC and business groups, but to date no legislation has been passed. Control repurchases can be challenged in court as a breach of the management's fiduciary duty to shareholders, but courts are generally reluctant to intervene unless the manager's decision serves to protect only his or her own interests. Many people think that there ought to be a law, but we need to ask first why control repurchases are considered to be unethical.

There are three main ethical objections to control repurchases.[43] First, control repurchases are negotiated with one set of shareholders, who receive an offer that is not extended to everyone else. This is a violation, some say, of the principle that all shareholders should be treated equally. The same offer should be made to all shareholders—or none. To buy back the stock of raiders for a premium is unfair to other shareholders. This argument is easily dismissed. Managers have an obligation to treat all shareholders according to their rights under the charter and bylaws of the corporation and the relevant corporate law. This means one share, one vote at meetings and the same dividend for each share.[44] Otherwise, there is no obligation for managers to treat shareholders equally. Moreover, paying a premium for the repurchase of stock is a use of corporate assets that presumably brings some return to the shareholders, and the job of managers is to put all corporate assets to their most productive use. If the $60 million that Disney paid to Saul Steinberg, for example, brings higher returns to the shareholders than any other investment, then the managers have an obligation *to all shareholders* to treat this one shareholder differently.

Second, control repurchases are criticized as a breach of the fiduciary duty of management to serve the shareholders' interests. One critic of greenmail makes the case as follows:

> Say you owned a small apartment building in a distant city, and you hired a professional manager to run it for you. This person likes the job, and when someone—an apartment "raider"—sought to offer you a good price for the building, the manager does everything to prevent you from being able to consider the offer. . . . When all else fails, the manager takes some of your own money and pays the potential buyer greenmail to look elsewhere.[45]

If managers use shareholders' money to pay raiders to go away merely to save their own jobs, then they have clearly violated their fiduciary duty. However, this may not be the intent of managers in all cases of greenmail. Managers of target corporations may judge that an offer is not in the best interests of shareholders and that the best defensive tactic is a repurchase of the raiders' shares. With $60 million, Disney might have made another movie that would bring a certain return. However, Disney executives might also have calculated that the costs to the company of continuing to fight Saul Steinberg—or allowing him to gain control—would outweigh this return. If so, then the $60 million that Disney paid in greenmail is shareholder money well spent. Other defensive tactics cost money as well, and the possibility of managers spending shareholders' money to preserve their own jobs exists with any takeover defense.[46] So there is no reason to believe that greenmail or control repurchases necessarily involve a breach of fiduciary duty.

Third, some critics object to greenmail or control repurchases on the grounds that the payments invite *pseudobidders* who have no intention of taking control and mount a raid merely for the profit.[47] The ethical wrong, according to this objection, lies with the raiders' conduct, although management may be complicitous in facilitating it. At a minimum, pseudobidders are engaging in unproductive economic activity, which benefits no one but the raiders themselves; at their worst, pseudobidders are extorting corporations by threatening some harm unless the payments are made.

Is pseudobidding for the purpose of getting greenmail a serious problem? The effectiveness of pseudobidding depends on the credibility of the threatened takeover. No raider can pose a credible threat unless an opportunity exists to increase the return to shareholders. Therefore, the situations in which pseudobidders are likely to emerge are quite limited. Even if a pseudobidder or a genuine raider is paid to go away, that person has pointed out some problem with the incumbent management and paved the way for change. Unsuccessful raiders who accept greenmail may still provide a service for everyone.[48] A prohibition on greenmail or control repurchases would increase the risk of attempting a raid and thereby discourage this potentially beneficial activity.

If it were possible for raiders to hold America's corporations hostage, then something should be done, and prohibiting greenmail would be one solution. Before taking action, however, more empirical research must be done on the incidence of pseudobidding, the conditions under which it occurs, and the actual consequences. Moreover, the distinction between a pseudobidder and a genuine raider is difficult to make, and provable pseudobidding could be prosecuted as a fraud because of false statements in mandatory SEC filings. Hence, even if pseudobidding is a problem, a ban on greenmail may not be the solution.

The role of the board of directors

In 1989, Paramount Communications made a tender offer for all outstanding stock in Time Incorporated. Many Time shareholders were keen to accept the all-cash, $175-per-share bid (later raised to $200 per share), which represented about a 40 percent premium over the previous trading price of Time stock. However, the board of directors refused to submit the Paramount offer to the shareholders. Time and Warner Communications, Inc., had been preparing to merge, and the Time directors believed that a Time–Warner merger would produce greater value for the shareholders that an acquisition by Paramount. Disgruntled Time shareholders joined Paramount in a suit that charged the directors with a failure to act in the shareholders' interests.

This case raises two critical issues. First, who has the right to determine the value of a corporation in a merger or acquisition? Is this a job for the board of directors and their investment advisers? Both boards and their advisers have superior information about a company's current financial status and future prospects, but they also have a vested interest in preserving the status quo. Should the task of evaluation be left to the shareholders, whose interests are the ultimate arbiter but whose knowledge is often lacking? Some of the shareholders are professional arbitragers, who are looking merely for a quick buck. Second, does the interest of the shareholders lie with quick, short-term gain or with the viability of the company in the long run? Acceptance of the Paramount offer would maximize the immediate stock price for Time shareholders but upset the long-term strategic plan that the board had developed.

The Delaware State Supreme Court decision in *Paramount Communications. Inc. v. Time Inc.* addressed both issues by ruling that the Time board of directors had a right to take a long-term perspective in evaluating a takeover bid and had no obligation to submit the Paramount proposal to the shareholders.[49] The court recognized that increasing shareholder value in the long run involves a consideration of interests besides those of current shareholders, including other corporate constituencies, such as employees, customers, and local communities.[50] One concern of the Time directors was to preserve the "culture" of *Time* magazine because of the importance of editorial integrity to the magazine's readers and journalistic staff.

The *Paramount* decision is an example of a so-called other constituency statute. A majority of states have now adopted (either by judicial or legislative action) laws that permit (and, in a few states, require) the board of directors to consider the impact of a takeover on a broad range of nonshareholder constituencies.[51] Other constituency statutes reflect a judgment by judges and legislators that legitimate nonshareholder interests are harmed by takeovers, and directors faced with a takeover do not owe allegiance solely to the current shareholders.[52] Whether other constituency statutes serve to protect non-shareholder constituencies or merely increase the power of management to resist takeovers is an unresolved question. However, they represent a rethinking of the market for corporate control. As a result of other constituency statutes, decisions about the future of corporations depend more on calm deliberations in boardrooms and less on the buying and selling of shares in a noisy marketplace.

Notes

1. *SEC v. Texas Gulf Sulphur*, 401 F.2d 19 (1987).
2. *Chiarella v. U.S.*, 445 U.S. 222 (1980); *Dirks v. SEC*, 463 U.S. 646 (1983); *U.S. v. Chestman*, 903 F.2d 75 (1990); *U.S. v. Willis*, 737 F. Supp. 269 (1990); and *U.S. v. O'Hagan*, No. 96–842.
3. Henry Manne, *Insider Trading and the Stock Market* (New York: The Free Press, 1966).
4. This point is argued in Jennifer Moore, "What Is Really Unethical about Insider Trading?" *Journal of Business Ethics*, 9 (1990), 171–82.
5. *Carpenter et al. v. U.S.*, 484 U.S. 19 (1987).

6.　*Report of the Presidential Task Force on Market Mechanisms* (Washington, DC: US Government Printing Office, 1988).

7.　"The Uses and Abuses of Chapter 11," *The Economist*, March 18, 1989, 72; and Paul G. Engel, "Bankruptcy: A Refuge for All Reasons?" *Industry Week*, March 5, 1984, 63–8.

8.　Anna Cifelli, "Management by Bankruptcy," *Fortune*, October 31, 1983, 69–72; and Harold L. Kaplan, "Bankruptcy as a Corporate Management Tool," *ABA Journal*, January 1, 1987, 64–7.

9.　Kevin J. Delaney, *Strategic Bankruptcy: How Corporations and Creditors Use Chapter 11 to their Advantage* (Berkeley and Los Angeles: University of California Press, 1992).

10.　One exception is that a plan may be imposed over the objections of one or more classes of creditors as long it is approved by at least one class of creditors whose claims are reduced and a court finds the plan to be "fair and equitable." The imposition of a nonunanimous plan is called a "cram-down."

11.　See Douglas G. Baird and Thomas H. Jackson, *Cases, Problems, and Materials on Bankruptcy*, 2nd edn. (Boston: Little, Brown, 1990); and Thomas H. Jackson, *The Logic and Limits of Bankruptcy Law* (Cambridge, MA: Harvard University Press, 1986).

12.　The need to force creditors to act collectively is called the problem of the common pool. See Baird and Jackson, *Cases, Problems, and Materials on Bankruptcy*, 39–42.

13.　Thomas H. Jackson, "Bankruptcy, Non-Bankruptcy Entitlements, and the Creditors' Bargain," *Yale Law Journal*, 91(1982), 857–907.

14.　*NLRB v. Bildisco*, 465 U.S. 513 (1984).

15.　Section 1113 of the Bankruptcy Code requires companies to attempt to negotiate with unions in good faith and, if an agreement cannot be reached, to demonstrate that any changes are "necessary to permit the reorganization" or that rejection is justified by a "balancing of equities." The courts enforced these more stringent standards in *Wheeling-Pittsburgh Steel Corporation v. United Steelworkers of America*, 791 F.2d 1074 (3d. Cir. 1986).

16.　"A Retailer's Chapter 11 Has Creditors Enraged," *BusinessWeek*, May 9, 1983, 71, 74.

17.　See Delaney, *Strategic Bankruptcy*, 162–8.

18.　Paul Brodeur, *Outrageous Misconduct: The Asbestos Industry on Trial* (New York: Pantheon Books, 1985), 257–8, 268, 270-1.

19.　Such asset shifts can be challenged by creditors as "fraudulent conveyances," that is, as transfers made to defraud creditors.

20.　Michael Bradley and Michael Rosenzweig, "The Untenable Case for Chapter 11," *Yale Law Journal*, 101 (1992), 1043–95.

21.　Bradley and Rosenzweig, "The Untenable Case for Chapter 11," 1049–50. This conclusion is controversial and has been challenged. See Elizabeth Warren, "The Untenable Case for Repeal of Chapter 11," *Yale Law Journal*, 102 (1992), 437–79.

22. Jackson, *The Logic and Limits of Bankruptcy Law*, 21–7.

23. Chapter 11 contains some mechanisms to counter these management rights and limit possible abuses. Thus, at any time during bankruptcy proceedings, creditors can file a petition for immediate liquidation, which permits a bankruptcy court to judge whether managers are "playing games" with the creditors. Because creditors can always hold out for liquidation or the opportunity to submit their own plan, and because management's plan must be approved by each creditor group, managers are forced to propose a plan that is reasonably fair and equitable. And in the event of a "cram-down," a court must determine that the reorganization plan is fair and equitable.

24. Joseph McCafferty, "Is Bankruptcy an Unfair Advantage?" *CFO*, June 1995, 28; and Stephen Neish, "Is the Revised Chapter 11 Any Improvement?" *Corporate Finance*, March 1995, 37–40.

25. Peter Drucker, "To End the Raiding Roulette Game," *Across the Board*, April 1986, 39.

26. Michel T. Halbouty, "The Hostile Takeover of Free Enterprise," *Vital Speeches of the Day*, August 1986, 613.

27. See Michael C. Jensen, 'The Takeover Controversy," *Vital Speeches of the Day*, May 1987, 426–9; "Takeovers: Folklore and Science," *Harvard Business Review*, November–December 1984, 109–21.

28. Jensen, "Takeovers"; Michael C. Jensen and Richard S. Ruback, "The Market for Corporate Control: The Scientific Evidence," *Journal of Financial Economics*, 11(1983), 5–50; and Douglas H. Ginsburg and John F. Robinson, "The Case Against Federal Intervention in the Market for Corporate Control," *The Brookings Review*, Winter–Spring 1986, 9–14.

29. F. M. Scherer, "Takeovers: Present and Future Dangers," *The Brookings Review*, Winter–Spring 1986, 15–20.

30. These points are made in Scherer, "Takeovers," 19–20.

31. Hostile takeovers are conducted less frequently by means of a proxy contest. A friendly merger or acquisition generally results from a proposal to the board of directors of the target corporation, which is submitted in due course to a vote by the shareholders. Shareholders are not asked to tender their stock, but if the takeover is approved, their shares are exchanged for some package that typically includes shares of the acquiring corporation or a newly created corporation. Even "friendly" mergers and acquisitions may involve heated proxy contests.

32. For a discussion of coercion in tender offers see John R. Boatright, "Tender Offers: An Ethical Perspective," in W. M. Hoffman, R. Frederick, and E. S. Petry, Jr, eds., *The Ethics of Organizational Transformation: Mergers, Takeovers, and Corporate Restructuring* (New York: Quorum Books, 1989), 167–81.

33. Section 13(d) requires a similar statement within ten days after any party acquires more than 5 percent of a corporation's stock. This statement provides notice of a possible takeover bid and facilitates an orderly response.

34. Philip L. Cochran and Steven L. Wartick, " 'Golden Parachutes': A Closer Look," *California Management Review*, 26 (1984), 113. A 1982 study by Ward Howell

International reported the number of Fortune 1000 companies with golden parachutes doubled between 1979 and 1982 to 25 percent. Ward Howell International, Inc., *Survey of Employment Contracts and Golden Parachutes Among the Fortune 1000*, company report, 1982. A study by Hewitt Associations in 1987 found that the figure among Fortune 100 industrial companies was 46 percent. Hewitt Associates, *Survey of Employment Contracts, Change-in-Control Agreements and Incentive Plan Provisions*, company report, June 1987.

35. Protection against job losses following a takeover has been extended by some companies to all employees in the form "tin parachutes." See Diana C. Robertson, "Corporate Restructuring and Employee Interests: The Tin Parachute," in Hoffman et al., *The Ethics of Organizational Transformation*, 195–202.

36. Michael C. Jensen, "The Takeover Controversy: Analysis and Evidence," in John C. Coffee, Jr, Louis Lowenstein, and Susan Rose-Ackerman, eds., *Knights, Raiders, and Targets: The Impact of the Hostile Takeover* (New York: Oxford University Press, 1988), 340.

37. One study reports that the announcement of golden parachutes raises the price of a company's shares by 3 percent, thus suggesting shareholder approval. However, this price rise could be due to the perception that the company is a takeover target. R. Lambert and D. Larker, "Golden Parachutes, Executive Decision-Making, and Shareholder Wealth," *Journal of Accounting and Economics*, 7 (1985) 179–204. See also Jensen, "The Takeover Controversy," 340.

38. Peter G. Scotese, "Fold Up Those Golden Parachutes," *Harvard Business Review*, March–April 1985, 170.

39. Cochran and Wartick, " 'Golden Parachutes'," 121.

40. Scotese, "Fold Up Those Golden Parachutes," 168.

41. Jensen, "The Takeover Controversy," 341.

42. J. Gregory Dees, "The Ethics of 'Greenmail'," in William C. Frederick and Lee E. Preston, eds., *Business Ethics: Research Issues and Empirical Studies* (Greenwich, CT: JAI Press, 1990), 254.

43. These arguments are developed and evaluated in Dees, "The Ethics of Greenmail."

44. However, different classes of stock can carry different voting rights and different dividends.

45. Quoted in Robert W. McGee, "Ethical Issues in Acquisitions and Mergers," *Mid-Atlantic Journal of Business*, 25 (March 1989), 25.

46. Some argue that managers should never attempt to defend against a takeover but allow the shareholders to decide. However, management generally has better information than shareholders and may be in a better position to determine what is in the shareholders' interests. See Frank H. Easterbrook and Daniel R. Fischel, "The Proper Role of a Target's Management in Responding to a Tender Offer," *Harvard Law Review*, 94 (1981), 1161–204.

47. John C. Coffee, Jr, "Regulating the Market for Corporate Control: A Critical Assessment of the Tender Offer's Role in Corporate Governance," *Columbia Law Review*, 84 (1984), 1145–296.

48. This is argued in Roger J. Dennis, "Two-Tiered Tender Offers and Greenmail: Is New Legislation Needed?" *Georgia Law Review*, 19 (1985), 281–341.
49. *Paramount Communications, Inc. v. Time Inc.*, 571 A.2d 1140 (1990).
50. In *Paramount*, the Delaware State Supreme Court cited a previous decision in which it had held that considering a takeover's "effect on the corporate enterprise" includes such concerns as "the impact on 'constituencies' other than shareholders (i.e. creditors, customers, employees, and perhaps even the community generally)." *Unocal Corporation v. Mesa Petroleum Co.*, 493 A.2d 946, 955 (1985).
51. See Eric W. Orts, "Beyond Shareholders: Interpreting Corporate Constituency Statutes," *George Washington Law Review*, 61(1992), 14–135.
52. Roberta S. Karmel, "The Duty of Directors to Non-shareholder Constituencies in Control Transactions – A Comparison of U.S. and U.K. Law," *Wake Forest Law Review*, 25 (1990), 68.

Chapter Six

The Financial Theory of the Firm

A business firm or corporation is an organization that brings together many different groups—most notably managers, employees, suppliers, customers, and, of course, investors—for the purpose of providing some product or service. Because these various corporate constituencies have different and sometimes competing interests, the question arises: In whose interest should the corporation be run? To this question, finance offers a simple, univocal answer. A firm should be run in the interests of the shareholders. The objective of the firm is to maximize shareholder wealth.

Finance textbooks seldom argue for this claim. It appears to function in finance like an axiom of geometry—an obvious truth that needs no support. The claim is not unsupported, however. The finance literature contains a well-developed, theoretical argument for what may be called the shareholder model of the corporation. In presenting this argument, finance theorists depart from the idea that finance is a purely factual, value-free science because they hold not merely that firms are run, in fact, in the interested of shareholders but that they *ought* to be so run. The word "ought" marks a moral claim that must be supported by some moral argument.

The claim that a firm ought to be run in the shareholders' interest or to maximize shareholder wealth—the two claims are equivalent—is almost universally accepted by finance theorists. However, it is widely challenged outside of finance by critics who contend that shareholder primacy unjustly neglects the interests of other corporate constituencies. In particular, so-called stakeholder theorists hold that corporations ought to be run in the interest of all those groups with a "stake" in them. These stakeholders include employees, suppliers, customers, and community members, as well as stockholders.

This chapter examines the argument in finance for shareholder control of corporations and concludes that the shareholder model of the corporation is morally justified. However, it is important to understand the argument for this model. Properly understood, this argument does not justify putting the interests of shareholders above all other corporate constituencies. The purpose of a firm—like that of a market, which firms resemble—is to serve the interests of everyone. However, the interests of stakeholders other than stockholders are served in other ways besides having control. The important question, then, is what forms of corporate governance or ownership structures enable firms to serve the interests of all.

Traditional Theories

The theory of the firm has a long and tangled history.[1] In economics, neo-classical marginal analysis regards the firm as a profit-maximizing unit, and for the purposes of economics there is no need to inquire into its internal workings. As the entry on the theory of the firm in the *New Palgrave* dictionary of economics observes: "*If* firms maximize, *how* they do it is not of great interest or at least relevant to economics." The marginalist theory has been challenged in economics, however, by behavioral and managerial theories of the firm, which are based on the operation of actual corporations.[2]

Legal theorists have also developed theories of the firm in order to answer the many puzzling questions that arise in corporate law. Debate rages to this day over the nature of the corporation: Is the corporation the private property of the stockholders who chose to do business in the corporate form, or is the corporation a public institution which is sanctioned by the state in order to achieve some social good?[3] On the former view (which may be called the property rights theory), the right to incorporate is an extension of the property rights and the right of contract that belong to everyone.[4] The latter view (let us call it the social institution theory) holds that the right to incorporate is a privilege granted by the state and that corporate property has an inherent public aspect.[5]

The theory of the firm that is prevalent in modern finance is the contractual theory, according to which a firm is viewed as a nexus of contracts among all corporate constituencies. On this theory, different groups, including investors, employees, suppliers, and customers, each contract with a firm to supply some needed resource in return for some benefit. The manager's role in the nexus-of-contracts firm is to coordinate the vast web of mutual agreements. The crux of the financial argument is that shareholders are different from other constituencies by virtue of being residual risk bearers and that, as such, they have peculiar problems of contracting that are best met by having control.

The contractual theory of the firm stands in sharp contrast to the social institution theory, in which the corporation is sanctioned by the state to serve the general welfare. In contrast to the property rights theory, which it more closely resembles, the contractual theory does not hold that the firm is the private property of the shareholders. Rather, shareholders, along with other investors, employees, and the like, each own assets that they make available to the firm. Thus, the firm results from the property rights and the right of contract of every corporate constituency and not from those of shareholders alone.

Whether corporations ought to serve the interests of shareholders alone or the interests of a wider range of constituencies depends on the theory of the firm that we accept. Even though holders of all three theories generally conclude that the interests of shareholders are primary, the arguments that they provide are different, and it is important to understand the logic of each argument, especially the argument provided by the contractual theory, given its importance for finance. But, first, we need to examine the arguments that proceed from the property rights and social institution theories.

Whose interests should be served?

The original form of the modern corporation was the joint-stock company, in which a small group of wealthy individuals pooled their money for some undertaking that they could not finance alone. In the property rights theory, this corporate form of business organization is justified on the grounds that it represents an extension of the property rights and the right of contract enjoyed by everyone. Just as individuals are entitled to conduct business with their own assets, so too have they a right to contract with others for the same purpose. Although individual shareholders in a joint-stock company or a corporation have exchanged their personal assets for shares of stock, they are still owners of property in the full sense of the term. They jointly own the common enterprise, and as owners, they are entitled to receive the full proceeds, as though it were a business conducted by one person alone.

The property rights theory prevailed in American law through the first two decades of the twentieth century, although elements of the social institution theory exercised some force. The law has been especially ambivalent as to whether the corporation is essentially a *private* association created for the purpose of personal enrichment, as the property rights theory suggests, or a *public* enterprise that is intended to serve some larger social good. The fact that the earliest joint-stock companies were special grants that kings bestowed on favored subjects for specific purposes fits the social institution theory. The property rights theory also raises a question about regulation: If the corporation is essentially the private property of the shareholders, then what justifies state regulation? The courts have attempted to solve this problem by holding, in decisions such as *Munn v. Illinois* (1877), that some property is "affected with a public interest" so that states can rightly regulate its use.[6] Corporations are thus not wholly private; they fill some public role.[7]

In a pure expression of the property rights theory, the Michigan State Supreme Court ruled in 1919 that the Ford Motor Company could be forced to pay out dividends to the shareholders, in spite of Henry Ford's view that the company had made too much profit and ought to share some of it with the public by reducing prices. In *Dodge v. Ford Motor Co.*, the court declared, "A business corporation is organized and carried on primarily for the profit of the stockholders."[8] The profit-making end of a corporation is set forth in its charter of incorporation, which represents a contract among the shareholders who have invested their money, and Henry Ford had no right to substitute another end by using corporate resources for an essentially philanthropic purpose.

The argument expressed in *Dodge v. Ford Motor Co.* could retain its validity as long as corporations had relatively few shareholders who actively controlled the business. However, the premise that shareholders are the owners of a corporation was challenged in 1932 in a book that profoundly changed all thinking about corporate governance. That book was *The Modern Corporation and Private Property*, by Adolf A. Berle, Jr, and Gardiner C. Means.

Ownership and control

The Modern Corporation and Private Property documented a dramatic shift that had occurred in American business.[9] The dispersion of stock ownership in large corporations among numerous investors with little involvement in corporate affairs, combined with the rise of a professional managerial class that exercised actual control, had resulted in a separation of ownership and control, with far-reaching implications. In particular, the separation of ownership and control changed the nature of corporate property as well as the ownership rights of shareholders.

Strictly speaking, property is not a tangible thing like land but a bundle of rights that defines what an owner can and cannot do with a thing, such as a piece of land. Shareholders provide capital to a corporation in return for certain rights, such as the right to vote and to receive dividends. But full ownership involves control over property and an assumption of responsibility, both of which shareholders have relinquished. By doing so, shareholders of large, publicly held corporations have ceased to be owners in the full sense and have become one among many providers of the resources needed by a corporation.

According to Berle and Means, "The property owner who invests in a modern corporation so far surrenders his wealth to those in control of the corporation that he has exchanged the position of independent owner for one in which he may become merely recipient of the wages of capital."[10] They continued:

> [T]he owners of passive property, by surrendering control and responsibility over the active property have surrendered the right that the corporation should be operated in their sole interest,—they have released the community from the obligation to protect them to the full extent implied in the doctrine of strict property rights. At the same time, the controlling groups . . . have in their own interest broken the bars of tradition which require that the corporation be operated solely for the benefit of the owners of passive property.[11]

Because of the separation of ownership and control, managers have assumed the position of trustee for the immense resources of a modern corporation, and in this new position, they face the question: For whom are corporate managers trustees?

Berle and Means recognized the possibility that managers could be trustees who operate corporations in the interest of society as a whole. Managers, they observe, "have placed the community in a position to demand that the modern corporation serve not alone the owners . . . but all society."[12] That society should make this demand—and that corporate managers should heed it—was advocated by E. Merrick Dodd, Jr, in a famous 1932 exchange with Berle in the *Harvard Law Review*.[13] Dodd saw public opinion and the law moving toward a view of the corporation as "an economic institution which has a social service as well as a profit-making function."[14] According to Dodd, the modern corporation had also become a public institution, as opposed to a private activity of the shareholders, and as such, it had a social responsibility that could include the making of charitable contribution.[15] Because a corporation is property only in a "qualified sense," it may be regulated by society so that the interests of employees, customers, and others are protected. And corporate managers have a right, even a duty, to consider the interests of all those who deal with the corporation without violating the property rights of shareholders.[16]

Berle cautioned against Dodd's position because of the dangers posed by unrestrained managerial power. In a response to Dodd in the *Harvard Law Review*, Berle wrote, "When the fiduciary obligation of the corporate management and 'control' to stockholders is weakened or eliminated, the management and 'control' become for all practical purposes absolute."[17] It would be unwise, in Berle's estimation, for the law to release managers from a strict accountability to shareholders, not out of respect for their property rights as owners of a corporation but as a matter of sound public policy. He wrote: "Unchecked by present legal balances, a social-economic absolutism of corporate administrators, even if benevolent, might be unsafe; and in any case it hardly affords the soundest base on which to construct the economic commonwealth which industrialism seems to require."[18]

Berle is fully in agreement with Dodd's contention that the corporation has a social service as well as a profit-making function, but this service to society requires an immense concentration of resources that must be very carefully restrained. Corporate law has evolved effective means for restraining managerial power by directing managers to act in the interests of the shareholders, but we lack effective means for ensuring that managers serve the interests of society as a whole. And there is no guarantee that managers will exercise their newly acquired control in any interests but their own. Berle described the rise of corporate managers as a "seizure of power without recognition of responsibility—ambition without courage."[19] In the absence of effective restraints on managerial power, Berle concludes, "[W]e had best be protecting the interests we know, being no less swift to provide for the new interests as they successively appear."[20]

Although the separation of ownership and control documented by Berle and Means undermined the property rights theory, a fully developed social institution theory did not replace it. Instead, a conception of the corporation as a quasi-public institution emerged, in which managers have limited discretion to use the resources at their command for the good of employees, customers, and the larger society. In a world of giant corporations, managers are called upon to balance the interests of competing corporate constituencies, and in order to fill this role, they developed a sense of management as a profession with public responsibilities. Managers ceased being the exclusive servants of the stockholders and assumed the mantle of public-spirited leaders.

With Berle's warnings in mind, legislators and judges have been reluctant, as a matter of public policy, to free managers from a reasonably strict obligation to run corporations in the interests of shareholders. However, in recognition of the public role of managers in leading major institutions, the law has loosened the restraints that were imposed in *Dodge v. Ford Motor Co.* and allowed corporations to expend some corporate funds for the good of society. In *A. P. Smith Manufacturing Co. v. Barlow* (1953), the New Jersey State Supreme Court ruled that the managers of the company were permitted by law to give $1,500 to Princeton University, despite shareholder objections, on the grounds that to bar corporations from making such contributions would threaten our democracy and the free-enterprise system. The court agreed with the testimony of a former chairman of the board of the United States Steel

Company that if American business does not aid important institutions like private universities, then it is not "properly protecting the long-range interests of its stockholders, its employees and its customers." After the decision in *A. P. Smith Manufacturing Co. v. Barlow*, Berle conceded defeat in his debate with Dodd: Public opinion and the law had accepted Dodd's contention that corporate powers ought to be held in trust for the whole of society.[21]

The Contractual Theory

The modern theory of the firm as a nexus of contracts originated in the work of the economist Ronald Coase.[22] One of Coase's many insights is that firms exist as less costly alternatives to market transactions. In a world where market transactions could occur without any costs (what economists call *transaction costs*), economic activity would be achieved entirely by means of contracting among individuals in a free market. In the actual world, the transaction costs involved in negotiating and enforcing contracts can be quite high, and some coordination can be achieved more cheaply by organizing economic activity in firms. Thus, there are two forms of economic coordination—firms and markets—and the choice between them is determined by transaction costs.

In the Coasean view, the firm is a market writ small in which parties with economic assets contract with the firm to deploy these assets in productive activity. Generally, an individual's assets are more productive when they are combined with the assets of others in joint or team production. And individuals will choose to deploy their assets in a firm instead of the market when the lower transaction costs of a firm combined with the benefits of team production yield them a higher return.

Deploying assets in a firm involves some risks, however, when those assets are *firm-specific*. Consider the situation of an employee who acquires skills that are needed by a particular employer. A worker with such skills will generally earn more than one with only generic skills, but only a few employers will value those special skills and be willing to pay the higher wages. An employee with special skills is also tied more closely to the firm because the skills in question are not easily transportable, and he or she would likely suffer a loss if forced to move to another employer. The assets of an employee who can be more profitably employed with one or a few firms are thus firm-specific. Firm-specific assets enable a worker to create more wealth, which makes possible the higher pay, but this wealth can also be appropriated by the firm itself. In economic terms, firm-specific assets create quasi-rents, some of which are distributed to employees with special skills in the form of higher pay. The risk to employees is that a disproportionate share of these quasi-rents will be appropriated by the firm, thereby leaving the employee without adequate compensation for acquiring special skills.

Not only employees but also investors, suppliers, customers, and other groups have firm-specific assets, and these groups will make their assets available to a firm only with adequate safeguards against misappropriation. That is, each group will seek guarantees to ensure that they are adequately compensated for any assets that cannot be easily removed from joint productive activity. Most groups protect themselves by means of contracts, both explicit and implicit. Thus, employees are often protected by employment contracts, suppliers by purchase contracts, consumers by warranties, and so on. Bondholders lend money to a firm with written agreements (called *indentures*) that specify the terms of repayment and other conditions. In the nexus-of-contracts firm, managers coordinate these contracts with the various corporate constituencies. The contracts with most corporate constituencies are relatively unproblematic, but one group raises special problems in both finance theory and corporate law, namely shareholders.

The role of shareholders

In the usual interpretation of the contractual theory, shareholders provide capital along with bondholders and other investors; but, more significantly, they also assume the residual risk of conducting business. Because capital can be raised by issuing debt in place of equity, adequately capitalized firms can exist without shareholders. Indeed, this is the case with an entrepreneur who goes into business with only a bank loan for capital. In addition to capital, firms need someone to bear the risk that is inherent in any business activity, which is to say the *residual risk* that remains after a firm has fulfilled all of its legal obligations. Residual risk could be borne by every group that contracts with a firm, but risk bearing can also be a specialized role in which one group bears the preponderance of risk. The lone entrepreneur assumes this role in the example just cited, *if* the bank loan is adequately secured; otherwise, the bank assumes this role as well. In the large, publicly held corporation, shareholders fill the role of residual risk-bearer, and it is this role, rather than the role of capital provider, that sets them apart from other groups in the nexus of contracts.

The assets that shareholders make available to a corporation are highly firm-specific. Bondholders invest for a fixed term, and employees, suppliers, customers, and other groups generally have the option of easy exit; but shareholders invest for the life of a firm. (True, individual shareholders can usually dispose of any given shares of stock, but a buyer must be found who is willing to take over the investment.) Like other constituencies with firm-specific assets, shareholders will contract with a firm only if their investment is adequately safeguarded.

In the contractual theory of the firm, the position of residual risk-bearer is difficult to protect by ordinary contractual provisions, such as those available to bondholders, for example. Some protection is provided by the opportunity to diversify and by the limited liability that shareholders enjoy. Shareholders are also rewarded for their investment with dividends and appreciation of their stock, although neither of these is guaranteed. In addition, shareholders have corporate control, which is a package of rights that includes the right to select the board of directors and approve important changes. However, the most important aspect of corporate control is the status of shareholders as the chief beneficiary of the firm's wealth-creating activity. Finance theory holds that maximizing shareholder wealth is the objective of the firm, and this financial view is given legal force by the *fiduciary duty* that corporate law imposes on the officers and directors of corporations to serve the shareholders' interests.

Although the right of control is an effective safeguard for residual risk-bearers, the contractual theory of the firm itself does not assign this right to shareholders—or to any other group, for that matter. Rather, corporate control is a benefit to be bargained for in the nexus-of-contracts firm, and through bargaining, any constituency or stakeholder group could conceivably make their interests the objective of the firm and the end of management's fiduciary duty. Indeed, other groups take control when a corporation becomes employee-owned or customer-owned. Employees have also successfully bargained for representation on boards of directors, and bond indentures sometimes give bondholders the right to vote on certain risky ventures. When corporations are in distress, creditors take control from shareholders and the creditors' interests become primary until the firm recovers.

Nevertheless, the current system of corporate governance assigns control, for the most part, to shareholders. Some further argument is needed, however, for this assignment of rights. Why should corporations be obligated to serve the interests of shareholders alone? Both finance theory and corporate law provide an argument for shareholder control, to which we now turn.

The argument for shareholder control

In the contractual theory, the argument for shareholder control turns on the fact that shareholders bear residual risk. Shareholders are not the owners of the firm according to the contractual theory because no group can be said to "own" the firm; shareholders are merely the providers of a needed resource, namely capital. Unlike bondholders, for example, who also provide capital, shareholders settle for a claim on residual revenues instead of a fixed return. That is, shareholders are willing to make their assets available to a firm in return for whatever remains after the claims of bondholders, employees, suppliers, and other groups are satisfied. However, the fact that shareholders are residual risk-bearers does not entail by itself that shareholders ought to have corporate control. Some further steps are needed to complete the arguments. Two such steps are the value of control to shareholders and the need to solve the problem of controlling agents.

The value of control to shareholders

One way of completing the argument is by holding that the right of corporate control is a protection that is of greater value to residual claimants than to other constituencies. Therefore, shareholders are more willing to pay for the privilege of having their interests be the objective of the firm. Bondholders, employees, and other groups generally prefer different contractual arrangements. The underlying assumption is that nonshareholder groups can better protect their firm-specific assets by other means that do not involve corporate control. Employees, for example, are protected by contracts, either explicit or implicit, that assure them a specific wage and other benefits, and these protections are more secure than payments that vary with a firm's fortunes. (Few employees would want to be paid entirely in stock options.) Bargaining for control rights, such as the right to a seat on the board of directors, would require employees to give up something else, and the reluctance of employees to bargain for such rights suggests that the gain is not worth the price.

The fixed claims of bondholders, employees, suppliers, and other groups will be satisfied as long as the firm remains solvent, no matter how poorly or how well the firm performs otherwise. However, shareholders, with their residual claims, will be compensated for providing capital only if the firm does *well.* The right of control, therefore, is better suited to the situation of residual risk-bearers because their main source of protection is the ability to spur the firm to a high level of performance. Without the right to control, shareholders would either refuse to assume residual risk or demand a higher price for doing so. From a corporate point of view, it makes sense to offer control rights to shareholders in order to raise capital more cheaply.

This argument is not very strong in the case of large, publicly held corporations. Not only do individual shareholders generally lack the ability to influence underperforming management (thus reducing the value of control as a source of protection), but there is little evidence that shareholders invest with this expectation. Studies show that investors buy shares of stock (and thereby assume greater risk) for the prospect of superior returns and that control rights have little bearing on their decisions.[23] Moreover, the liquidity of the stock market enables shareholders to dispose easily of disappointing stocks, and though this step may result in some loss, the cost of selling is generally less than the cost of attempting to exercise control.[24] Liquidity, in short, is an alternative to control that offers much the same protection.[25] The limited liability of shareholders reduces the risk from any one firm to the amount invested. Finally, properly diversified shareholders can eliminate all of the unique risk of individual firms from their portfolios and incur only systemic or market risk. Limited liability and diversification thus reduce further the value of control to individual shareholders. The argument for shareholder control based on their assumption of residual risk founders on the fact that shareholders, in truth, bear relatively little risk.

Solving the agency problem

A stronger argument for shareholder control can be constructed by addressing the problem, raised by Adolf Berle, of restraining managerial power and ensuring that managers make decisions that maximize the wealth-creating powers of the firm. Wealth is created any time a firm pursues projects with a positive net present value (NPV), and choosing projects with the highest NPV will result in the maximum creation of wealth. Assuming that maximum wealth creation is the goal of business activity, control should go to the group with the appropriate incentives for making weath-maximizing decisions.

This group—according to the standard argument—is the shareholders. Bondholders, employees, and other corporate constituencies with fixed claims tend to favor decisions that secure their claims and no more. Therefore, some profitable investment opportunities might not be pursued if these groups had control. Managers, too, lack the incentives to pursue all profitable ventures, especially those that would reduce their power or place them at risk. Wealth-maximizing decisions are more likely to be made by the residual risk-bearers, because they incur the marginal costs and gain the marginal benefits of all new ventures. Shareholder control, therefore, is the most efficient form of corporate governance.

That shareholders would run a corporation most efficiently is of little importance, however, if managers not shareholders, have control. The separation of ownership and control noted by Berle and Means thus creates an agency problem: How can managers be induced to run a corporation in the same way that the shareholders would? The problem, in other words, is to make managers act as though they were agents of the shareholders at the least cost. Again, shareholder control solves this problem because shareholders have the incentive not only to monitor managers' performance but to reduce agency costs. On the contractual theory, then, control rights should be held by residual risk bearers, not because they are owners or because they are at risk but because they are in the best position to monitor the managers who have actual control. More precisely, structuring the nexus of contracts in such a way that residual risk bearers have control rights enables a firm to maximize wealth creation with the lowest agency costs. Insofar as shareholders bear residual risk, they should have control.

This account of the argument for shareholder control in the contractual theory is obviously incomplete. Control rights themselves are varied, and a fuller discussion would focus on specific details of corporate governance. Although firms do not actually bargain with individual shareholders over the terms of the contractual relation, they are free to experiment in the terms that they offer, and so there is some variation in governance forms. Much of the contractual relation between shareholders and firms is determined by the law on corporate governance. This law consists, to some extent, of the terms that shareholders and the firm would agree upon if they could negotiate face-to-face. However, it also reflects experimentation by legislators and judges to create effective forms of corporate governance. A complete account of the argument for shareholder control, then, would consist of a justification of the whole system of corporate governance based on the main principles of the contractual theory.

Efficiency and morality

The contractual argument for shareholder control or shareholder primacy is based largely on considerations of efficiency. Under most conditions, the shareholder model of the corporation is more efficient than the alternatives. Thus, in an economy in which corporate governance is determined largely by the market, this form of governance is the most likely to be chosen. However, to say that a form of governance is efficient is not to say that it is morally justified. Some additional steps in the argument must be supplied to complete the argument.

Before completing the argument, some clarifications are needed. First, the contractual argument does not entail that only the shareholder-controlled firm is justified. Many forms of corporate governance are possible, and under certain conditions, other forms beside the shareholder model may be more efficient. The crucial question is, in forming a nexus-of-contracts firm, what governance structure would be mutually agreed upon by all constituencies.

Under some conditions, firms will be owned by the employees. This is especially true when an enterprise is human-capital intensive and has little need for financial capital. Indeed, the partnership, which is the dominant governance form for accounting and law firms, represents a kind of employee ownership. When suppliers, such as dairy farmers, are subject to a single buyer, they can protect themselves by jointly owning their customer, which, for dairy farmers, is the dairy processor. Thus, the dairy processor (Land O'Lakes is an example) becomes a supplier-owned cooperative. A food cooperative is an example of a customer-owned firm. Mutual insurance companies are owned by the policy holders. Henry Hansmann suggests that the shareholder-owned firm can be viewed as a "capital cooperative."[26]

Second, it follow from the first point that shareholders are not always the investors in a firm. Shareholders may be any group. As a matter of definition, shareholders are whatever group that possesses two important rights: the right of control and the right to residual revenues or profit. In addition, shareholders are the exclusive beneficiary of the fiduciary duty of management, which is to say that they are the group whose interest management has a fiduciary duty to serve. So to the question of why shareholders should have the right of control and a right to profit there is a simple answer: This is a matter of definition. The more relevant question is why, in most firms, equity capital providers are the shareholders. That is, why has the investor-owned firm become so dominant?

The answer provided by the standard financial argument is that equity capital providers typically assume the residual risk of an enterprise—that is, accept profits or residual revenues as the return for their input of capital—and, for this reason, insist on control as a means for protecting their return. Just as customers buy a company's products, equity capital providers "buy" the future profits of a firm; or, alternatively, in order to raise capital, a firm "sells" its future profits to investors. Equity capital providers may also be said to "sell" their risk-bearing and decision-making services to a firm in return for a right to profits.

The moral justification for the shareholder model of the corporation consists, then, of two related arguments. First, in the nexus-of-contracts firm, the form of governance is determined by contracting among all the concerned parties. Thus, if one group "buys" the right of control and the right to profits, it is with the consent of the other groups. Since contracting in a firm is largely a matter of supplying some asset to a firm for some return, the main aim of each group is to secure the expected return on the asset it supplies. In general, the right of control and the right to profits are of little value to employees, suppliers, customers, and bondholders, each of whom is usually better able protect its input to the firm by other means. Whatever form of governance results from contracting among all corporate constituencies, it is justified, like any market outcome, because it represents the mutual consent of all the parties.

Second, each corporate constituency is willing to give its consent because, in general, shareholder control is in the interest of every other group. First, society as a whole benefits when business organizations are maximally profitable because of the greater wealth creation. If control were exercised by groups whose only interest is that a firm be merely solvent and not maximally profitable, then less wealth would be created. Second, every nonshareholder group benefits when shareholders assume much of the risk of an enterprise because their return is all the more secure. Shareholders are willing to assume this risk—in return for some compensation, of course—because they are better able to diversify their risks among a large number of companies. Employees, by contrast, are very undiversified inasmuch as their fortunes depend wholly upon the employing firm. The willingness of shareholders to assume residual risk thus provides a kind of insurance for employee's wages. Third, without the right of control, equity capital providers would require a greater return to compensate for the increased risk to their investment. This, in turn, would drive up the price of capital, thus increasing the cost of production for everyone and reducing the amount of wealth created.

The economic case for corporate governance not only explains why investor ownership is, in fact, the dominant form of corporate governance but also why it is morally justified. Because, under most conditions, this form of governance is the most efficient, it benefit all corporate constituencies, who, in turn give their consent to it. The investor-owned corporation thus represents the best cooperative arrangement that can be negotiated among the various corporate constituencies in a free market.

The Objective of the Firm

A fundamental tenet of finance theory is that the objective of the firm is shareholder wealth maximization (SWM). The argument for SWM is easily constructed on the contractual theory as part of the case for shareholder primacy. Accepting this objective, however, raises questions about what constitutes SWM. The objective of SWM is not as clear as may first appear, and clarifying it requires some value judgments. A more serious problem arises from the fact that SWM is not, in fact, the sole objective of most corporations, and for practical reasons, SWM is an inadequate guide for corporate managers. Even managers committed to SWM still face questions about how best to serve shareholders' interests. Doing this involves pursuing many objectives other than the wealth of shareholders. A manager can serve the shareholders, in other words, only by fulfilling a wide-ranging set of responsibilities to all corporate constituencies, that is, by exercising corporate social responsibility.

Initially, it is difficult to see why the interest of shareholders should be the sole aim of all business activity. Shareholders are not owners in any meaningful sense but are merely one among many constituencies with firm-specific assets. They are entitled to have these assets protected, but this could be accomplished by interest payments on their "loan" of capital to the corporation and a certain risk premium. The important role of shareholders in the contractual theory is not that of capital provider but that of residual risk-bearer. Corporate control is an effective safeguard for residual risk-bearers, but, as we have observed, well-diversified shareholders of most corporations bear relatively little risk. Moreover, other constituencies sometimes bear residual risk and thus have a claim to control rights as well.

The main argument for shareholder control, then, is that corporations will be more efficient if major investment decisions are made with only the shareholders' interests in mind. What is important to note about this argument is that the *ultimate* objective of the firm is not shareholder wealth maximization but the maximization of wealth for the whole of society. The objective of SWM is merely a means to this larger end.

What is shareholder wealth?

Before SWM can be accepted as the objective of the firm, we need to clarify the concept. Even determining what is a share of stock and who is consequently a shareholder is complicated by the existence of ordinary and preferred stock, convertible stock, and myriad other financial instruments that blur the boundary between equity and debt. Shareholders, too, are a diverse group with different risk preferences and time horizons, and so decisions that raise the value of the firm for one group could lower it for another. The interest of the shareholders is assumed to be identical with that of the firm, but the correlation is not perfect. Thus, well-diversified shareholders might prefer a firm to take risks that threaten the survival of the firm, whereas managers, as well as employees and other constituencies who have a greater stake in the firm as an ongoing entity, are generally more risk-averse. No one group's interest is identical to the interest of the firm itself.

Finance theory suggests that shareholders' risk preferences and time horizons ought to be ignored by management. The irrelevance theory, developed by Franco Modigliani and Merton Miller, holds that decisions about financial policy (such as capital structure and dividends) do not affect firm evaluation because investors can make changes in their own portfolios to achieve any desired outcome.[27] Thus, an investor who would prefer that a corporation have a different debt-to-equity ratio or a different level of dividends can make other investments that offset the financial policy of the corporation in question. Therefore, managers should concentrate on nonfinancial decisions that affect share price. However, this conclusion overlooks the fact that shareholders are not always able to invest under the same terms as corporations, and hence they may incur greater cost in satisfying their own risk and return preferences.

The most common measure of shareholder wealth is stock price, rather than accounting profits, which are subject to manipulation. However, stock price is also influenced by many nonfundamental factors, including investor psychology, economic trends, and market irrationality, all of which are beyond management's control. Insofar as stock price reflects the risk preferences of shareholders with little stake in the firm, it is not always a good guide for managing a firm in the long run. For all these reasons, managing to maximize stock price may not result in maximum firm value.

As an alternative to accounting profits or stock price as a measure of wealth maximization, Henry Hu proposes the "blissful-shareholder" model, in which the management of large, publicly held companies with actively traded stock and well-diversified shareholders seek to maximize "what the share price would be in a stock market that is completely omniscient and fully efficient."[28] Under this model, management has a fiduciary duty to pursue worthwhile (positive NPV) projects, even if doing so results in a reduction of the price of a company's stock because of market mispricing.

Bradford Cornell and Alan C. Shapiro propose that the objective of the firm be measured by an "extended balance sheet," which includes, in addition to the usual assets and liabilities, the value to the firm of implicit claims to various constituencies and the costs to the firm of honoring these claims.[29] These constitute "organizational capital" and "organizational liabilities" respectively, and the difference between them is "net organizational capital," which represents a form of wealth that is not recorded by traditional financial accounting practices. This proposal reflects the view that the value of a firm consists not merely in its financial state but in its organizational abilities. (And the failure of some financially restructured firms to perform lends some credence to this view.)

The "blissful shareholder" model and the "extended balance sheet" model each addresses the fact that maximizing wealth for shareholders is not a clear objective for managers. Deciding which shareholders to favor and resolving differences between shareholders and the firm both involve some value judgment about the worth of the respective claims. Short-term profits benefit well-diversified shareholders with a strong preference for risk and a short time horizon. By contrast, a decision to promote the long-term prospects of the firm considers the interests of a risk-averse shareholders as well as the various constituencies with a stake in the survival of the firm. For example, Hu considers other constituency statutes to embody a "blissful shareholder" view because they permit directors to choose long-term value over short-term shareholder gain in responding to a takeover bid. The long-term value of a firm has been understood by the courts in some cases to include its value to employees, consumers, and society in general.[30] Moreover, SWM is subject to differing interpretations, and the choice between these interpretations requires the use of value judgments. If the value of a firm is taken to be its value as an ongoing entity that is capable of creating wealth for society indefinitely into the future, then managers cannot consider the interests of individual shareholders or current stock price, but must take into account the interests of all of the groups that make up the corporation.

Do firms seek to maximize?

It is no secret that most business firms do not seek to maximize shareholder wealth. If all corporations did, there would be no extravagant headquarters or fleets of corporate jets; prices would be the highest possible and costs the lowest, so that neither could be changed if the need arose to improve profitability; and every legal stratagem would be employed, no matter how unconscionable, in order to extract the full return from every dollar invested. Some regard this failure to maximize shareholder wealth as a regrettable shortcoming of a system in which managers are able to consume perquisites, collude with employees and customers against the interests of investors, and salve their consciences and gain public approval with good works. Others hold that SWM is a theoretical ideal that cannot and should not be realized in practice.

In a 1960 article in the *Harvard Business Review*, Robert N. Anthony contended that most large, publicly held corporations do not attempt to maximize profits but seek only a *satisfactory* level of profit—and that this is a good thing![31] First, profit maximization is an impractical goal that, if pursued single-mindedly, would have counterproductive consequences. Pricing, for example, is not done by comparing demand and costs at all volumes—which is a formidable task that is seldom attempted outside economics classrooms; rather pricing is done by developing a "normal" price based on a conventional cost-accounting system. Similarly, capital budgeting does not commonly consist of comparing every investment opportunity in order to select the one with the greatest return over the marginal cost of capital. Typically, promising projects are selected if they exceed a minimum expected return.

Although decisions are often made by inexact means that still aim at profits, ethics also plays a role in these decisions. Business people have learned, for example, that pricing is only one aspect of marketing and that higher prices can be charged if there is a high degree of consumer trust. Some opportunities are pursued and others rejected for reasons of a corporation's social responsibility.

The main implication for ethics if firms deliberately seek only a satisfactory return is that a surplus remains to be distributed. Whether managers divert the surplus to themselves, as many maintain, or confer it upon employees, customers, suppliers, or other groups is immaterial to the point that a distribution is being made by some criteria other than SWM. These distributions are often justified on the grounds that they ultimately benefit shareholders, but such claims are partially true at best. (It is unfortunate that corporate managers feel compelled to justify decent treatment of employees—offering generous severance packages to those laid off, for example—as indirectly benefiting shareholders when, in truth, they believe that this is the compassionate thing to do.) These criteria for distribution are varied, but some include ethical standards which are considered a part of responsible business conduct.[32]

Contracts and social responsibility

Does the contractual theory of the firm allow for corporate social responsibility? Although the responsibility of business firm to serve social ends is much debated, corporations typically devote some resources to philanthropy and worthwhile social initiatives.[33] However, the objective of shareholder wealth maximization and the fiduciary duty of management to act in the shareholders' interest seem to be incompatible with the pursuit of corporate social responsibility. Corporate social responsibility also includes addressing the social costs of production, also known as externalities. Social costs or externalities are costs of production, such as pollution, that are not *internalized* (factored into the price of a product) but *externalized* (passed on to society). On the contractual theory of the firm, what should firms do with regard to social costs?

First, some contractual theories reject the idea of corporate social responsibility. Michael C. Jensen and William H. Meckling, in their seminal paper on the contractual theory of the firm, assert that it makes no sense to talk about corporate social responsibility because the firm is not an individual.[34] The nexus-of-contracts firm functions like a market, and just as it would be a mistake to speak of the social responsibility of the wheat market, so too should we dismiss any talk of the social responsibility of General Motors.

This claim fails to address the truly perplexing conundrums of corporate activity that have been addressed in philosophy and the law. It may be useful in finance to think of the firm as if it were merely a nexus of contracts; but actual corporations are like persons in some respects and unlike them in others, and the way we treat them reflects this ambivalence. Thus, the law recognizes corporations as legal persons for some purposes, and if this were not so, then individuals and not the corporation itself would be the subject of legal actions, such as suits and criminal prosecutions. We say that General Motors has a responsibility to pay taxes, so why can we not also say that it has a responsibility to prevent pollution, for example?

Friedman's argument

The economist Milton Friedman has argued against the idea of corporate social responsibility by saying:

> This view shows a fundamental misconception of the character and nature of a free economy. In such an economy, there is one and only one social responsibility of business—to use its resources and engage in activities designed to increase its profits so long as it stays within the rules of the game, which is to say, engages in open and free competition without deception or fraud.[35]

Friedman's argument proceeds mainly from the premise that when managers make decisions in their capacity as agents of the corporation and not as private citizens, they have an obligation to serve the interests of the corporation alone. Otherwise, they are taking on the role of public officials with the power to tax, and as such they ought to be elected through the political process and not by the shareholders of private business firms. He writes:

> What does it mean to say that the corporate executive has a "social responsibility" in his capacity as businessman? If this statement is not pure rhetoric, it must mean that he is to act in some way that is not in the interest of his employers. For example, that he is to refrain from increasing the price of the product in order to contribute to the social objective of preventing inflation, even though a price increase would be in the best interests of the corporation. Or that he is to make expenditures on reducing pollution beyond the amount that is in the best interests of the corporation or that is required by law in order to contribute to the social objective of improving the environment. Or that, at the expense of corporate profits, he is to hire "hardcore" unemployed instead of better qualified available workmen to contribute to the social objective of reducing poverty.
>
> In each of these cases, the corporate executive would be spending someone else's money for a general social interest. Insofar as his actions in accord with his "social responsibility" reduce returns to stockholders, he is spending their money. Insofar as his actions raise the price to customers, he is spending the customers' money. Insofar as his actions lower the wages of some employees, he is spending their money.[36]

In presenting this argument, Friedman acknowledges that there are "rules of the game," but these rules may impose more obligations on corporations than he realizes. The operation of a free market requires an extensive set of rules that we often overlook. These include common understandings, background institutions, the legal system, and government regulations. (Consider, for example, the fundamental changes that are required in order to introduce free markets in the formerly socialist countries of eastern Europe.) In addition, corporations, like government and other institutions in society, gain the legitimacy needed for survival by meeting people's legitimate expectations. This point has been expressed as the Iron Law of Responsibility: "In the long run, those who do not use power in a manner which society considers responsible will tend to lose it."[37] Friedman accepts the need to consider matters of social responsibility in order to serve the ultimate interests of the corporation, but he appears to underestimate the attention to such matters that this long-term perspective requires.

Friedman charges that acts of social responsibility, such as spending money to prevent pollution beyond the amount that is in the corporation's best interest, takes money away from shareholders, employees, and other groups. To be sure, acting in a socially responsible manner involves trade-offs between the interests of different constituencies, and managers must be careful not to exceed their authority and assume the powers of elected officials. However, managing trade-offs is a task that is assigned to managers in the nexus-of-contracts theory of the firm. Thus, spending money on pollution might be described not as spending other people's money without authority but as bargaining with environmentalists who have the power to affect the corporation as consumers (who can boycott the company's products), as citizens (who can lobby for government regulation), and even as employees and shareholders, who favor environmental protection and are willing to accept less in wages or dividends in order to achieve this goal.

Friedman would not object to an expenditure to prevent pollution as long as the expenditure is in the best interest of the corporation. However, the best interest of the corporation is not merely what the shareholders of the moment prefer, because managers of a nexus-of-contracts firm must manage relations with all constituencies on whose cooperation the corporation depends. Short-term shareholders might complain that managers are spending *their* money in preventing pollution, and they might respond by driving the price of the stock down. But we have already noted that stock price is not always a reliable indicator of shareholder value. Acting in the best interest of the corporation requires a long-term perspective, such as the "blissful shareholder" model, and taking such a perspective leads to more socially responsible behavior than Friedman's argument suggests.

The contractual theory poses another challenge to Friedman's argument because the exercise of social responsibility affects the contracting process itself. For example, bondholders who do not trust management may insist on restrictive bond covenants; employees who do not trust management may form unions in order to achieve a collective-bargaining agreement; and customers who do not trust management may insist on more explicit warranties. In other words, responsible business conduct can facilitate the contracting among all constituencies by substituting informal expectations for more formal agreements, and in the absence of any trust, contracting would be impossible. So even if the objective of the firm is shareholder wealth, this objective cannot be achieved without attending to the matters that are considered to be a part of corporate social responsibility.

Social costs

One response of contractual theorist to externalities or social costs is that problems such as pollution tend to be corrected as the wealth of a society increases, and the more efficient business firms are, the greater the wealth that is created. Thus, problems like pollution are best addressed by focusing on efficient production. Easterbrook and Fischel make the point in the following way:

> A successful firm provides jobs for workers and goods and services for consumers. The more appealing the goods to consumers, the more profit (and jobs). Prosperity for stockholders, workers, and communities goes hand in glove with better products for consumers. Other objectives, too, come with profit. Wealthy firms provide better working conditions and clean up their outfalls; high profits produce social wealth that strengthens the demand for cleanliness. . . . [W]ealthy societies purchase much cleaner and healthier environments than do poorer nations—in part because well-to-do citizens want cleaner air and water, and in part because they can afford to pay for it.[38]

Thus, a wealthier society is better able to afford the cost of pollution because it has both the desire and the resources to clean up the environment. However, this response does not address the question of who pays. The problem remains: Should corporations bear the cost by internalizing it? Or is it permissible for them to externalize the cost by passing it on to society? Furthermore, if the socially responsible course of action is for firms to internalize the cost, can this be reconciled with the pursuit of shareholder wealth maximization and a fiduciary duty for managers to serve the shareholders' interest? If not, then problems of social cost, such as that posed by pollution, can be resolved only by making some change in the system of corporate governance entailed by the contractual theory, or else by government regulation.

An assumption of the contractual theory is that any voluntary agreement between two persons is just for the reason that both have given their consent. However, a contract that is optimal for two parties may not be socially optimal if it has third-party effects by adversely affecting the interests of other persons. This is the case with pollution when a resource, such as air or water, can be used without cost. A factory that can dispose of waste in a nearby stream uses the water without cost to itself but imposes a cost on all other users of the water. Thus, its contracts with employees, suppliers, and others that facilitate production have third-party effects.

Easterbrook and Fischel recognize this possibility but deny that it has any bearing on corporate governance. They write:

> We do not make the Panglossian claim that profit and social welfare are perfectly aligned. When costs fall on third parties—pollution is a common example—firms do injury because harm does not come back to them as private cost. . . . Users of the stream impose costs on the firm (and its consumers) as fully as the firm imposes costs on the users of the stream. No rearrangement of corporate governance structures can change this. The task is to establish property rights so that the firm treats the social costs as private ones, and so that its reactions, as managers try to maximize profits given these new costs, duplicate what all of the parties (downstream users and customers alike) would have agreed to were bargaining among all possible without cost. To view pollution . . . or other difficult moral and social questions as *governance* matters is to miss the point.[39]

The crucial point in this argument is that a clear assignment of property rights would force firms to internalize what would otherwise be external costs. For example, if third-party victims of pollution could demand compensation for damage to their property caused by the pollution in the stream, then firms would be forced to include this compensation in their cost calculations, thereby internalizing the cost of pollution. This cost could be paid by a company either by cleaning up the discharge into the stream or by paying compensation, whichever is cheaper.

This argument exemplifies the Coase Theorem, which holds that externalities do not cause a misallocation of resources provided that there are defined and enforceable property rights and no transaction costs—that is, that the affected parties could form contracts at no cost.[40] The flaw in the argument, however, is the absence, in many cases of social costs, of both property rights and zero transaction costs. Although steps can be taken to remedy both of these factors, they are likely to remain insurmountable obstacles to solution that Easterbrook and Fischel propose. Indeed, Ronald Coase, the creator of the Coase Theorem in a 1960 paper, claimed more than 28 years later that his main message, that economic analysis must take transaction costs into account, had been misunderstood.[41]

The conclusion to be drawn, then, is that contracting or market transacting is unlikely to allow managers to address the problem of externalities or social cost in a way that is consistent with profit maximization and a fiduciary duty to serve shareholder interests. If corporations are to be socially responsible in addressing this problem, there must be either some relaxation of these central tenets of the contractual theory or else more extensive government regulation (Friedman's "rules of the game"). Easterbrook and Fischel are probably right that the problem of externalities is not appropriately addressed by changes in corporate governance.[42] If so, then government regulation is the remaining alternative.

The Stakeholder Challenge

The shareholder or stockholder model of the corporation has been challenged by those who believe that an exclusive focus on shareholder interests is morally unjustified. The objective of shareholder wealth maximization, they contend, unjustly neglects the interest of other corporate constituencies. In particular, stakeholder theorists generally hold that corporations ought to be run in the interests of all stakeholders, which commonly include, employees, suppliers, customers, and community members, in addition to shareholders.[43]

On one point, the shareholder and stakeholder models are in agreement: the purpose of the firm is to enable each corporate constituency or stakeholder group to obtain the maximum benefit from their involvement. The economic approach to the firm expresses this purpose in terms of realizing the full benefits of engaging in joint production. Although the advocates of the stakeholder model speak in terms of having each group's interest taken into account and balanced one against the other, it must be recognized that all benefits result from wealth-creating economic activity and that stakeholders can receive no more benefits than this activity creates. In short, wealth must be created before it can be distributed.

However, two questions remain. One question is how best to protect or serve each stakeholder group's interests. On the contractual approach, what each group is due is a return on the assets that they provide for joint production. There are many means for securing each group's return, one of which is reliance on management's decision-making powers. In the prevailing system of corporate governance, this means is utilized by giving shareholders control, making them the beneficiaries of management's fiduciary duty, and setting shareholder wealth as the objective of the firm. The question, then, is whether the means of relying on management's decision making would better serve the interest of nonshareholder groups or whether they are better served by other means.

The second question is: What are the interests of each group that ought to be protected or served? Stakeholder theorists contend that even if the market return due to each group is adequately protected by other means, they are sometimes due more, and that these additional, nonmarket benefits can be best provided in the stakeholder model. This position is a challenge to the use of the market to determine how the benefits of economic activity are to be distributed. Instead of using the market alone to make this determination, the stakeholder model would make this a task of management.

Protecting stakeholder interests

The first question—how best to serve each stakeholder's interest—is largely an empirical one about the effectiveness of the available means. One way to answer this question is by conducting a thought experiment. Suppose that the stakeholder model were adopted by a great many firms or even all firms in an economy. In such a system of corporate governance, all groups would share control of a firm; managers would have a fiduciary duty to act in the interests of all groups; and the objective of the firm would be to maximize the return of every group. The resulting economy would exemplify the stakeholder model.

Now, add one more condition: That each group is free to opt out of such a system of governance and choose other means for protecting their interests. That is, they would have the opportunity to forgo the protection of management acting in their interests and to seek different contracts with a firm or different legal rules for protecting their interests. This could be achieved by allowing new firms to spring up that would offer different employment opportunities for workers, different purchasing opportunities for customers, different investment opportunities for investors, and so on. Governments could also experiment with different legal rules that promise to provide better protection.

Although opinions may different on the system of corporate governance that might emerge from this thought experiment, there is good reason to believe that each group would prefer the shareholder model.

First, management decision making is a weaker form of protection than legally enforceable contracts or legal rules. When such contracts and rules are available, they are more likely to be preferred than a reliance on management's fiduciary duty. Shareholders are forced to rely on the protection of a fiduciary duty because of problems that prevent them from utilizing fully specified contracts or precise legal rules. Fiduciary duty should be viewed, accordingly, not as a special privilege that shareholders enjoy but as an imperfect substitute when more effective means for protecting a group's interests are not available.[44]

Second, corporate decision making is more efficient and effective when management has a single, clearly defined objective, and shareholder wealth maximization provides not only a workable decision guide but one that increases the total wealth creation of the firm.[45] This, in turn, enables each group to obtain a greater share. That is, each group can get a larger piece of pie if the pie itself is larger. Thus, employees who seek greater job security or expanded benefits—which advocates of the stakeholder view would support—are more likely to get these goods if the employing company is prospering. A similar argument can be developed for customers, suppliers, investors, and every other stakeholder group. The benefits of a single objective would be compromised if other groups sought, like shareholders, to protect themselves with claims on management's loyalty.

If the disagreement between shareholder and stakeholder advocates is an empirical one about the most effective means for protecting or serving the interests of each stakeholder group, then a definitive resolution is not easy. What the argument for the shareholder model shows, however, is that reliance on management decision making, as the stakeholder model proposes, is but one means and that many other means are available. Therefore, from the premise that corporate activity should benefit all stakeholder groups, it does not follow that ensuring this outcome is a task for *management*. It is an outcome that should be achieved by some means, but the alternative of contractual agreements and legal rules, which do not involve management decision making, may secure this end more effectively.

Securing fairness for stakeholders

The second question about the interests that ought to be protected or served assumes that some stakeholders are due more than a secure return on the assets that they contribute to joint production. Stakeholder advocates might contend that the prevailing system unduly favors one group, namely shareholders, and that more of the wealth created by firms ought to flow to other groups, such as employees, customers, and the community, even if this introduces some inefficiency and hence less wealth creation. In other words, the shareholder model may be efficient, critics complain, but it is not fair. This is a charge to take seriously, and it is recognized in economics as the familiar equity–efficiency trade-off.

Without question, there are many ways in which stakeholders could be treated unfairly, and such unfair treatment might increase efficiency or it might merely benefit one stakeholder group at the expense of another. It is morally required that any economic system ensure basic fairness and, where necessary, make a morally defensible trade-off between fairness (or equity) and efficiency. Just as corporations should protect and serve the interests of all stakeholders, they should also treat all stakeholders fairly. The question, as before, is how best to do this. Is this a task for management or should it be handled in some other way?

Two points should be observed. One is that there is no reason to believe that contractual agreements and legal rules are any less adequate to ensure fairness than they are to secure each group's rightful return. Just as reliance on management's decision making to protect each group's return on its assets is generally inferior to other, more effective means, so, too, is it inferior for ensuring that the wealth created by firms is fairly distributed. In short, there are better ways than adopting the stakeholder model to ensure fairness.

Second, a case can be made that ensuring fairness is not a task of management. Aside from the question of efficacy—whether management decision making is an effective means for achieving this—there is a more fundamental question about who or what should determine the distribution of wealth. Broadly speaking, an economy faces two questions: How to *produce* wealth and how to *distribute* it. Generally, decisions about production are made in a market where managers, like employees, customers, and other participants, make decisions primarily on the basis of economic considerations. The market also determines how wealth is to be distributed, but the resulting distribution may not be fair or otherwise desirable. When it become necessary or advisable to interfere in the operation of a market and alter the distribution of wealth, this task usually falls, and rightly falls, to government. Because the interests involved bear so heavily on people's welfare, decisions about the distribution of wealth that depart from market outcomes should be made, for the most part, through the political process. It is not only unreasonable to expect managers, who have enough responsibility making decisions about how to produce wealth, to handle questions about how it should be distributed, but it is also dangerous in a democracy to allow unelected managers to make such crucial decisions.

Summary

Viewed in terms of an economic approach to the firm, the stakeholder model offers managerial decision making as a means for protecting and advancing stakeholder interests. Insofar as it proposes that managers have a fiduciary duty to serve the interests of all stakeholders and that maximizing all stakeholder interests be the objective of the firm, it seeks to extend the means used to safeguard shareholders to benefit all stakeholders. In short, the stakeholder view proposes that all stakeholders be treated like shareholders.

The fundamental mistake of the stakeholder model is a failure to see that the needs of each stakeholder group, including shareholders, are different and that different means best meet these needs. The protection that shareholders derive from being the beneficiaries of management's fiduciary duty and having their interests be the objective of the firm fit their particular situation as residual claimants with difficult contracting problems, but employees, customers, suppliers, and other investors (such as bondholders) are better served by other means, which include contractual agreements and various legal rules. Management decision making is a relatively ineffective means for protecting the interests of nonshareholder stakeholders. In any event, the choice of means for protecting each stakeholder group's interest is mainly an empirical one about what works best in practice, and the evidence tends to support the prevailing stockholder-centered system of corporate governance.

Finally, insofar as the stakeholder model assigns to managers the task of ensuring that the wealth created by a firm is distributed in a fair way that departs from the distribution that results from purely market forces, this task, too, is better done by other means, most notably through the political process. Managers lack both the ability and the legitimacy that are required to fulfill this task.

Notes

1. See G. C. Archibald, "Firm, Theory of," *The New Palgrave* (London: Macmillan, 1987); Richard M. Cyert and Charles L. Hedrick, "Theory of the Firm: Past, Present, and Future; An Interpretation," *Journal of Economic Literature*, 10 (1972), 398–412; Fritz Machlup, "Theories of the Firm: Marginalist, Behavioral, Managerial," *American Economic Review*, 62 (1967), 1–33; and Philip L. Williams, *The Emergence of the Theory of the Firm* (New York: St Martin's Press, 1979).

2. William J. Baumol, *Business Behavior, Value, and Growth* (New York: Macmillan, 1959); Richard M. Cyert and James G. March, *A Behavioral Theory of the Firm*

(Englewood Cliffs, NJ: Prentice Hall, 1963); Robin Marris, *The Economic Theory of Managerial Capitalism* (New York: Free Press, 1964); and Oliver E. Williamson, *The Economics of Discretionary Behavior: Managerial Objectives in a Theory of the Firm* (Englewood Cliffs, NJ: Prentice Hall, 1964).

3. The distinction between the property rights and the social institution conceptions of the corporation is due to William T. Allen, "Our Schizophrenic Conception of the Business Corporation," *Cardozo Law Review*, 14 (1992), 261–81. See also William T. Allen, "Contracts and Communities in Corporate Law," *Washington and Lee Law Review*, 50 (1993), 1395–407.

4. Because the right to incorporate is alleged to "inhere" in the right to own property and to contract with others, this view is also known as the *inherence theory*.

5. The view that incorporation is a privilege "conceded" by the state in order to achieve some social good is also known as the *concession theory*.

6. *Munn v. Illinois*, 94 U.S. 113; 24 L. Ed. 77 (1876).

7. This solution in *Munn* still involves an acceptance of the property rights view, however, since the justification of regulation relies on the right of the state to protect people from others' use of property rather than on the right of the state to charter corporations. Regulating corporations by means of state chartering laws would be more consistent with the social institution theory. The acceptance of the property rights theory was furthered by the decision of the US Supreme Court in the *Santa Clara* case, which concerned the power of the state to tax railroads. In ruling that corporations are entitled to the equal protection clause of the Fourteenth Amendment, the court recognized their status as persons with property rights and some other constitutional protections. *Santa Clara Country v. Southern Pacific R.R.*, 118 U.S. 394 (1886).

8. *Dodge v. Ford Motor Co.*, 170 N.W. 668, 685 (1919).

9. Adolf A. Berle, Jr and Gardiner C. Means, *The Modern Corporation and Private Property* (New York: Macmillan, 1932).

10. Berle and Means, *The Modern Corporation and Private Property*, 3.

11. Ibid., 355.

12. Ibid., 355.

13. E. Merrick Dodd, "For Whom Are Corporate Managers Trustees?" *Harvard Law Review*, 45 (1932), 1145–63.

14. Dodd, "For Whom Are Corporate Managers Trustees?" 1148.

15. Ibid., 1161.

16. Ibid., 1162.

17. Adolf A. Berle, Jr, "For Whom Corporate Managers *Are* Trustees: A Note," *Harvard Law Review*, 45 (1932), 1367.

18. Berle, "For Whom Corporate Managers *Are* Trustees," 1372.

19. Ibid., 1370.

20. Ibid., 1372.

21. Adolf A. Berle, Jr, *The 20th Century Capitalist Revolution* (New York: Harcourt, Brace & World, 1954), 169.

22.   Ronald M. Coase, "The Nature of the Firm," *Economica*, NS, 4 (1937), 386–405. The contractual theory has been developed by economists using an agency or transaction cost perspective. See Armen A. Alchian and Harold Demsetz, "Production, Information Costs, and Economic Organization," *American Economic Review*, 62 (1972), 777–95; Benjamin Klein, Robert A. Crawford, and Armen A. Alchian, "Vertical Integration, Appropriable Rents, and the Competitive Contracting Process," *Journal of Law and Economics*, 21(1978), 297–326; Michael C. Jensen and William H. Meckling, "Theory of the Firm: Managerial Behavior, Agency Costs, and Ownership Structure," *Journal of Financial Economics*, 3 (1983), 305–60; Eugene F. Fama and Michael C. Jensen, "Separation of Ownership and Control," *Journal of Law and Economics*, 26 (1983), 301–25; Steven N. S. Cheung, "The Contractual Theory of the Firm," *Journal of Law and Economics*, 26 (1983), 1–22; and Oliver E. Williamson, *The Economic Institutions of Capitalism* (New York: The Free Press, 1985). An authoritative development of the theory of the firm in corporate law is Frank H. Easterbrook and Daniel R. Fischel, *The Economic Structure of Corporate Law* (Cambridge, MA: Harvard University Press, 1991). See also William A. Klein, "The Modern Business Organization: Bargaining under Constraints," *Yale Law Journal*, 91 (1982), 1521–64; Oliver Hart, "An Economist's Perspective on the Theory of the Firm," *Columbia Law Review*, 89 (1989), 1757–73; and Henry N. Butler, "The Contractual Theory of the Firm," *George Mason Law Review*, 11 (1989), 99–123.

23.   See Robert A. Naby and Robert W. Obenberger, "Factors Influencing Investor Behavior," *Financial Analysts Journal*, July–August 1994, 63–8. An earlier but more comprehensive study is M. E. Blume and Irwin Friend, *The Changing Role of the Individual Investor* (New York: John Wiley, 1978).

24.   As exception is institutional investors with large blocks of underperforming stocks, who are often unable to sell without driving down the price further and who find it less costly to exercise their control rights in an effort to improve performance. This effort by some large institutional investors is called *relationship investing*. See Robert A. G. Monks and Nell Minow, *Corporate Governance* (Oxford: Blackwell, 1995), 160–3.

25.   Whether the use of liquidity as an alternative to the exercise of control rights results in effective corporate governance is an other matter. Amar Bhide argues that it does not. Amar Bhide, "The Hidden Costs of Stock Market Liquidity," *Journal of Financial Economics*, 34 (1993), 31–51. For a shorter version of this article see Amar Bhide, "Deficient Governance," *Harvard Business Review*, 71 (November–December 1994), 129—39.

26.   Henry Hansmann, *The Ownership of Enterprise* (Cambridge, MA: Harvard University Press, 1996), 13–14.

27.   Franco Modigliani and Merton H. Miller, "The Cost of Capital, Corporation Finance, and the Theory of Investment," *American Economic Review*, 48 (1958), 261–97; and Merton H. Miller and Franco Modigliani, "Dividend Policy, Growth, and the Valuation of Shares," *Journal of Business*, 34 (1961), 411–33.

28. Henry T. C. Hu, "Risk, Time, and Fiduciary Principles in Corporate Investment," *UCLA Law Review*, 38 (1990), 282.
29. Bradford Cornell and Alan C. Shapiro, "Corporate Stakeholders and Corporate Finance," *Financial Management*, 16 (1987), 5–14.
30. This point is made explicitly in *Unocal Corporation v. Mesa Petroleum Co.*, 493 A.2d 946, 955 (1985), and in *Paramount Communications v. Time, Inc.*, 571 A.2d 1140, 1152 (1990).
31. Robert N. Anthony, "The Trouble with Profit Maximization," *Harvard Business Review*, 38 (1960), 126–34.
32. That such standards should be part of the objective of business corporations is recommended in the as-yet-unaccepted *Principles of Corporate Governance* drafted by The American Law Institute. Section 201 states that in addition to "enhancing corporate profit and shareholder gain," a business corporation "may take into account ethical considerations that are reasonably regarded as appropriate to the responsible conduct of business."
33. See David Vogel, *The Market for Virtue: The Potential and Limits of Corporate Social Responsibility* (Washington, DC: Brookings, 2005); Craig C. Smith, "Corporate Social Responsibility: Whether or How?" *California Management Review*, 45 (2003), 52–76; and David Hess, Nikolai Rogovsky, and Thomas W. Dunfee, "The Next Wave of Corporate Community Involvement: Corporate Social Initiatives," *California Management Review* (2002), 110–25.
34. Jensen and Meckling, "Theory of the Firm," 311.
35. Milton Friedman, *Capitalism and Freedom* (Chicago: The University of Chicago Press, 1962), 133.
36. Milton Friedman, "The Social Responsibility of Business Is to Increase Its Profits," *New York Times Magazine*, September 13, 1970, 33.
37. Keith Davis and Robert L. Blomstrom, *Business and Society: Environment and Responsibility*, 3rd edn. (New York: McGraw-Hill, 1975), 50.
38. Easterbrook and Fischel, *The Economic Structure of Corporate Law*, 38.
39. Ibid., 39.
40. Ronald H. Coase, "The Problem of Social Cost," *Journal of Law and Economics*, 3 (1960), 1–44.
41. Ronald H. Coase, *The Firm, the Market, and the Law* (Chicago: The University of Chicago Press, 1988), 15.
42. See Ian Maitland, "Distributive Justice in Firms: Do the Rules of Corporate Governance Matter?" *Business Ethics Quarterly*, 11 (2001), 129–43.
43. R. Edward Freeman, *Strategic Management: A Stakeholder Approach* (Boston: Pitman, 1984); R. Edward Freeman and William M. Evan, "Stockholders and Stakeholders: A New Perspective on Corporate Governance," *California Management Review*, 25 (1983), 88–106; R. Edward Freeman and William M. Evan, "Corporate Governance: A Stakeholder Interpretation," *Journal of Behavioral Economics*, 19 (1990), 337–59; and Thomas Donaldson and Lee E. Preston, "The Stakeholder Theory of the Corporation: Concepts, Evidence, and Implications," *Academy of Management Review*, 20 (1995), 65–91.

44.   Jonathan R. Macey, "An Economic Analysis of the Various Rationales for Making Shareholders the Exclusive Beneficiaries of Corporate Fiduciary Duties," *Stetson Law Review*, 21 (1999), 23–44; Richard Marens and Andrew C. Wicks, "Getting Real: Stakeholder Theory, Management Practice, and the General Irrelevance of Fiduciary Duties Owed to Shareholders," *Business Ethics Quarterly*, 9 (1999), 273–93.

45.   Michael C. Jensen, "Value Maximization, Stakeholder Theory, and the Corporate Objective Function," *Business Ethics Quarterly*, 12 (1992), 235–56; Anant K. Sundaram and Andrew C. Inkpen, "The Corporate Objective Revisited," *Organizational Science*, 15 (2004), 350–63.

Index

DH